Being There, Being Here

Contemporary Issues in the Middle East
Mehran Kamrava, *Series Editor*

Select Titles in Contemporary Issues in the Middle East

Generations of Dissent: Intellectuals, Cultural Production, and the State in the Middle East and North Africa
Alexa Firat and R. Shareah Taleghani, eds.

In the Wake of the Poetic: Palestinian Artists after Darwish
Najat Rahman

The Lost Orchard: The Palestinian-Arab Citrus Industry, 1850–1950
Mustafa Kabha and Nahum Karlinsky

Ottoman Children and Youth during World War I
Nazan Maksudyan

Political Muslims: Understanding Youth Resistance in a Global Context
Tahir Abbas and Sadek Hamid, eds.

Readings in Syrian Prison Literature: The Poetics of Human Rights
R. Shareah Taleghani

Turkey's State Crisis: Institutions, Reform, and Conflict
Bülent Aras

Understanding Hezbollah: The Hegemony of Resistance
Abed T. Kanaaneh

For a full list of titles in this series, visit https://press.syr.edu/supressbook-series/contemporary-issues-in-the-middle-east/.

Being There, Being Here

PALESTINIAN WRITINGS IN THE WORLD

MAURICE EBILEENI

Syracuse University Press

First Edition 2022

22 23 24 25 26 27 6 5 4 3 2 1

∞ The paper used in this publication meets the minimum requirements of the American National Standard for Information Sciences—Permanence of Paper for Printed Library Materials, ANSI Z39.48-1992.

For a listing of books published and distributed by Syracuse University Press, visit https://press.syr.edu.

ISBN: 978-0-8156-3765-3 (hardcover)
978-0-8156-3760-8 (paperback)
978-0-8156-5557-2 (e-book)

Library of Congress Control Number: 2021951781

Manufactured in the United States of America

For my sons, Jude (جود), Rai (راي), and Maas (ماس)

Where should we go after the last frontiers?
Where should the birds fly after the last sky?

—Mahmoud Darwish

Contents

Preface

In 1868, the unknown "nine years old or thereabouts" Konrad Korzeniowski, "while looking at a map of Africa of the time," put his finger on "the blank space then representing the unresolved mystery of the continent" and promised himself, "When I grow up, I shall go there!" It seems now to be common knowledge in literary circles that many years later, Korzeniowski's adult alter ego, Joseph Conrad, immortalizes this call in *Heart of Darkness* (1902) through the fictional Charlie Marlow before he engages on his journey to the Congo and confronts the "dangers" of the continent. I am beginning with this reference to Conrad because while writing *Being There, Being Here*, Marlow's words resonated to me in former head of the Misgav Regional Council in the north of Israel Erez Kreisler's descriptions of the Galilee in a recent *Ha'aretz* article about the monitoring of Israeli housing regulations to maintain a dividing line between the area's Jewish and Arab inhabitants.[1] Kreisler, who claims to be "in favor of life together, but on the basis of some sort of structure and framework," explains that he arrived in the Galilee in 1989 when "the image of the Galilee was that of an enfeebled, wretched, even dangerous region." With these few words, Kreisler transformed the birthplace of my parents, my wife, and my three children into—to put it in Conradian terms—"one of those dark places on earth" and severely inflamed my awareness of my status as a "person of color."

It is not to claim that I had not stood face-to-face with my "otherness" before. Nonetheless, for many years, the repercussions of those encounters were remarkably faint. Born and raised in Copenhagen by Arab immigrants, my "color" was a constant mark of distinction, but it was the 1980s and my presence among my Danish peers was still viewed as "exotic" rather than "threatening." I grew up as a native speaker of Danish, a devout lover of *leverpostej* and remoulade, and a loyal fan of Dennis Jürgensen's youth novels. Surely, I was occasionally reminded of "where I originally came from," insofar as my Danish education could, of course, never be fully realized owing to my "exotic" roots. I can, however, not recall a single instance of such evocations that stuck or caused any recognizable long-term damage to my character (if such a thing is possible). It was a relatively happy childhood, and, although I was rarely targeted, it is only in retrospect that I understand the severity of derogatory colloquialisms such as *fremmedarbejder*, *indvandrer*, and *perker*. During those years, I possessed an innate ability to brush off the impact of such verbal assaults—that same ability that I, in adulthood, have further honed to brush off the tremors of terms and expressions employed in the mainstream Israeli discourse regarding the country's Arab citizens (the community with which I am affiliated today). For some enigmatic reason, I have never felt that I belonged in those targeted minority groups. Kreisler's words did not exactly unsettle this ability, but rather they complemented a process that had started some years earlier. My so-called ability was severely diminished during the period between 2014 and 2017 when I won a Martin Buber postdoctoral fellowship at the Hebrew University and had to stay overnight in Jerusalem during weekdays to work from my office. Daily interactions with Jewish and German colleagues at the Hebrew University revealed an Israeli reality that I had not encountered while living in Tarshiha since I had moved to Israel nearly two decades earlier.

Although Israel always configured as a major presence ever since I can remember, up until the point of my postdoctoral studies, I had somehow succeeded in not really seeing or understanding what Israel represents. The annual three-hour trip from the Lydda airport (Ben Gurion Airport) to Tarshiha—which marked the start of the summer vacation—never opened my eyes to the complex reality between Tel Aviv and this distant Galilean village since I always managed to sleep through the ride. As far as how my young mind conceptualized the world then, Tarshiha was Israel and Israel was Tarshiha. Herzilya, Netanya, Haifa, Acre, and Naharyia did not exist, insofar as they never entered my field of vision or imagination. I recall my mother waking me up when we'd arrive at the entrance to Tarshiha and ascend the curvy main street past the mosque, the Roman Catholic church, and then the Greek Orthodox one, before we reached our destination—the upper quarter of the village where both my paternal and my maternal families resided and where we would stay for the next four weeks.

Years later when I, as a young adult, moved to Israel for my university studies, my decision was based in those childhood memories—the joy associated with those summer vacations. Strange as it may seem, I simply did not think about the political implications of what it would be like to live in Israel as an Arab. During my undergraduate studies at the University of Haifa, I stuck with my Danish peers between classes. I arrived during a period when the glamour of the signing of the Oslo Agreement was still at large and political activity on the mixed campus in Haifa appeared more or less civilized. The controversial Arab (and today exiled) intellectual Azmi Bishara was being courted by the Israeli media as the next big thing, and this first actual encounter with Israel of the '90s outside Tarshiha convinced me that the place seemed by and large habitable.

In 1995 I stood among the crowds outside the Church of Nativity on Christmas Eve witnessing Yasser Arafat's historic arrival in Bethlehem. To be honest, I felt excited, but my excitement was not rooted in national sentiments; it was, rather, a sensation a tourist might experience, like seeing the Sistine Chapel for the first time. During the following years, my impressions remained intact despite having experienced the October Riots and the Second Intifada in 2000 as well as the Second Lebanon War (with short-range missiles raining over the Galilee while I was carrying my then one-year-old son) in 2006. On television I watched the Israeli military declare three consecutive wars on the population of Gaza, killing thousands of Palestinians. I saw the mainstream Israeli political discourse moving further and further to the right, anticipating the election of one extreme government after another, and still I did not get it. It was only when I arrived in Jerusalem as a postdoctoral researcher that I started to understand my place in all of it. In Tarshiha among relatives and friends, I was *al-danimarki* (the Dane). In Jerusalem, I became the Arab—a Palestinian Arab.

This identity was a far cry from the "exotic" one I had been allotted in Copenhagen. The Jerusalem climate cornered me into assuming the role of the Arab in the Zionist narrative. Moving about, on and off, the campus and engaging in conversations during coffee breaks and lunches with my Jewish colleagues—less about politics and more frequently about trivialities of parenthood and postdoctoral anxieties of never getting a university position—I, nevertheless, received a world-class education on the Zionist character of Israeli culture. Consequently, I also began to comprehend the trouble I had gotten myself into by moving to Israel as a young man and, worse, the trouble I am passing on to my sons in raising them there. At this point in my life, the prejudices of my mostly well-meaning peers and mentors stuck, and I understood it was time to significantly update my outdated navigation system that I had brought with me from Denmark. The European character of Zionist ideology (in Israel academia is mainly an Ashkenazi institution) boxed me into specific categories to which I became increasingly sensitive. Israel views its Arab citizens as a "demographic problem" and as "a potential threat to national security"—a fifth column—but Jerusalem transformed me into something different. Seeing myself through the eyes of many of my Jerusalem peers, I understood that everything about me would be exclusively defined by my Arabness. Rather than coping with midlife and job-search crises head-on, a new venue opened up during those days. I started to understand, or perhaps imagine, that my sophisticated level of English might be viewed as a scam and my intellectual output as fake, and—returning to Conrad—I might have appeared as nothing more than "an improved specimen." On more than one occasion, I have had to answer questions by "well-meaning" Israeli academics about whether I am the first person in my village or in my family to receive a PhD and so on. Such questions position me in an

Orientalist Israeli discourse of "pioneering" Arab citizens—the first Arab beauty queen in Israel, the first Arab winner of the Israeli version of *MasterChef*, the first Arab minister in an Israeli government, the first Arab lecturer of literature in an Israeli English Department, and, perhaps sooner than we might expect, the first Arab head of the Israeli Mossad. To some of the brightest minds in Israeli academia, I was conspicuously the first member of my village or extended family to have earned a doctoral degree.

Certainly, I had never felt straightforwardly comfortable in my Arab skin. However, growing up in Copenhagen and eventually settling down in Tarshiha did not develop the rashes I procured in Jerusalem. My constant outsider status, my "exotic roots," and my "color" were now partaking in a vicious political narrative that required I radically reassess my identity. I could no longer merely indulge in my Danish cultural tastes. Rather, I became conscious of the second-generation immigrant character framing those tastes. My belonging to the Arab minority in Israel could no longer be separated from the history of this minority's relationship to the Israeli establishment and its relationship to other Palestinian communities. Rather, I started to comprehend its political character and understand that the future of this relationship is all but simple. And finally, viewing my decision to settle down in Tarshiha as some kind of successful story of returning to the roots has completely dissolved. My occasional estrangement to local customs and deep dislike of familial, sectarian, homophobic, and misogynistic attitudes toward almost everything between earth and sky have also brought me face-to-face with my "otherness" among my own.

Notwithstanding the complexities of how I (still) struggle to identify, Kreisler's words cut through loud and clear. My childhood summer vacation playground, my parents' village where my wife grew up and where I am raising my children—my home today—were "enfeebled," "wretched," and "even dangerous" before *he* arrived in 1989?! Tarshiha had been part of that "blank space" in the north of Israel until the government implemented its plan to "Judaize the Galilee"—a cornerstone of the Zionist project. My so-called roots belonged in that "dangerous" region where aunts, uncles, and cousins welcomed me to their homes every summer. Between playing soccer on the street in front of Abu and Um Shadi's house, having Manaqeesh from the clay ovens in the family yard between my uncles' homes, and devouring delicious charcoal grilled pork chops in the evening, people seemed, to me, content amid the dust and heat covering their beloved Tarshiha. But of course, back then what did I know of the "dangers" of the area. At the end of the vacation, I would always return to my safe, chilly Copenhagen, and, to be honest, going home was like returning to the real world. Tarshiha was my childhood summer vacation playground—a place of make-believe that evaporated from my mind just before returning to school in mid-August. I felt effortlessly comfortable in Denmark, since I could leave some of my Arab roots in Tarshiha and lock up the rest in our apartment on Ryesgade with my parents, and Palestine—well, at the time, Palestine was a place on Mars.

Since *Being There, Being Here* is to a great extent a study of Palestinian literature in languages other than Arabic, a personal note on language is warranted here. Arabic is unconditionally the Palestinian national language. However, for many, it is no longer their mother tongue. My own relationship with Arabic remains vexed. Today, I enjoy an advanced level of proficiency, but I still find it emotionally challenging to either write or read in Arabic. I rarely pick up an Arabic novel (despite my profession as a professor of literature) and feverishly avoid writing in Arabic. Any such direct engagement immediately brings back memories of my uphill battle learning to read and write Arabic during those early years growing up in Copenhagen. It was a battle I did not choose. It was forced upon me by my parents every evening when I had completed my Danish school homework and they would wait for me with the Arabic textbooks to teach me the basics. It was forced upon me with every lash of the cultural whip at my preference for speaking Danish at home rather than Arabic—at every transgression of the conventions of our Arab ways.

I do not believe that my relationship with the Arabic language is unique. It is telling, I think, of how second-generation immigrants relate to their parents' heritage in general. We spend a lifetime negotiating, occasionally accepting, and mostly rejecting what our parents represent. I have yet to meet someone who has not stood next to their parents at some supermarket, embarrassed while listening to them speak in the local foreign language that is native to their children. In addition to language, my rebellion against my parents' heritage became most vocal during epic arguments over food. While I have always adored my mother's *mujadarrah*, *mloukhieh*, and *maqloobeh*, I constantly made sure to express my preference for the Danish cuisine in reply to her lectures of how much better and healthier the Arabic one was in comparison to anything else in the world. My biases against everything Arab became increasingly radical. I wanted to assimilate. As far as I was concerned, I was already Danish—although with the "exotic" twist—while my parents offered what seemed to me the option to be an immigrant. At the time, I was completely ignorant of the ongoing public discussions about defining "Danishness" and the general notion that "brown skin" could never become genuinely Danish. In my uncompromising adolescent battles against my parents, it was "me" against "them." Although I today live in Tarshiha with my family and my parents have by now retired and moved back here as well, I cannot honestly claim that these battles have ended. They may be different in character, but the substance of our constant arguments remains more or less the same, and I, today a middle-aged man, adamantly continue to express my preference for everything Danish and dislike for everything Arab in their presence.

My family and I frequently go to visit my former homeland. My sons and my wife do not speak a word of Danish—except for sometimes intentionally mispronouncing things they hear me say for the purpose of making fun of me—yet they have developed a bond with the place and generally look forward to our trips. I selfishly enjoy adding this dimension to my sons' upbringing, in the hope that they will grow up to become less localized individuals and better prepared for our increasingly globalized world (with a twist of some Nordic culture). However, I also recognize as we walk through the streets of Copenhagen that the place no longer houses the notion of home for who I have become in Israel. I am still intimately familiar with every minute detail and nostalgically savor the smells emitted from the butchers and bistros. I make it a ritual to walk to the local bakery in the morning to pick up *Politiken*, a *spandauer*, and a coffee. I enjoy shopping for Danish groceries in the local Netto, but I am also aware that my head is elsewhere at this point in my life. At the end of our trip, we return to Israel, to Tarshiha, to the awful "Nation-State Law," back to claim our position in the Arab minority among those individuals who miraculously managed to survive and stay on their land despite impossible odds in 1948.

The point of describing this journey is not to present a coming-of-age narrative and declare that I have finally arrived—to the contrary. My national sentiments remain compromised. Surely, I would like to see the end of the siege on Gaza, the occupation of the West Bank, and the discriminatory policies toward Arabs in Israel. I would also like to see refugees return and reclaim their homes, although I doubt that these homes may still house the notion of home for the majority of today's refugees and their descendants. However, these positions are not definitively Palestinian, insofar as many—not necessarily Palestinians—would support them. Personally, the only flag I own is a rolled-up Dannebrog, hidden away on the shelf in my kids' room. I still prepare various versions of *smørrebrød*, cook a delicious *flæskesteg* for Christmas, and keep my stash of Piratos licorice safely locked away for my own private enjoyment. I still follow the news in Denmark and am excited whenever I receive anything from my former homeland. The purpose of this preface is to explain that the writing of this book is motivated by the idea of creating room in the Palestinian story for people like myself. Although my experience is that of a second-generation immigrant, I am confident that other different itineraries of displacement have led to the development of similar liminal identities that need to be incorporated into the Palestinian context.

My modest library in Tarshiha somewhat represents these sensitivities. Erez Kreisler would perhaps be relieved (or not) to know that it does not solely hold titles in Arabic. In this "enfeebled, wretched, even dangerous region," there exists a private book collection composed of titles in languages that he would probably consider less unsettling. In addition to the Hebrew, Arabic, and Danish (as well as other Nordic languages), the majority of the books are in English—my language of profession. It is a far cry from Jorge Luis Borges's universal library, but kind of reminiscent of Mustafa Saeed's—from Tayeb Salih's *Mawsim 'al-Hijrah 'ila 'al-Shamal* (*Season of Migration to the North*, 1966)—in the village of Wad Hamid next to the Nile in northern Sudan. Hidden away, far from the Israeli reality comprising the kibbutzim, the moshavs, and the developmental cities in the Galilee, in a lonely house on the south side of the Mujahed hill in Tarshiha, situated among olive groves and sheep, this collection of books represents not only my personal story but also those stories of Palestinians and their descendants today residing in different locations around the globe. Adding to the titles that reflect my training in English and American modernist literature and Lacanian psychoanalysis, names such as Naomi Shihab Nye, Diana Abu Jaber, Nathalie Handal, Susan Muaddi Darraj, Randa Jarrar, Ibrahim Fawal, Selma Dabbagh, Lina Meruane, Mischa Hiller, and Ahmad Mahmoud—among so many others—have authored texts that more or less express my predicaments regarding identity in ways that Arabic texts could not sufficiently do. This book is about our Palestine(s).

Acknowledgments

Being There, Being Here, like most books before it, would of course not have been possible without the support and contributions of colleagues, family, and friends. So many helped shape the ideas of *Being There, Being Here*—some by taking the actual time to read and generously comment on drafts of the manuscript and others by debating its ideas or sharing their own at conferences and workshops. I don't think there was a moment when I was not writing this book during these various encounters, and I will always be indebted to them for making this book into what it is today. However, surprisingly—yet perhaps not so surprisingly—I have been constantly dreading and, thus postponing, the writing of acknowledging my vast debts to so many people. It is not because I wish to ignore or dismiss some of these contributions. Rather, from the outset of this project, I understood that there would come a moment when I had to officially come to terms with the contradictions of being an Arab in Israel and of being a Palestinian scholar in the Israeli academia.

How is it possible to write a book on Palestinian literature and culture within the framework of Israeli academic institutions and accept fellowships and grants from Israeli research organizations while millions of Palestinians still live in refugee camps or under the Israeli military occupation or in exile? How might I accept that the academic institutions that have in the first place made my career possible present me—and my fellow Arab academics across Israeli universities (we seem to occupy between 1 and 3 percent of senior positions)—as proof of Israel's "unquestionable" democratic character while they remain committed to substantiating an exclusivist Zionist agenda (lately also, in the wake of the horrible "Nation-State Law")? The truth is that I live with these questions (and many more) every day, and I am unable to offer a satisfying answer to any of them. This quandary is, I guess, my—along with more than 1.5 million Arab citizens in Israel—Palestinian predicament. However, notwithstanding this predicament, I am also aware that I am unable to deny the debt that I have accumulated over the years to the institutions that supported this project and to the many people whose invaluable insights and support have made *Being There, Being Here* what it is today.

The story of this book begins in the spring of 2014 while in New York City for a conference and David Shulman, sitting in Jerusalem, interviewing me over Skype for a much-coveted Martin Buber postdoctoral position at the Hebrew University. In hindsight, I don't think my academic career in Israel would have been possible if I had not won that fellowship. I will always be indebted to Professor Shulman for giving me this opportunity that literally changed my life. I also wish to thank Ruth HaCohen and Yigal Bronner (Shulman's successors as the directors of the Buber Society) and Yael Baron (the former program coordinator) for turning the Buber Society into a thriving academic home while we (my fellow postdocs and myself) were still learning the ropes. The early chapters of this book were written there, in the Martin Buber Society of Fellows at the Hebrew University, while in dialogue with colleagues and friends. The many lunches and coffees on campus and over the counter in the office kitchen with Eitan Grossman, Assaf Nativ, Liat Hasenfratz, Yoni Moss, Shai Secunda, Orit Gazit, Nitzan Rothem, Antonio Kalatzis, Daphne Oren-Megidor, Jan Kühne, Jose Maria Sanchez de Leon Serrano (better known as Chema), and Tawfiq Da'adli, chatting about life, careers, and family, were personally gratifying and shaped many of my ideas about Palestinian literature and culture in ways that I won't dare to try to describe here. I am especially grateful for the friendships with Ruthie Abeliovich and Nadeem Karkabi, who are today also my colleagues at the University of Haifa. At the Hebrew department a cool place. I especially wish to thank Zoe Beenstock for constantly reading, commenting, and offering advice on different parts of the manuscript and last, but not least, Ayelet Ben Yishai, a dear friend who has been a tireless mentor—reading, commenting on, and discussing my work as well as constantly challenging me to always aim an inch higher.

To end, I want to express my gratitude for the friendships of Nabil Armaly, Norma Musih, Manar Makhoul, Ella Elbaz, Hans Shakur, Shadi Roahana, Nahum Karlinsky, Shuli Barzilai, Bashir Abu Manneh, Talia Trainin and Gabi Lanye; you've probably heard more than enough about the contents of this book. And last, there is nothing I can write here that will adequately describe my wife Rasha's boundless support and love all those years. This book is her second with me, and she, more than anyone, understands the kind of labor that has gone into this project—my partner in the journey of life and intellectual discovery. Finally, I want to dedicate *Being There, Being Here*, to my sons, Jude, Rai, and Maas. I hope this one will make you proud.

Parts of the following were published in *Interventions: International Journal of Postcolonial Studies* 19, no. 2 (2017); *Comparative Literature* 69, no. 2 (2017); *Ot* 7 (Spring 2018); and *Journal of Postcolonial Writing* 55, no. 5 (2019). Many thanks to the editors for granting me the permissions to reuse some of the material in the publication of this book. Also, many thanks to the Israel Science Foundation for supporting this research.

Being There, Being Here

Introduction

> To listen to the world now is to wake up from a romantic enchantment whose spell cast human subjects into vessels of one language, made language seem almost identical to nation, and made nation practically indistinguishable from state. . . . But today, *home* means not a here but a there, somewhere else.
>
> —Doris Sommer, "Language, Culture, and Society"

In 2009, twelve years after the publication of Palestinian poet Mourid Barghouti's acclaimed prose work *Ra'aytu Ramallah* (*I Saw Ramallah*, 1997), describing the poet's first-time visit to his hometown, Deir Ghassanah, after more than two decades of exile, he published the sequel, *Wulidtu Hunak, Wulidtu Huna* (*I Was Born There, I Was Born Here*).[1] Barghouti tells the story of his second visit and of his son Tamim's rite of passage. Barghouti narrates Tamim's transition from a second-generation refugee who grows up inside his father's memories of the homeland into a Palestinian who returns for a short period, ironically as a tourist, to claim his identity card. While meditating on this ceremonial initiation and gradually heading toward his place of birth, Barghouti's narrative frequently moves back to the moments of Tamim's birth, twenty years earlier, in Cairo. He anticipates the moment when he will be able to tell his son, upon arriving at his parents' former house, that he himself "was born *here*," instead of stating that he "was born *there*," as he has done for many years while in exile. At the climactic moment of being able to utter the long-awaited sentence "I was born here, Tamim" (89), Barghouti is overwhelmed by the realization of viewing his life in exile as having occurred "there" rather than "here." Like its predecessor, *I*

Saw Ramallah, I Was Born There presents a complex perspective of the exile's relationship to the idea of location, of origin, and of his diasporic existence. Barghouti insightfully mixes up the referents "there" and "here" to delineate this complexity and, as a result, offers a relevant platform for the inevitable encounter between first-generation refugees and upcoming generations of displaced Palestinians both in exile and in the homeland.

Being There, Being Here—this book—critically explores this encounter by way of reading together mainly textual and, to a lesser extent, filmic productions by Palestinians from the various locations that they have come to refer to as both "there" and "here" in the various areas both "inside" and "outside" Israel-Palestine. However, whereas Barghouti problematizes the liminal relationship of these referents in the context of his and his son's respective moments of birth in Deir Ghassanah and Cairo, I wish to make the transition from the term "born," featured in the title of Barghouti's book, to the term "being" in the title of this book. The purpose is to show that the polylingual literary branch whose establishment I intend to call forth is grounded in the idea of imagining a Palestinian homeland from a variety of positions that are not primarily dependent upon the artists' notion of birth or birthplace. "Being," in the Palestinian context, refers to the position of feeling present in a certain place ("here") while cultivating a relationship to the homeland through memories and narrations of previous generations without necessarily perceiving it as "home" ("there"). Although this relationship may appear relatively straightforward in the diasporic context, it is, as Barghouti demonstrates, far from simple. Indeed, this relationship is no less complex in local Palestinian contexts. In the case of Palestinian citizens of Israel and those individuals subject to Israel's military administration in the occupied Palestinian territories, these referents do not unconditionally attach a connotation of a "homeland" to the concept of "home." To the extent that the presence of Israeli institutions has rendered the cultural and lingual landscape relatively "strange" for the majority of both groups, displacement refers not only to the historic dispossession and mass transfer of the Palestinian population from one area to another but also to the irreversible transformation of a certain area, rendering it alien to its native population. Hence, while members of diasporic Palestinian communities may not always feel at home when visiting the homeland, those persons who have remained may probably never feel they possess a homeland in the only place they consider to be their home. My point is that meditations on being "there" or "here" problematize the positions that contemporary Palestinian authors occupy in their respective locations while writing about Palestine.

In the May 2015 issue of the online periodical *Words without Borders*, the guest editor, poet and playwright Nathalie Handal, presents a variety of works composed in languages other than Arabic by Palestinians and descendants of Palestinian refugees and immigrants from across the globe. Handal argues that the existence of these literary productions in multiple languages, of different nationalities and cultural influences, as well as of diverse aesthetics, demonstrates the ongoing dynamic and fluid character of Palestinian literature.[2] Though written in multiple languages, all these works stem from mutual memories and narrations of a lost homeland. I believe, like Handal, that it is by now plausible to ascertain that Palestinian literary productions have surmounted their circumscribed position within the Arab cultural context. The ongoing cultural diversification among displaced Palestinian communities running through several generations since 1948 (and even prior to 1948) has become conspicuous in literature because of the increasing production of Palestinian writing in Hebrew, English, Spanish, Italian, and Danish, among other languages. Up-and-coming—as well as some already established—Palestinian writers or authors of Palestinian descent who may have grown up as second- or third-generation exiles or immigrants in Western countries, or as citizens of Israel, have not, in many instances, enjoyed the choice of writing in Arabic. Rather, as a number of the authors—whose works I will focus on in this book—have remarked at some point in their careers, growing up in their respective societies, they have had to write in the language of the majority in their host nations because they were unable to write in their parents' native tongue.[3]

These authors are bringing their national heritage and personal stories into a variety of languages through different literary media. Depending on lingual and cultural contextualization, their writings engage varied political, social, and aesthetic conditions, contributing to the Palestinian national narrative while also determining its multiple prospective transnational proliferations. For example, the status of Palestinian authors in Israel differs from the status of their counterparts from Europe and the Americas. They are a special case in that they belong not to a migrant community but to the country's indigenous Arab population.[4] They enjoy citizenship under Israeli law. However, while enduring the perils of relative cultural and geographic isolation from their Palestinian counterparts "outside" Israel, they are also generally viewed as culturally and nationally inferior by the country's Jewish majority. In this context, the language of Hebrew Palestinian texts such as Anton Shammas's *Arabesqot* (*Arabesques*, 1986) or any of Sayed Kashua's novels is fueled with these political sensitivities related to both the underprivileged status of Arab citizens since the foundation of the State of Israel and the local mainstream view of these authors' "chutzpah" for making themselves comfortable in a basically Jewish language. Similarly, Anglophone Palestinian writings are inseparable from the instrumental role played by the British (territorial) Empire and the US-led (nonterritorial) powers—respectively, since the mid-eighteenth century and World War II—in shaping the history as well as the current conditions of the Israeli-Palestinian conflict, according to long-standing Orientalist discourses. Novels such as Susan Muaddi Darraj's *The Inheritance of Exile: Stories from South Philly* (2007), Randa Jarrar's *A Map of Home* (2008), and Susan Abulhawa's *Mornings in Jenin* (2010) both resist and explore this Anglophone legacy in their respective portrayals of Palestinian displacement.

In comparison, writings from Latin America differ yet again from their counterparts in Europe and North America. The majority of

Palestinian communities in Latin America were founded as a result of the waves of Arab emigration from Palestine between 1870 and 1930. Migrants were predominantly Christian merchants from the Bethlehem region, Jerusalem, Taybeh, and Ramallah who wished to escape Ottoman rule. Today's descendants of these migration waves generally belong to middle- and upper-social classes and are well represented among political and business elites (representing, for once, a "successful" Palestinian story). Consequently, they do not easily fit into the national narrative shaped by experiences of exile in the Arab world, dispossession, and life under the Israeli military occupation.[5] Writings by Palestinian-descended authors in the Spanish language such as Lina Meruane's *Volverse Palestina* (*Becoming Palestine*, 2014) or Rodrigo Hasbún's *El lugar del cuerpo* (*The Place of the Body*, 2012) cannot be separated from the cultural nuances and sensitivities that have developed over a century since the first waves of immigration from Ottoman Palestine. Furthermore, whereas Palestinian writers residing in Europe and the Americas may generally be defined as exiles or émigrés, they basically belong to historically different waves of migration. Europe and North America variedly host exiles who have escaped either the perils of Israeli occupation or the dire conditions of refugee camps in the Arab countries. Last, the narratives of recent Danish texts—such as the late Yahya Hassan's two self-titled poetry collections *Yahya Hassan* (2013) and *Yahya Hassan 2* (2019), Ahmad Mahmoud's *Sort Land: Fortællinger fra Ghettoen* (Black Nation: Stories from the Ghetto, 2015), and Abdel Aziz Mahmoud's *Hvor Taler Du Flot Dansk* (How Wonderfully You Speak Danish, 2016)—cannot be separated from contemporary public discussions on the problems of immigration, assimilation, and the "parallel societies" evolving in certain "ethnic" neighborhoods, such as Nørrebro in Copenhagen, Vollsmose near Odense, and Gellerrup at the heart of Århus. My point is that as a result of decades of displacement, the Palestinian story has—within distinct lingual and social environments—proliferated in multiple directions and, as a result, was compelled to grapple with different cultural and political conditions.

The number of Hebrew, Latinate, Anglophone, and Nordic writings by Palestinian authors began to "flourish" between the late 1980s and the second decade of the twenty-first century, following a nearly quarter-century interval since Jabra Ibrahim Jabra's pioneering and sole English novel, *Hunters in a Narrow Street* (1960), and Atallah Mansour's *Beor Hadash* (*In a New Light*, 1966)—the first Hebrew-language novel by an Israeli-Palestinian writer. Accordingly, if we look beyond the Gaza Strip and the West Bank, or the Arab diaspora, and make an in-depth analysis of literature produced in Israel and the West, it is a sine qua non condition to recognize contemporary artistic expressions of Palestinian experiences presented in languages other than Arabic alongside their Arabic counterparts. Moreover, rather than argue for the prioritization of the Arabic literary branch at the expense of another, the primary aim of this book is to explain the necessity for—and the problems of—establishing a polylingual category of Palestinian literature that could comprehend the ongoing cultural and literary implications of displacement in the various contexts "inside" and the variety of locations "outside" Israel-Palestine.

The critical move of interlacing literary productions by authors from Israel-Palestine with those works of diasporic writers is necessary in the case of Palestinian literature, since it amalgamates works that represent a diversity of deterritorialized experiences in the absence of a successful nation-building project. Rather than define literary works as Palestinian according to criteria of theme, content, language (Arabic), and the author's identity, I deem it crucial to further problematize the canon by including critical considerations for territoriality and languages other than Arabic as basic factors for the demarcation of liminal spaces of artistic creation among culturally diverse Palestinian authors in the global context. As I hope to make clear in the following chapters, the literary productions under discussion might, on the one hand, conform to a scripted national narrative that describes the history of a shared origin and the making of the Palestinian people and its culture while confronting, for centuries, the authority of various foreign occupying forces. On the other, they no longer conveniently acquiesce to this narrative's constant call for shared collective needs and ambitions. That is, this more or less immutable scripted narrative certainly stores passions of allegiance and delineates the sense of a distinct moral being across borders, but owing to the appearance of linguistically distinct Palestinian writers around the globe, its monolingual character does not adequately encompass the diversity and ambitions of literary and cultural productions in general from the various contexts of both the diaspora and the homeland.[6] The long-term implications of displacement overflow the edges of this curricular national framework and necessitate the creation of new spaces to expand the scope of Palestinian literature and cultural production (as well as the field of Palestine studies in general). Therefore, rather than develop a line of criticism based upon the political notion of an unrescinded historic injustice committed against the Palestinian people in 1948, I suggest that the critic needs to emphasize the cultural significance of the past century in order to seriously consider the consequences of displacement on the production and consumption of literature as well as cultural production in general. It is pertinent to emphasize that this critical move does not express a political (defeatist) position of "forgetting," "letting go," or "moving on"—to the contrary. My point is that given the geographical and cultural fragmentation of Palestinians since the early waves of migration to the Americas at the end of the nineteenth century and after 1948 as well as 1967, it seems critically fruitful to keep our finger on the pulse of historic progression in order to explore how Palestinian themes are evolving in these various habitats of displacement.

A contemporary demographic account of Palestinian displacement may shed light on the various contexts addressed here: at the end of 2018, the Palestinian Central Bureau of Statistics reported that approximately 80 percent of nearly 13.05 million Palestinians live nowadays within a hundred miles of the borders of historical Palestine, in or within the enclosures of the fifty-eight recognized refugee camps in the Hashemite Kingdom of Jordan, Lebanon, the (once united) Syrian Arab Republic, and the Palestinian Authority (including East Jerusalem). These geographical locations demarcate scattered communities that have framed the larger part of Palestinians' experiences up to today. Some 4.91 million reside in the West Bank and the Gaza Strip, where they have, respectively, lived under two different occupational administrations since 1948 and under Israeli and Egyptian siege since 2007. Approximately 5.85 million reside in neighboring Arab countries, of which more than 3 million live in Jordan as naturalized citizens. The rest remain relatively deprived of basic civil rights and are disallowed from purchasing land or homes and, in some cases, acquiring a proper education. In addition to these two largest branches of the dispersed Palestinian population, the remaining 20 percent—1.57 million Israeli citizens and close to 1 million exiles and immigrants around the world—are concentrated mostly in Europe and the Americas (both North and Latin Americas) and daily partake in languages and cultures other than Arabic.[7]

This current scattered state of Palestinian communities is the ongoing outcome of more than a century of displacement. Sari Hanafi, former director of the Palestinian Refugee and Diaspora Center, divides the dispersion of Palestinians into three historical phases. The first refers to the early waves of immigration that began in the late nineteenth century and continued in the early decades of the twentieth century, mainly owing to economic reasons and to evade the Ottoman military draft. Arabs of Palestine migrated, in particular, to the Americas, while a few of them moved to neighboring Arab—at the time—provinces of the Ottoman Empire. The founding of the State of Israel in 1948 perpetuated the British policy instituted during the Mandate period that disallowed these immigrants from freely returning to Palestine, turning these newly established immigrant communities into diasporic ones. The second category concerns the 1948 exodus of Palestinians who also lost their right to return to their homes. In this category, Hanafi also includes the approximately 350,000 Palestinians who left during the 1967 war and lost their residence rights by "being absent," according to an Israeli census. The third refers to recent immigration based on economic reasons that are also related to political events such as the Lebanon War in 1982, the Gulf War in 1991, the First Intifada in 1987, as well as the second one in 2001.[8] Hanafi's categories show that current dispersed Palestinian communities were mainly created or perpetuated as a direct or a long-term consequence of the events of 1948.

Yet I do not seek to contend that these events mark the destruction of a single culturally uniform Palestinian society. The initial historical context for my argument is framed by the understanding that at the time of the establishment of the State of Israel, variegated indigenous groups and traditions prevailed in the region (I refer to the entrenched multiple social and geographical affiliations, religions, and dialects prior to 1948), and the realization of the Zionist project destroyed the majority of these communities in a single stroke and irrevocably altered the few left.[9] Consequently, between 1948 and 1967, new contexts emerged and demarcated subsequent phases of the Palestinian experience: the Arab-populated areas within the Green Line became subject to martial law, the Egyptian military ruled the Gaza Strip and Jordan annexed the West Bank, while the majority of refugees were confined to the newly established United Nations Relief and Works Agency (UNRWA) camps scattered around the territories, the Jerusalem area, and neighboring Arab countries. The founding of the State of Israel did not destroy one Palestinian entity to create a single Palestinian problem, but rather marked the end of a culturally heterogeneous era and generated several fragmented contexts, as proposed by Lauren Banko and Joseph Massad, among others.[10] The historic dispersion of Palestinians and the consequent ramifications of their experiences may seemingly have dispelled the sense of cultural homogeneity—a notion that obliterates not only the cultural nuances of the currently splintered Palestinian reality but also those characteristics of the population in Palestine prior to the establishment of Israel.

Nonetheless, as Julianne Hammer contends in *Palestinians Born in Exile: Diaspora and the Search for a Homeland* (2005), despite the diversity of personal stories, Palestinians everywhere experience a ubiquitous sense of *communitas*—of belonging to one another. Certainly, Palestinians—irrespective of age and location—would relate to one another through memories (according to generation) or narrations of recent historical events, such as the Nakba as well as the Sabra and Shatila massacre of 1982, or the First and Second Intifadas in 1987 and 2000, respectively, sharing a deep sense of a mutual destiny. Or, more nostalgically, as Ghada Karmi depicts, first-generation exiles bond through the process of re-creating the geography and genealogical charts of Palestinian villages while scattered in the diaspora.[11] The claim for self-determination and the "Right of Return" are tenets embraced by Palestinians worldwide, but I believe that it is becoming increasingly important to look beyond these pillars of the national script and begin to acknowledge the developing cultural differences among Palestinian communities in order to critically comprehend the ongoing repercussions of their historic displacement. The various geographical, cultural, and social settings housing today's Palestinians have yielded multiple lifestyles and value systems based upon widely different socioeconomic conditions. Such cultural diversities call for the emergence of new venues in order to reassess and redefine the notion of a modern Palestinian (trans)national identity. Steeped in different languages and cultures other than Arabic, the more than two million Palestinians who currently reside in Israel and in the Western world at large have—through their idiosyncratic experiences—significantly expanded the definition of this identity that stems from more or less shared memories and narrations of a lost homeland.

In the following chapters, I will speculate on specific literary consequences of Palestinian displacement. Because of the authors' daily engagement in the languages of local majorities in Israel and other varied locations in the West, works stemming from these distinct contexts are commonly characterized by the authors' attempts at preserving cultural boundaries and reproducing national sentiments both against the backdrop and under the influence of external cultural elements. Another aim of my argument is to highlight several of the problems deriving from the inclusion of such exchanges (among these polylingual processes) in the national canon. To the extent that Hebrew, Latinate, Anglophone, and Nordic Palestinian literary productions may respectively present linguistically and culturally distinct narrations of deterritorialization, among other leitmotifs, they also challenge the fundamental idea of an immutable Palestinian identity that lies at the core of the national script—an unsettling crisis that largely frames the argument of this book.

Prior to the events of 1948, the development of Palestinian literature partook in the literary movements that flourished in the Arab world through cultural centers such as Cairo, Beirut, Damascus, and Baghdad. However, it is not to claim that it did not already assume a local character, addressing the political and economic crises reverberating throughout Palestine during the 1930s. Ghassan Kanafani explains in *Thawrat 36–39 Fi Filistin* (*The 1936–39 Revolt in Palestine*, 1972) that the political repercussions of the peasants' revolt in 1936 also marked a turning point in Palestinian letters. Poets such as Ibrahim Tuqan, Abu Salma, and Abdrahim Mahmoud joined the struggle and became the leading voices in the creation of what Kanafani refers to as a "popular culture," countering the alliance between British imperialism and Zionist settler-colonialism as well as the complicit Arab elites.[12] Following the suppression of the revolt in 1939 and the destruction of the multifaceted reality of Palestine in 1948, the generation of new fragmented ones necessitated the invention of new themes, motifs, and techniques.[13] During nearly two decades of collective confusion in these new contexts of displacement, and following the events of 1967 with the revival of a national consciousness across borders, intellectuals took to "arms" again and revived the Palestinian "popular culture"—this time defying a new world order that had not left room for Palestinians on the map.[14]

Mainstream Palestinian writings assumed an anticolonial tenor and variedly combined representations of a nostalgic craving for the lost homeland and renderings of the apathetic present reality of displacement with a sense of heading toward an uncertain future. On the one hand, poetry composed by distinguished literary figures such as Abu Salma, Salem Jubran, Fadwa Tuqan, Sameeh al-Qasem, and

Mahmoud Darwish established a thematic bond, rooted in nature, between people and land.[15] Such literary motifs not only emerged as a result of the exiled poets' need to romanticize their bond to the homeland, but were also inspired by a historical relationship between Palestinian peasants and their environment. As Barbara McKean Parmenter argues, although Western pilgrims and early Zionist settlers thought of the local population as backward and the general state of agriculture as poor, Palestinians cherished the fruits of their hard work and marked the end of harvest seasons with songs and joyous festivities.[16] Poets have immortalized this relationship through descriptions of, perhaps, one of the most characteristic topos: the olive tree. Enduring for hundreds of years, its fruits supporting generations of the same family, the olive tree has potently served as the ultimate symbol in a poetry reflecting the Palestinians' inextricable bond to the land.

Conversely, prose writers such as Ghassan Kanafani in *Rejaal fil-Shams* (*Men in the Sun*, 1963) and Emile Ḥabiby's *Al-Waqa'i' al-Gharib fi ikhtifa' Sa'id Abi al-Naḥs al-mutasha'il* (*The Strange Facts in the Disappearance of Saeed the Ill-Fated Pessoptimist*, henceforth *The Secret Life of Saeed the Pessoptimist*, 1974)—a masterpiece of the tragicomic—developed and connected a political consciousness to Palestinians' sense of existential futility and estrangement in the respective contexts of displacement following their historic uprooting.[17] Eventually, such literary productions have perpetuated founding principles of the national script for the dispossessed populations and facilitated a literary framework that has, since, comprehended the production of subsequent texts. During those early years, Palestinians, in their distinct situations of displacement, have craved a token of recognition from the outside world, and literature—particularly poetry—became the medium through which the dispossessed called out to the world as a people.

The publications of Kanafani's *'Adab 'al-Muqawama fi Filistin 'al-Muḥtalla, 1948–1966* (Literature of Resistance in Occupied Palestine, 1948–1966) and *Adab 'al-Filistini 'al-Muqawem taht 'al-Ehtelal, 1948–1968* (Palestinian Resistance Literature: Under

Occupation, 1948–1968) in 1968 feature as crucial documents that have established the parameters that single out Palestinian from the rest of Arabic literature in the wake of the Nakba. In the former, Kanafani describes an artistic break from the Arab world through the concepts of "exile" and "resistance" that thematically came to frame the national canon for several decades:

> After 1948, Palestinian literature succeeded in laying the foundations of a new literary movement which may be better described as the literature of Exile rather than Palestinian or Refugee literature. Poetry, the chief element of this movement, has been able during recent years to witness a remarkable progress in quality and technique. The short period of silence after the 1948 war was followed by a great awakening, and national poetry poured out reflecting the people's national fervor. It interacted with Arab and foreign literary trends and gradually broke the traditional rules of technique, rejected the old sentimental outbursts and emerged with a unique feeling of profound sadness more commensurate with the realities of the situation.[18]

Focusing on poetry, which embodies the crux of this movement, Kanafani points out that this departure in Palestinian writing is manifested through the changes that began to take place in form and technique. The employment of modern techniques bespoke a rejection of tradition that would also characterize the creation of (novel) motifs and themes that comprehend Palestinians' dire straits. Kanafani lists several literary elements that distinguish this leap: the love for a woman became an allegory for love of the homeland, satire became necessary for ridiculing the enemy and expressing a sense of bitter irony, and poetry, in general, became a configuration of pride, expressing defiance in confronting the enemy.[19]

Nonetheless, the emergence of these leitmotifs in both poetry and prose by the aforementioned poets and authors substantiated the story of a dispossessed nation, and Kanafani's concomitant meditations delineated a framework that has seemed to determine the "essence" of the Palestinian literary canon and, implicitly, compromised the possibility to include works that do not correspond thematically with literary representations of "exile" or "resistance." Ironically, although Kanafani's own works definitively represent the genre he advocates, they scarcely fit into this narrow framework, insofar as his writings connect to literary currents that transcend the particularly Palestinian as such. As Hilary Kilpatrick maintains, "Kanafani is far from being simply a politically committed author, wedded to his cause." His writings also demonstrate a deep interest in philosophy, metaphysics, and superstition, as well as Arabic literary tradition. Other more or less canonical writers also barely fit into the genre of "exile" and "resistance." Salah Hassan mentions Ghareeb Asqalani, Mahmoud Darwish, Emile Habiby, Akram Haniyyeh, Jabra Ibrahim Jabra, Sahar Khalifeh, Hisham Sharabi, Anton Shammas, and Fadwa Tuqan as only a few who foreground Arab culture, third-world solidarity, feminism, Marxism, or Islam in their Palestinian works. In *The Palestinian Novel: From 1948 to the Present* (2016), Bashir Abu Manneh, focusing on the birth of the Palestinian novel, highlights this point. He explains that the bureaucratization of the national liberation movement in the early '70s during the tenure of the Palestinian Liberation Organization (PLO) created an elitist framework ignorant of literary ambition. The political and cultural rise of the Palestinians after the Nakba was always about much more than statehood, and the Palestinian novel has emerged in the "ebb and flow of revolution." Abu Manneh warns against viewing the text exclusively through the prism of statehood, insofar as such a move would suppress "the history of revolution, modernization, and cultural renaissance." He contends that authors such as Kanafani, Jabra, Habiby, and Khalifeh composed their major works not only at a distance from the canonic national script but also as scrutinizing testimonies against its basic tropes: armed struggle and statehood.[20] In this vein, I also wish to add to this illustrious list recent Arabic-language Palestinian writers such as Adania Shibli, Raji Bathish, and Alaa Hlehel who have, through their works, headed toward aesthetically experimental destinations and significantly diverged from the national script.[21] Nonetheless, Kanafani's words—which primarily emblematize the revolutionary anti-imperialistic outlook of the PLO between 1967 and 1993—continue to resonate, to some extent, in contemporary thematic definitions of Palestinian literature.[22]

To move from theme to context, Salma Khadra Jayyusi—poet and editor of *Anthology of Modern Palestinian Literature* (1992)—regards Palestinian literature as an exclusively integral part of the modern Arabic literary canon that has, from 1948 to 1967, mainly been produced by exiles in Arab countries and residents of the occupied Palestinian territories. Eventually, the opening of the borders between the territories and Israel for the first time in the aftermath of the Six-Day War allowed for unprecedented encounters between distinct groups of Palestinians since 1948—Arabs "inside" Israel were now relatively able to establish relations with the rest of the Arab world. As a result, prominent works from Israel by authors such as Mahmoud Darwish, Sameh al-Qasem, Emile Habiby, and Tawfiq Ziad, who had previously been isolated from their counterparts across the borders, were introduced into the canon.[23] According to Jayyusi, despite geographical and political distinctions, oeuvres issuing from these three locations—the occupied Palestinian territories, neighboring Arab countries, and Israel—represent the official branches that have composed the modern Palestinian canon since the establishment of the State of Israel and the consequent dispersion of the indigenous Arab population. Israeli critic Ami Elad-Bouskila narrows down the definition to two areas: writings from Israel or abroad.[24] However, these models were presented in the 1990s, and both Jayyusi and Elad-Bouskila acknowledge the marginal position of emerging literary writings in languages other than Arabic by Palestinian authors. Owing to the scarcity of such works at the time they conducted their studies, Jayyusi may have found that their classification as a distinct category was unwarranted, whereas Elad-Bouskila, focusing on Hebrew-language writings by Arab authors, pursues the tradition of placing them exclusively within the Israeli context.

Like a number of oeuvres written in Arabic, some of the works I will focus on in the following chapters explore canonical themes, such as Palestinians' "tragic and heroic steadfastness" (Sumud), asserting faith in the ultimate triumph of justice; others variedly focus on problems of displacement (and the concomitant sense of homelessness) and the search for new ways of redefining the Palestinian heritage within local contexts while being personally haunted by memories and narrations of a spectacular "catastrophe"—the Nakba. Some texts present experiences of exile and migration within familiar cultural frameworks; others portray them in contexts that hitherto have remained alien to the majority of Palestinians who still remain in the Middle East. Moreover, to reiterate an earlier crucial point, although some of these authors may not have had an alternative, others have opted to write in the language of the local majorities rather than adopt Arabic—their own or their parents' native speech—for artistic creation. Hence, they have remained relatively obscure in the Arab world. Despite the "peripheral" status of this heterogeneous branch of Palestinian literature, my contention is that these writings are critically important, since they expand the scope of the linguistic and cultural framework, thereby making it is possible to express and interpret today's increasingly diverse Palestinian experiences.

A few notes are warranted before outlining the structure of this book. As mentioned, the Palestinian text is a political one. The question is whether it necessarily must demonstrate a kind of unconditional loyalty to the national script that seems to prioritize the story line of an unrescinded historic injustice over the distinct ongoing political and cultural consequences of this injustice in the various contexts of displacement. I believe that the relevance of studying Palestinian writings composed in languages other than Arabic is grounded in the tension between the idea of remaining loyal to a more or less fixed national narrative and the desire to understand the ongoing lingual and cultural proliferations of the Palestinian story. Insofar as the national narrative has hitherto inadequately framed the Palestinian novel to encompass the experiences of the second and third generations in manifold locations such as Chile, the United States, the United Kingdom, Denmark, Italy, and Israel, I think it is necessary to reiterate that the Palestinian story is no longer a single story (and I wonder if it ever was). It is altogether crucial to emphasize the relevance of the ongoing cultural consequences of Palestinian displacement at the expense of a seemingly static national script in order to narrow the distance between the story and its people in the various parts of Israel-Palestine and the various diasporas.

Second, defining literary productions in languages other than Arabic by Arab authors residing in Israel and the West as Palestinian literature is not a straightforward move and may expectedly raise objections, although several Anglophone works, such as Susan Abulhawa's *Morning in Jenin* and Selma Dabbagh's (UK) *Out of It* (2010) have already been unanimously defined as Palestinian. Nonetheless, to accept the inclusion of the literary works discussed here into the national canon may entail the acknowledgment that these authors have carried their Palestinian stories in different directions, severely unsettling the curricular national script because of their adopted language of artistic creation. Nonetheless, my strategy in this work is not dissimilar from the approach of Lital Levy and Allison Schachter, who define Jewish literature between local and transnational contexts. They follow—like I do—David Damrosch's suggestion of a new mode of reading that illuminates receptions of the translingual and cross-cultural circuitry of texts within new contexts. As Levy and Schachter have it, "This approach is germane to the study of minor literatures in broader world-literary contexts."[25] I also think that this approach is pertinent to the study of Palestinian literature in languages other than Arabic, which for too long has not been accessible to the Arab reader, insofar as it has not transcended its position as a minority genre.

Ruba Salih and Sophie Richter-Devroe's meditations on Palestine beyond the guiding logic of "national frames" are particularly inspirational in how they challenge the sacrosanctity of "the cause" and dispel metaphors of rootedness. Such critical moves are called for in the study of the polylingual Palestinian literary category, insofar as we recognize that the long-term implications of displacement running through several generations transgress the curricular national framework and that it is crucial to invent new spaces for expanding the scope of Palestinian writings. Following Salih and Richter-Devroe's line of logic, I suggest that our reading of such literary developments must transcend the national syntax of the postcolonial context and account for today's—to borrow Liisa Malkki's concept—"new awareness of the global social fact" to seriously consider the ongoing repercussions of Palestinian displacement.[26] Similar to Salih and Richter-Devroe, I identify the possible ideological fissures of this strategy. It is not my intention to ignore Israel's consistent procedures for oppressing Palestinians and appropriating Palestinian land for the purpose of celebrating a postmodern free-floating notion of diaspora narratives—on the contrary. I recognize the violent "fragmentation and deterritorialization of Palestinian nationhood" as an ongoing process that constitutes the proliferation of Palestinian experiences.[27] The concept of homeland remains inextricable to Palestinian experiences notwithstanding generation and location, but, as my argument in *Being There, Being Here* suggests, it may—or can no longer—straightforwardly house the notion of home for those Palestinians who were born and raised in a world where the state of Palestine has yet to come into existence.

Yet whereas a majority of the texts I discuss here by and large uniformly adhere to a political context based on the historic injustices committed against Palestinians, the intention is to unsettle this relationship for the purpose of yielding further possibilities of reading the Palestinian literary text. For instance, the aim of discussing the concept of "return" in the final chapter is not to question the legitimacy of the national principle of the Palestinians' "Right of Return," but rather to problematize it in order to demonstrate that matters are not as simple as they may have seemed during the early decades following the Nakba. Neither do I intend to discuss the historic settler-colonial foundations of the Zionist project, insofar as it is the present ostensibly unified State of Israel in opposition to the current demographic fragmentation of Palestinians that frames my argument. The Israeli presence in Palestinian consciousness is not a one-dimensional other. Rather, different contexts present different projections of this presence. For example, whereas Palestinian exiles in New York City may coexist with their Israeli-born Jewish neighbors on fairly equal terms, the experiences of their Israeli-citizen Palestinian compatriots are framed by an Israeli reality that is largely unknown to exiles. My key point is that the creation of multiple fragmented contexts of displacement since 1948 has led to multiple developments of the Palestinian story. The intention of this book is to bring these developing story lines into a challenging and fruitful dialogue.

The first and second chapters of this book are theoretically based and describe the relation between the local and transnational axes of the polylingual framework. In these chapters, I explore the multiple literary itineraries of Palestinian displacement across generations through a variety of writings in Hebrew, Danish, and English. In the first chapter, I explain the cultural significance of Palestinian writings in languages other than Arabic as minority literatures in their respective contexts. Drawing on the theories of Gilles Deleuze and Felix Guattari's minor literature, I show how these texts distinctively bring narrations of a shared national and cultural heritage into local mainstream through different gateways. The first part of this chapter will focus on the Danish and Israeli contexts. In the second part, I draw on Françoise Lionnet and Shu-mei Shih's theory of "minor transnationalism," as well as the globalization theories of Paul Jay, Simon Gikandi, Arjun Appadurai, and Jan Nederveen Pieterse, in order to set in motion a polylingual process of transnational intertextuality through these Palestinian minority writings in a contemporary global context. My point is to connect distinct lingual and cultural streams in localized Palestinian literatures in their respective searches for new ways to examine and reimagine their people's plight both locally and globally.

The aim of the following chapter is twofold: First, it investigates the development of the Anglophone branch of Palestinian literature. Second, focusing on Palestinian American authors Susan Abulhawa's and Susan Muaddi Darraj's novels, this chapter explores representations of future Palestinian generations in English-language literary texts. The choice to focus on these authors' works is primarily based on the contention that they represent distinct imaginings of the cross-generational implications of Palestinian displacement in the US context. While Abulhawa maintains the tenor of third-world anticolonial discourses in her writings, Darraj's novels generate new challenging cosmopolitan dimensions to the Palestinian narrative. However, this encounter between the unfulfilled national voice and the language of the former colonizer is not straightforward. The instrumental roles played by the British Empire and the United States in shaping the history and today's circumstances of the Israeli-Palestinian conflict structure the ways that Palestinian narratives are formulated in the English language.

The remaining chapters focus on specific thematic cruxes that reveal these ongoing literary consequences of Palestinian displacement in Israel-Palestine, Europe, and the Americas. Chapter 3 critically examines the unique literary trope in Palestinian literature of Arab characters who, under unusual circumstances, impersonate or literally acquire Israeli Jewish identities. My analysis focuses on linguistically distinct texts such as Susan Abulhawa's English-language *Mornings in Jenin* (2010), Sayed Kashua's Hebrew-language *Goof Sheni Yaheed* (*Second Person Singular*, 2010), and Ghassan Kanafani's Arabic *'Aed Illa Haifa* (*Returning to Haifa*, 1969) against the backdrop of poetic and philosophical meditations on the relationship between Jews and Arabs by distinguished literary figures such as Mahmoud Darwish and Anton Shammas. This chapter specifically demonstrates how the consequences of historic displacement impact Palestinian authors' diverse imaginings of the other through projections of Arab and Jewish motherhood, as well as ponders the meaning of experiencing the Jewish Arab conflictive reality through the eyes of adversarial counterparts.

The fourth chapter turns to Randa Jarrar's novel (US) *A Map of Home* (2008) and Maysaloun Hammoud's (Israel) film *Bar Bahar* (*In Between*, 2017) for the purpose of exploring how the sexualization of the female body in fictional representations of Palestinian women unsettles conventional discourses on their participation in the nation and opens new venues for rethinking gender politics in the national framework. Jarrar and Hammoud confront the mutually exclusive challenges of liberation and traditionalism while maintaining conflictual sentiments regarding cultural and social practices in the homeland and in the diaspora. In sexualizing the Palestinian woman through their respective fictional works, they alter her role as the maternal symbol of the nation and allow her the privileges of choice, enjoyment, and empowerment.

The final chapter presents an extended discussion of texts by Palestinian writers and intellectuals who took advantage of the Oslo climate during the 1990s and seized the opportunity to visit the homeland and those works composed by recent "returnees" who arrived in Israel-Palestine following the eruption of the Second Intifada in 2000. I open with a discussion of the history of the concept of *al-awdah* (return) in the formation of a national consciousness since the early waves of immigration from Palestine to the Americas until its current manifestation that came about as a result of the Nakba in 1948. Although contemporary Palestinian pilgrimages to the homeland seem to virtually fulfill a basic national desire, they also represent a token for cultural distinction among today's various Palestinian communities vis-à-vis the notion of Palestine and of who Palestinians have become in exile.

Last, I wish to comment on the title and the structure of *Being There, Being Here* in order not to mislead the reader. First of all, it will become clear that my argument does not solely focus on written texts as suggested in the title but also concentrates on visual ones. My readings of Palestinian writings will be extensively fused with analyses of Palestinian film. It might, therefore, appear as if the argument of this book focuses on cultural production in general rather than exclusively on literature. However, although the polylingual framework I call forth might certainly comprehend productions of various media, in *Being There, Being Here* its design will primarily address my requirements for literary analysis. Second, from the outset, I have expressed an interest in focusing on Palestinian writings in languages other than Arabic. While this goal will remain my primary interest, I do not think it is possible to seriously discuss Palestinian writings without considering writings in Arabic. It is, therefore, only expected that we read non-Arabic texts along with the Arabic ones to present a comprehensive overview of Palestinian letters. At the end, I think it is necessary to clarify that the following chapters mainly focus on Anglophone and Hebrew productions and less on Arabic, Danish, and Spanish. The reason for this structural imbalance is the quantitative surge in Anglophone Palestinian novels and memoirs published in the past two decades. This branch of Palestinians literature has superseded any other branch (even Arabic), and I have therefore found it important to emphasize how this particular development has influenced the proliferation of cultural production. However, I do not wish to make it appear as if the polylingual framework presents a platform for bringing Palestinian productions in different languages into dialogue on unequal footing. Although the situation, so far, is that less has been written and produced in Spanish, Danish, Italian, and so on (whereas Palestinian writers in English and Hebrew have been more prolific), this balance might change in the future, and the aim of the book is to demonstrate the potential and importance of the polylingual framework for accurately assessing the dynamic condition of Palestinian cultural production in the global context.

1

Palestinian Writings in the World

A Polylingual Literary Category

> The dispossessed, diasporic nature of Palestinian existence means that Palestinians are writing not just in different languages (English, Hebrew and French as well as Arabic), but that they are also representing different accents, experiences and outlooks.
>
> —Selma Dabbagh, quoted in "A Conversation with Selma Dabbagh" by Lindsey Moore

The purpose of presenting a polylingual analytical framework is twofold. First, it presents a critical space that allows for the exploration of cultural heterogeneity of writings in languages other than Arabic by Palestinians in Israel, Europe, and the Americas under the auspices of corporate and imperial homogeneity in today's globalized world. Second, this category will, hopefully, generate critical possibilities that challenge the established tendency to consider these texts as rooted exclusively in localized cultural and lingual contexts, disavowing an interconnectedness across borders, languages, and generations. For delineating the theoretical perimeters of this analytical approach, it is primarily necessary to recognize the bilateral character of Hebrew, Latinate, Anglophone, and Nordic Palestinian writings. Namely, the polylingual framework is constituted by both local and transnational axes. The *local* axis accounts for the minority status of Palestinian writings in the respective locations of production. Palestinian texts variedly portray the experiences of indigenous, ethnic, or immigrant Palestinian communities in relation to the "host nation." The *transnational* axis accounts for analyses of transnational intertextuality across political and linguistic borders. These very texts also portray experiences of displacement, exile, and diaspora in relation to the notion of a homeland. The local and transnational axes of the polylingual category intersect at a point that brings together various contexts framing Palestinian writings in the world today, necessitating the fashioning of a relational analytic strategy that would enable exploration of their similarities and distinctions. Ultimately, the aim of this twofold strategy is to reveal the global proliferation of Palestinian writings from the various locations across the globe.

This chapter is divided into three parts. In the first section, I focus on the issue of language in the postcolonial context in order to examine how works written in tongues other than Arabic qualify as a literary canon that originally developed from the Arabic literary tradition. Certainly, this phenomenon is not entirely unique to the peripheral branches of Palestinian literature in languages other than Arabic. Following more than a century of French colonial rule, several North African and Lebanese writers, such as Tahar Ben Jelloun and Amin Maalouf, have controversially adopted the French language for artistic production, rather than Arabic or other local languages. Although I do not intend to survey these writings here, I relate to several critics' opposing positions vis-à-vis Arab Francophone literary experiences as a framework for my own discussion. In the second part, I draw on Gilles Deleuze and Felix Guattari's theory of "minor literature" to define certain characteristics of works written in languages other than Arabic by Palestinian authors who artistically explore the implications of displacement. By and large, these authors belong to indigenous, exiled, or immigrant Arab minorities. Nonetheless, they write in the language of the majority, thus respectively introducing their minority discourse into the local mainstream culture. The final section of the chapter explains how recent global dynamics have linked works by Palestinians from various areas in the West with those works by authors who have remained in Israel-Palestine and write in Hebrew, ultimately setting in motion a (trans) national, polylingual literary process. I demonstrate the limitations of Deleuze and Guattari's theory and the need to supplement the concept of "minor literature" with recent discussions of the cultural consequences of globalization for the study of transnational Palestinian literature. Since critics rarely assess these writings beyond their respective local contexts, my aim is to bring them together and classify the works under a single category that can account for both their minority status and their transnational relations.

It is pertinent to add a note regarding my use of the term "minority" in reference to Palestinians in Israel, since it delineates a political outlook rather than a mere adherence to facts on the ground. As outlined in the previous chapter, approximately 4.5 million Palestinians reside in the occupied territories, while nearly 1.57 million Arabs live inside the Green Line as Israeli citizens. With approximately 300,000 Palestinian residents in Arab East Jerusalem, the total number of Palestinians currently inhabiting the area we refer to as Israel-Palestine amounts to around 6.48 million—a population size that roughly equals the number of Jews living in this region. Therefore, rather than demarcate majority and minority groups according to political divisions of the area, de facto, approximately 13 million people live in Israel-Palestine, and the demographic division between Arabs and Jews is nearly equivalent. However, I do not seek to claim that the displacement of Israel's Palestinian citizens is similar to the dislocation of their counterparts in the West Bank or the Gaza Strip; whereas the former are still an (unacknowledged) national minority, the latter have endured the rule of different military administrations since 1948. Furthermore, as long as the two-state solution remains on the agenda, this division continues to be relevant, since the various Palestinian groups in the area will confront distinct political realities regarding their status. If the idea of a binational state or a system of confederates should become the consensus, the term "minority" will no longer properly describe the reality of any Palestinian group in Israel-Palestine. As for the present study, at this point in history when, despite the current dire political climate consistently undermining the establishment of a sovereign Palestinian state and

President Trump announcing the United States' recognition of Jerusalem as the capital of Israel on December 6, 2017, the two-state solution continues to surface. In light of the above, I will, therefore, allow myself to refer to Israel's Arab citizens as a minority. My point is not to endorse one political vision over another but to highlight the daily engagement with and participation of this particular community in Israeli "culturalization" for the past seven decades.[1] Their familiarity with the Israeli landscape, as well as their command of the Hebrew language, has set them apart from other Palestinian communities in ways that are fundamentally relevant to a comparative study of Palestinian literatures.

On Language and Nationalism

The argument of this book raises a particularly problematic question: If literature is rooted in language, and language is a *differentia specifica* of national distinction, is it a legitimate critical move to identify Hebraic, Latinate, Anglophone, and Nordic literary productions as "Palestinian"? I believe so. A polylingual branch of Palestinian literature may seem seditious in relation to canonical writings in Arabic, since it seems to betray the very idea of the endurance of the Palestinian identity. My point is that language is certainly a defining element in the fashioning of a national identity. However, in the absence of an independent and functional national home, so is its gradual loss for second- and third-generation exiles or immigrants in the West—particularly for Palestinians in Latin American countries—or its political marginalization for Palestinian citizens of Israel.

The purpose of this section is to show how distinct literary productions in languages other than Arabic written by Palestinians—or authors of Palestinian descent—definitively represent developing cultural nuances in Israel-Palestine and in the diaspora. Critical controversies surrounding Francophone writings by Algerian authors have set a precedent in the discussion of identifying literary productions based on the languages adopted for artistic creation.[2] Certainly, there should be reservations regarding the application of the Algerian

Francophone framework to the particular branch of Palestinian literature I discuss here. First and foremost, the former emerged as a result of a long-standing colonial experience that ended with Algeria's independence in 1962, whereas the latter came about as a reaction to decades of international attempts to exclude Palestinians from the right of self-representation. Furthermore, it is pertinent to point out the different character of the British mandatory rule in Palestine and the French colonial sway in Algeria. The British-style system of education established for the local Arab population during the temporary mandatory administration in Palestine following World War I did not share the French colonial policy of assimilation, as it had for many decades in the West Indies, Africa, and the Indian subcontinent.[3] Its curriculum aimed to domesticate the local population by focusing on "pragmatic" topics—such as hygiene and sanitation—rather than culture.[4] The French, however, pursued a different policy in Algeria and its other colonial administrations in the Middle East and North Africa. As Geoffrey Nash explains, the French derived their policy from the notion of *mission civilisatrice*, in the expectation that a local class would emerge among the colonized that was "Francophile in taste and culture and predisposed towards French colonial rule."[5] These different conditions of British and French colonial policies in Palestine and Algeria led to substantially different local attitudes regarding the language of the colonizer and should not be overlooked when we engage in the critical controversies surrounding Algerian Francophone writings.

To begin with, Yasir Suleiman's essay "The Betweenness of Identity: Language in Trans-national Literature" (2006) surveys contesting positions regarding Francophone Algerian literary productions in the Arab world that may serve as a useful framework for developing a polylingual category in the Palestinian canon. Challenging the national legitimacy of Hebraic, Latinate, Anglophone, and Nordic Palestinian writings, I shall turn to Suleiman's reference to the renowned Egyptian novelist and critic Edwar al-Kharrat, who does not regard the identity of a literary work as inseparable from the author's choice of language for artistic production.[6] According to al-Kharrat, language determines the lexical, semantic, and intertextual ethos and vision of the literary production. Invoking the lexical similarity between *qalb* (core, essence, content) and *qaleb* (template, form, shape), al-Kharrat maintains that form determines content—that is, *qaleb* supersedes *qalb*. Drawing on his expertise in both Arabic and French literary traditions, al-Kharrat also alludes to Algerian writer Malek Haddad's promulgation that French is his exile. He interprets this statement as the author's admission of belonging not to the modern canon of Arabic literature but rather to a tradition of Francophone works of exile. Al-Kharrat does not deem it possible to preserve the Arab essence of idiomatic and fossilized expressions when transferred into French or any other language. Meanings are inevitably lost in relation to the Arabic language, while new meanings emerge in the acquired language.[7]

At the other end of the spectrum stands Mahmud Qasim, whose perspective is poised in diametrical opposition to al-Kharrat's. According to Qasim, Francophone writings by Arab authors should not be considered French literature—the language of a literary text does not define the literary identity of its author. He argues that content ranks higher than form (that is, he values *qalb* over *qaleb*) and that it is voice, settings, characters, and the worldviews presented in the text that determine identity. Even if Qasim's argument may seem a reversal of al-Kharrat's, the dependence upon a third element should not be overlooked. Adding a further dichotomy to the distinction between *qalb* and *qaleb*, Qasim prioritizes the national or ethnic identity of the author. Although Suleiman regards this shift from product to author as an ontological transgression, he still maintains that the identities of these two domains are inextricably intertwined. As Suleiman observes, the ambiguity in the meaning of the word *Arabī*, referring to both "Arab" and "Arabic," leaves Qasim's argument open for two interpretations. Qasim seems to favor the former—prioritizing *qalb* over *qaleb*—that is, he endorses the development of an Arab literary category rather than of Arabic. According to Qasim, as well as al-Kharrat, the author's ethnic or national identity is not inseparable from the identity of the literary work.

Nonetheless, it is legitimate to ask if it ought to be prioritized. If the answer is negative, it follows that the author's identity is secondary to the identity of the literary work, and language remains the litmus test that sifts the works that should be included from the ones that ought to be excluded from the canon. If the answer is affirmative, then literary canons may include writings in different languages, insofar as their authors come from an apposite background. I believe that although al-Kharrat's position is widely accepted in the Arab world, Qasim's stance may partly represent the current increasingly hybridized cultural experiences in postcolonial contexts.

However, Suleiman points to a mutual problem in Qasim's and al-Kharrat's arguments: both critics refer to the issue of literary identity in absolute terms—that is, they regard literature as *either* French *or* Arabic.[8] Neither addresses or invokes Homi Bhabba's idea of "the third space" in *The Location of Culture* (1994), to further develop an already complex issue made manifest in the problematic areas of literary production in the "postcolony."[9] Suleiman contends that Qasim and al-Kharrat may have consciously eschewed the idea of literary hybridization lest they provoke controversies of "cultural bastardy or treason" or incite heavily charged connotations of "political, economic, and cultural hegemony" associated with the French colonial rule.[10] He does refer to other critics, such as Ghalib Ghanim and Amin Malak, who add creative dimensions to the discussion—in their focus on literary heterogeneity in postcolonial Lebanon and Egypt—but concludes that literary classification cannot be performed without exercising some level of reservation. Countering Edward Said's rhetorical question "Who cares about the labels of national identity anyway?" Suleiman both acknowledges the increasing influence of the Arab diaspora and regards Arabic as an indigenous and dominant language that should not entirely go unacknowledged in defining the identity of a literary work in the Arab context.[11] This ambiguous position does not leave the problem of classifying a literary text free of contradictions.

Nonetheless, turning to Hilary Kilpatrick, Suleiman finds a sensible framework that acknowledges the equal importance of both language and content but also propounds systems of individual assessment in defining the identity of a text. That is to say, Kilpatrick's model both respects the integrity of a literary text in its own right and relates it to the context of the author's corpus of works, thereby granting it a bilateral identity.[12] However, the balance—Kilpatrick argues—between language and content in critics' classification of the identity of a text must be evaluated individually. In some instances, the language of the text supersedes content; in others, content takes precedence, depending on critical contextualization. Such flexibility, I think, is fruitful in identifying literary texts, but I also agree with Suleiman that although Kilpatrick's argument offers a sensible model, serious criticism will continue to defy "neat and contradiction-free classification."

Bilateralism might effectively characterize the conceptual framework for the dual status of the Palestinian text. Certainly, the critical and artistic value of language and content varies in both Arabic and non-Arabic Palestinian writings. However, such variations, I argue, depend upon the different positions of the respective texts along the local and transnational axes of the polylingual framework. As I shall demonstrate in the following section, representations of themes that might seem to be related exclusively to a particular local context—owing to the geographical location and language of creation—should also be pitted against relatively similar configurations in texts emerging from other Palestinian contexts of displacement. Such a critical move requires a systematic mode of reading that primarily acknowledges the different political problems that the respective authors grapple with when opting to write in local languages. Second, it also brings together linguistically distinct literary productions by Palestinian authors from these respective contexts and sets in motion polylingual processes of intertextuality that both demonstrate the increasing cultural diversities among present-day Palestinians and their continuing but varied commitments to the pillars of the national narrative.

My point is that it is critically crucial to come to terms with the fact that Palestinian writings have never been composed in an autonomous Arabic context. Insofar as different parts of Palestine, in the past century alone, were subjected to the rule of different governments, it is important to recognize that Palestinian writings were always composed in subordinate contexts. World War I ended four centuries of Ottoman rule and kicked off the British Mandate rule that would last for three decades, and, as mentioned in the introduction, the realization of the Zionist project in 1948 created new contexts that would demarcate subsequent phases of the Palestinian experience. That is to say, Palestinian writings have always existed under some form of foreign administration: Ottoman, British, or Israeli. Moreover, to borrow Edward Said's term, it has always been "out of place"—variedly shaped by experiences of dispossession, military occupation or siege, as well as itineraries of exile or immigration. Consequently, Palestinian writings in various languages, including Arabic, have in many contexts configured as minority literature and have had to carry a variety of citizenships—Israeli, European, American, and so forth.

The Local and Transnational Axes in Today's Globalized World

Following decades of displacement, with the increasing availability of the World Wide Web, it appears that the Palestinian nation has bonded online. Palestinians everywhere are connecting through online social networking and digital communication, developing virtual matrices of solidarity that have seemingly brought their scattered communities closer. By virtue of the "global village" phenomenon, they share genealogical charts, historic and current photographs of their respective villages, and general daily updates about "home" and "diaspora," both narrating and partaking in various ideological scripts (political, cultural, and national, among others) of local lives and imagined ones of those persons living elsewhere.[13] Although most exiles of the older generation have not seen their childhood homes since 1948 or 1967, and the younger generation may only imagine the "homeland," based on their parents' and grandparents' narrations, these virtual spaces have, nonetheless, developed the "illusion of simultaneity" (to borrow Pnina Werbner's term), prompting a sense of sharing in events of their native places from afar—expanding, thus, Benedict Anderson's conception of the "imagined community."[14] Under "normal" circumstances, the internet presents new possibilities for acquiring and disseminating information that may challenge the authority of state-funded media, as evinced during the "Arab Spring" across several Arab nations. Rather than assimilate into disappearance in their respective locations, or fall prey to the homogenizing forces of globalization, in the Palestinians' (paradoxical) case, it is precisely because of their stateless(ness) and demographically fragmented condition that online social networking has fostered the future generations' awareness of their heritage, thus enhancing their sense of national belonging.[15] This process is certainly not unproblematic, since sentiments of belonging based upon virtual notions of intimacy and straightforward sociality between the homeland and the diaspora eschew the question, as Werbner argues, of how intimate knowledge is conceived over discontinuous space and time. Online networking not only buttresses feelings of collective belonging but also facilitates possibilities of an epistemological homeland toward which inhabitants of diasporas direct these feelings. This online notion of a nation strengthens the sense of sharing along a coherent and continuous virtual space among diasporas, while suppressing inconsistencies that may issue between the idea of the homeland and the homeland itself. Miriyam Aouragh warns that the online nation is not a voluntary substitute for its physical counterpart. The motivation of Palestinians' online activity is grounded in feelings of exclusion, isolation, oppression, and an inherited desire to meet offline. In this sense, these online communities are merely tactical means for creating national sentiments among distinct displaced groups.[16]

However, while the development of online national sentiments is inextricably connected to the facilitation of an epistemological nation, it does not mean that the Palestinian identity has similarly developed in the various scattered communities over several generations. To the contrary, whereas a strong sense of *communitas* pervades among Palestinians everywhere, their cultural identities have evolved along different lines. One must consider that the pillars of the national script (that is, "the Right of Return," "national liberation," and so forth) no longer—seven decades after the Nakba—realistically comprehend collective needs and aspirations of diverse Palestinian communities in Israel-Palestine and the West, but offer their constituents a historic-mythical narrative of origin that does not explicitly influence their daily lives. The point is that the dynamics of recent global networking may enhance the semblance of a homogeneous national identity and reinforce the sense of unity among Palestinians, but it is, paradoxically, also revealing the constantly evolving cultural diversities among the various Palestinian communities whose literary opus is the subject of this book. Hypothetically, one child may live under Israeli occupation in the West Bank, whereas another, residing in the Shatila refugee camp in Lebanon, is deprived of basic civil rights. A third-generation Palestinian girl may grow up in Stockholm, Sweden, far away from the chains of a conservative patriarchy at "home," while her counterpart resides in Israel as an inferior second-rate citizen. In contradistinction to past generations, who dwelled in relatively isolated displaced communities, currently available virtual spaces allow present-day as well as future generation(s) to share textual, visual, audio, and other forms of data at light speed, effectively enhancing the sense of an imagined communal space and seemingly suppressing the "melancholia" of exile. However, its virtual members lead basically different lives, revealing a deep gap between what Aouragh describes as online and offline affiliations.[17]

My contention is that the polylingual analytical framework offers a major site for the exploration of these paradoxical currents, and to begin I wish to first focus on the local axis. Hebrew, Latinate, Anglophone, and Nordic Palestinian writings may be theorized as minor literatures, following Gilles Deleuze and Felix Guattari's definition in *Kafka: Toward a Minor Literature* (1986): "A minor literature does not come from a minor language; it is rather that which a minority constructs within a major language." Although relatively problematic, as I will demonstrate later, this theory does offer insights into the basic characteristics of minority literatures that may prove useful even for the assessment of works written by nationally distinctive authors such as the Palestinians in the West and Israel. Whereas the choice of language for artistic creation may pose problems of literary identification, as argued in the previous section, it provides a defining criterion within a theoretical framework that positions such literary productions in relation to local majorities. Deleuze and Guattari present three characteristics of minor literature: "the deterritorialization of language, the connection of the individual to a political immediacy, and the collective assemblage of enunciation."[18] Affiliated with ethnic or national minorities in their respective locations of residence, the authors discussed here mostly write in the language of the majority.

Several Palestinian literary productions written in languages other than Arabic emerging from the West and Israel may similarly be defined by these characteristics. First, Palestinian authors writing in the language of local majorities variedly infuse this language with ideological intentions and linguistic configurations and patterns that represent the ethnic or national shared worldview of the minority group. They destabilize the major language by thrusting their different marginal realities upon mainstream culture. Second, given the marginal status of minor literature, the political dimension of individual exile—a major concern for an immigrant minority—becomes thus ingrained in its worldview. The political status of the minority group is inextricable to individual meditations. In this context, Palestinians and authors of Palestinian descent residing in Israel and the West gravitate and work in narrow social spaces that force them to relate, first and foremost, to their respective political situations. The "cramped space" of minor literature, argues Waïl Hassan, "forces each individual intrigue to connect immediately to politics. The individual concern thus becomes all the more necessary, indispensable, magnified, because a whole other story [that of the minority group] is vibrating within it." As Palestinian American critic and poet Lisa Suhair Majaj puts it, "Whether we wish it or not, Palestinian memory, like Palestinian history, is always already political." Third, in the same vein as the second feature of minor literature, individual concerns are inseparable from the collective. Personal utterances already express experiences expectedly shared by others: "Everything takes on a collective value."[19] It seems nearly impossible to separate individual Palestinian literary odysseys from political and collective concerns.

To exemplify, I wish to focus on the late second-generation immigrant and Danish Palestinian poet Yahya Hassan—a "New Dane," as Danish periodicals and newspapers have dubbed second-generation youngsters of ethnic backgrounds. Growing up under dire circumstances in a predominantly immigrant suburb of Denmark's second-largest city, Århus, Hassan's poetry offers Danish audiences a window into the inner workings of an underprivileged ethnic immigrant family in what Anja Kublitz refers to as the "Danish camps."[20] In poems such as "Barndom" (Childhood), "Parabol" (Satellite Dish), and "Mor til Tre Fremmede Søskende" (Mother to Three Alien Siblings) from his first collection, Hassan shocks his readers by revealing daily rituals of violence, religious hypocrisy, social fraud, and arranged marriages on the verge of statutory rape.[21] Despite criticism issuing from ethnic communities similar to the one he grew up in, Hassan's overnight rise to fame and his narration of the migrant experience in Denmark entered the mainstream and have ultimately altered the cultural landscape. In Deleuze and Guattari's terms, he both destabilizes the Danish language and touches upon the highly politicized issue of immigrants' social status in the Danish context. Also, writing from within the cramped space of the minority as a "New Dane," Hassan's poetry portrays an immigrant individual's experience growing up in a so-called isolated parallel society, struggling with vague integration policies while dismissing his parents' socially dysfunctional generation. Ultimately, Hassan's depictions are inseparable from the ongoing political controversies surrounding communities such as his own.

Certainly, Hassan's scrutiny of his own community in the Danish language may imply that he confirms ethnic prejudices rather than creating a discourse of incisive self-criticism. Danish audiences may generalize Hassan's depictions and become susceptible to accusations of stereotyping, but Hassan is, indeed, not alone in his positions and, like his counterparts, is not capable of writing in his parents' native tongue. Recently, an increasing number of "New Danes" have begun to share experiences similar to (and some different from) the ones described by Hassan. Ahmad Mahmoud's memoir *Sort Land: Fortællinger fra Ghettoen* (Black Nation: Tales from the Ghetto, 2015) presents a particularly dark narrative of growing up in a violent immigrant community in Denmark. Like Hassan, he focuses on dire experiences of social injustice and hypocrisy. *Black Nation* does not present a familiar Palestinian narrative. It does not mourn the loss of the homeland. Rather, Mahmoud focuses on the problems of Palestinian immigrants in integrating into Danish society, explicitly blaming his parents' generation for this failure: "Although there is not much philosophizing on education methods in our culture, the endeavor is to stave off Arab children from becoming Danish." Mahmoud does not search for answers through reclaiming Palestinian roots and establishing an exilic identity. To the contrary, addressing Arab immigrant parents, he calls for total assimilation: "Confront your children and tell them that they are Danish. It is not racism. It is caring."[22]

Abdel Aziz Mahmoud's *Hvor Taler Du Flot Dansk* (How Wonderfully You Speak Danish, 2016) presents a somewhat different story. Whereas Yahya Hassan's and Ahmad Mahmoud's paths to assimilation in the Danish society came about in their respective rejections of their communities and families, Abdel Aziz Mahmoud's experience is made up of ongoing attempts at merging between his family's middle-class lifestyle and the experiences of Danish families. Abdel Aziz presents a heartwarming story about growing up in a supportive, hardworking immigrant family and becoming a popular television correspondent, accepted and loved by the Danish public. This seemingly perfectly synchronic relationship between family and society culminates when Abdel Aziz—following the publication of his book—comes out as being gay. Contradicting the expected stereotypical reaction of a Muslim family, the Mahmouds accept their son's sexual identity and remain supportive of him. The Danish public continues to be enamored by Abdel Aziz's appearances, particularly as he takes local Muslim leaders to task for condemning the gay community. Abdel Aziz's experience stands in stark contrast to Ahmad Mahmoud's, who has also come out as gay since the publication of his book. Ostracized by his community and disowned by his family, Ahmad's tale of escaping the "ghetto" continues in his columns, as he now identifies as gay.

It may seem unreasonable to qualify these writings for the Palestinian canon since they do not explicitly connect to established themes such as the Nakba, the suffering of their compatriots in the occupied Palestinian territories, or the refugee camps in Arab countries. Nonetheless, they narrate experiences that concern an entire second generation of immigrants in Denmark—including Palestinians. In the Danish language, they reveal the violence of a traditional and damaged patriarchal social structure that is struggling to preserve its authority in a foreign milieu and against an emerging second generation of Arabs torn between Eastern and Western cultural forces. Locally, in what may be seen as expressions of youthful rebellion against society and their parents' generation, these young writers indeed present an unsettling self-reflexive criticism of their own ethnic cultural stagnation and project mistrustful perspectives on their parents or their parents' generation.

However, contemporary Danish writings by Palestinians should not be read only as representations of the immigrant experience in Denmark. In order to engage them in the (trans)national dialogue, it is also necessary to address the historic conditions framing these narrations. On June 1, 2014, Denmark's leading newspaper, *Politiken*, published a revealing article titled "Nydanske Forældre: Vi her Begået alt for Mange Fejl" (New Dane Parents: We Have Made Too Many Mistakes), which discussed first-generation Palestinian refugees and their reflections on how they had failed as parents in Denmark. The interviewees painfully admitted to having been unsuccessful at securing a healthy upbringing for their children and guaranteeing them a proper education, pulling them off the streets and away from the instant, if short-lived, "glories" of criminality. The majority ground their parental and personal deficiencies in their unsettling and detrimental refugee experiences. Traumatized by the events of the Lebanese Civil War, most of them arrived in Denmark uneducated and illiterate—a direct outcome of the Lebanese government's decades-long discriminating policies toward the Palestinian refugee community.[23] Such reflections may or may not effectively explain the malfunction of this "welfare generation" toward their children. Nonetheless, the fact remains that these failures originate from major political events unfolding in recent Palestinian history: the Nakba that turned them into refugees in Lebanon, the local government's maltreatment of this community, and the Lebanese Civil War that led to the total defeat of the PLO in 1982. The testimonies of this generation represent a specific itinerary of displacement in the Palestinian narrative that not only confirm but also motivate and frame the artistic and critical output of individuals such as Yahya Hassan and Ahmad Mahmoud as well as the seemingly exceptional story of Abdel Aziz Mahmoud.

Yahya Hassan's, Ahmad Mahmoud's, and Abdel Aziz Mahmoud's writings radically diverge from canonical themes of exile, but they insist on defining themselves and their writings in a Palestinian context, thus redefining the boundaries of the canon. In the chapter "Uden Rødder" (Without Roots), Ahmad Mahmoud describes a complex relationship to his Palestinian heritage. Growing up in the ethnic community of Askerød, Mahmoud learned to identify himself as Palestinian. Time and again, he declares that he is Palestinian, until a local shop owner asks where exactly he is from in Palestine. Surprised at the question, Mahmoud admits that he does not know. This discovery leads to yet another revelation. Mahmoud realizes that he is not alone; the narrative voice shifts from the individual "I" to the collective "we": "We are the stateless generation, the lost generation and the splintered generation. Our parents escaped to Denmark, we were born in Denmark, but we do not belong in any place. We are neither real Palestinians nor real Danes, but then what are we, where do we belong, and most importantly: who are we?" (138; my translation). It is Mahmoud's meditations on the loss of national identity that lead to his pondering the development of an ambiguous Danish identity. Less confused, and as if in response to Mahmoud's question, Hassan makes a straightforward declaration. On the back cover of Hassan's poetry collection, he identifies himself as follows: "Yahya Hassan, born 1995. Stateless Palestinian with Danish Passport." His experience may be that of an immigrant residing in Denmark, but he ultimately defines it as Palestinian.[24]

Shifting from the Nordic Palestinian experience, I wish to turn to a different Palestinian context: Israel. Writings by Israeli-Palestinian authors Sayed Kashua and Anton Shammas further problematize the ongoing cultural fragmentation of Palestinian communities owing to the fact that they were composed in Hebrew.[25] Unlike their Danish counterparts, Shammas and Kashua do not hail from an immigrant community but rather come from the country's indigenous population. Their autobiographical Hebrew-language novels *Arabesqot* (*Arabesques*, 1986) and *Araveem Rokdeem* (*Dancing Arabs*, 2002) present unsettling projections of a distinctive Palestinian reality. Whereas characters in diasporic Palestinian fiction exist abroad, or in a setting construed out of the ruins that for several decades remained buried underneath the Israeli landscape, Shammas's and Kashua's protagonist-narrators, respectively, reside in Arab villages in the Galilee and the Triangle area on the margins of Israeli reality. Shammas and Kashua are not refugees but citizens of Israel. They have, during different periods, engaged in the Israeli reality outside their villages: Shammas moved to Haifa at the age of twelve with his family and attended a local Jewish school; at approximately the same age, Kashua enrolled in the Israel Arts and Science Academy (a prestigious Israeli Jewish junior high school in Jerusalem)—both acquiring superb command of the Hebrew language. As Palestinian authors holding Israeli citizenship and writing in Hebrew, their respective novels explore problems of identity in a dynamic cultural minefield.

Although held in high regard by certain Israeli audiences, Kashua remains markedly unpopular among his Arab compatriots. Many are offended by his satirization, in the Hebrew language, of social and national Palestinian imagery. In *Dancing Arabs*, Kashua portrays an entirely different experience than the life of an exile, positing Israeli Palestinians in a tragicomic scenario. The unnamed protagonist's father represents a generation that may not have experienced the Nakba firsthand but suffers the repercussions of the humiliating Arab defeat in 1967. At home, before his wife and children, he constantly rants about the corruption of Arab rulers and, indeed more cautiously, about Zionist American conspiracies. However, when his son, the protagonist, wins a scholarship to a prestigious Israeli boarding school in Jerusalem, he expresses pride in having been accepted by the ruling establishment. On the one hand, he immerses himself in patriotic Palestinian discourse, but only in the privacy of his home. On the other, he also reveals the need for acceptance by the ruling Jewish majority. Kashua thus portrays his parents' generation's ambivalent relationship to Israel. Aimed at the Hebrew-reading audience, Kashua inscribes in the Israeli consciousness how Arabs in Israel both politically and collectively move in two opposing directions. They are Palestinians, but, then again, not entirely. They are also Israelis, but, then again, not entirely. They are victims of a tragic predicament that Kashua's predecessor Shammas incisively explored in the '80s.

About two decades prior to the publication of *Dancing Arabs*, Shammas the author frames the story of protagonist-narrator Anton Shammas against the backdrop of the newly found State of Israel (1948) and the Israeli occupation of the West Bank and the Gaza Strip (1967) in his celebrated Hebrew-language novel *Arabesques*. Exploring the facets of his own identity, he tunnels into the history of the Shammas clan, beginning with the family patriarch's move from Syria to the Galilean Christian village of Fassuta at the onset of the nineteenth century. The setting of the story eventually shifts from Fassuta to the United States, where the protagonist attends the International Writing Program held at the University of Iowa. While studying there, the Israeli Arab Shammas seeks the opportunity to track down his former namesake and Palestinian doppelgänger

Michel Abyad, who had originally been named Anton Shammas but was kidnapped shortly after his birth from his biological mother, Almaza, to be raised by a childless couple in Beirut. Shammas had previously learned of Michel Abyad's story from Layla Khouri, who had worked as a servant in the Abyad household while Michel was growing up. However, during Shammas's emotionally charged meeting with Michel himself in Iowa City many years later, he discovers small but significant discrepancies between Layla's version and Michel's. Years earlier, following his return to Beirut to join the Center for Palestinian Studies in 1978, Michel meets Nur, Shammas's cousin. As Nur tells Michel about the tragedy of Almaza, Michel completely identifies with her son and is inspired to write a fictional autobiography of Anton Shammas. These revelations cast the novel in a new light. Suddenly, the reader and Shammas the protagonist realize that everything that took place prior to this point does not necessarily belong to Shammas's narrative. Michel Abyad may be the authoritative narrator, and the entire Shammas-Abyad affair, as told by Layla Khouri, could actually be the product of his narrative design.

The narrative structure of *Arabesques* follows, indeed, the complex patterns of the arabesque; seemingly linear, it constantly breaks off into cyclical shapes. Narration in Shammas's novel is anything but straightforward, and its aesthetic dimension deserves and has been the subject of several studies. Culturally, *Arabesques* is a Hebrew-language novel by a Palestinian author and, as such, has entered the Israeli canon under the category of minority literature. Shammas steers his story from the geographically peripheral Fassuta in the Galilee toward the West Bank and then toward an international gathering of young writers in Iowa City. Yet, beyond the fictional world of the novel, the themes gravitate from a minority space on the margins of the Israeli society toward the country's cultural center and then en route to Iowa in the American Midwest—a provincial state but, nonetheless, considered for decades a hub for young writers. Although widely acclaimed by Israeli critics for its aesthetic and cultural value, a question arises: What has Shammas's novel contributed to the Israeli mainstream, and how does it link to the Palestinian experience?

While in Iowa, the protagonist's refusal to label himself a Palestinian according to his Jewish compatriot Yehoshua Bar-On's definition is telling of Shammas's experimentation: "Shammas's compatriot [Paco] here speaks much more to my heart than he does. He forces me to respond and take a stand toward him. You have to bear in mind that he is still a pure Palestinian, whose strength resides in his simplicity and his lack of cynicism." Bar-On opts to model the Arab protagonist in his novel after his Palestinian colleague from the territories rather than after Shammas, whose identity as both a Palestinian Arab and an Israeli citizen defies any clear-cut definition and challenges any hope of returning to an "original" state. In positioning himself between the Israeli Jew and the Palestinian Arab, Shammas points to a liminal space that challenges both Arabs' and Jews' Israeli identities. To employ Emile Habiby's neologism, *pessoptimistically*, the author regards this space as the unreachable utopia whereby Arabs may become Israelis and Jews may prioritize their Israeli identity over a Jewish one. It is this idea that Shammas controversially advances in relation to the Israeli cultural mainstream by deliberately choosing to write in Hebrew. He both deterritorializes the Hebrew language and subverts Israeli assumptions by claiming a place in the language of the majority and creating a text that, in Shammas's own words at the time, aims to "un-Jew the Hebrew language, making it more Israeli."[26]

Having lived in Israeli society for decades, relatively cut off from their compatriots in Arab countries and abroad, history as well as the sociopolitical and cultural reality have pushed Shammas and Kashua beyond their national narrative and wedged an unbridgeable gap between the Israeli-Palestinian Arab they have inevitably transformed into and the national Palestinian agent they can no longer return to become. They hover, as both Shammas's and Kashua's works suggest, in this liminal space, unable to go back to a previous state and incapable of deciding where to advance from here. Still, it is pertinent to ask, "Where does this clear-cut Palestinian identity exist that neither Shammas nor Kashua seems able to acquire through their Hebrew-language works?" It may appear that such an entity is currently being cultivated in the occupied Palestinian territories, whereas previously it was nurtured in refugee camps. However, this reading only highlights the hegemonic dynamics in the Palestinian context and does not account for the ongoing diversification taking place away from these political centers of gravity and under distinct cultural and linguistic circumstances. Therefore, whereas it may seem that Israeli-Palestinian Hebrew-language writers are moving away from canonical projections of the Palestinian, they are also, through their unique experience, creating new cultural spaces—spaces whereby Shammas and Kashua (as well as Atallah Mansour and Ayman Sikseck) have expanded and continue to do so through their writing.

Beyond the Local

The local axis of the polylingual framework addresses the problems of Palestinian minorities in relation to respective majorities, as revealed through Danish Palestinian writings as well as Kashua's and Shammas's Hebrew novels. These texts assume an "oppositional" stance, aiming not only to resist but also to alter hegemonic local discourses. According to Deleuze and Guattari, they "no longer designate specific literatures but the revolutionary conditions for every literature within the heart of what is called great (or established) literature." The integrity of Yahya Hassan's, Ahmad Mahmoud's, and Abdel Aziz Mahmoud's Danish as well as Kashua's and Shammas's Hebrew writings should be respected in its own right, both linguistically and culturally (following Kilpatrick's model of dual identification). Nevertheless, in addition to local context, the authors' national heritage should not be ignored, since it is a principal marker that distinguishes them from the local majority and binds them together and to other authors of Palestinian origins worldwide.

In the vein of this latter observation, I find Chana Kronfeld's criticism leveled at the assessment of deterritorialized writings as exclusively "oppositional" within a major language relevant and worth mentioning in my proposal to establish a polylingual framework for Palestinian writings in the world. Rather than squeeze diverse literary productions under a procrustean bed consisting of basic classifying conditions that fit a work into the category of minority literature, Kronfeld draws on David Lloyd's more nuanced and historicized interpretation to suggest a strategy that further develops Deleuze and Guattari's approach. Lloyd reinterprets and expands the conditions for the emergence of minor literature in an attempt to render the existing model more coherent. He ultimately shifts this category closer to the position of the historic reception of modernist literature, in that it represents experimental writings that are critical or oppositional to the canon, whereby they only marginally belonged. In this context, Deleuze and Guattari may have "conveniently" chosen one of the major authors of the modernist canon to develop a theory of minority literatures. Certainly, their choice exposes the discrepancy between Kafka's international canonic status and his more ambivalent position within the German literary context. Kronfeld regards Deleuze and Guattari's view of Kafka as a Jewish author writing in the hegemonic German within a Czech environment as reductive in that they erase other non-Germanic dimensions of his literary affiliations. Lloyd's thesis on the modernist characteristic of minor literature draws Kafka closer to contemporary minimalist writings in Hebrew and Yiddish that emerged at the time from Vienna and Berlin but also from Moscow, Warsaw, Kiev, and Tel Aviv, among others. Relevant to my study is Kronfeld's suggestion of emphasizing the cross-cultural character of Kafka's writings, in addition to their status in the German context, to highlight their contradictory and ambivalent multiple literary affiliations.[27] Similarly, in the development of a polylingual category, Deleuze and Guattari's theory should be superseded by postcolonial theories of contemporary global forces, first and foremost, in order to surmount the common tendencies in literary criticism of confining analyses of these works exclusively to local frameworks and, second, to explain the processes of literary and linguistic hybridization that connect works by Palestinian writers of different generations from various displaced minorities seven decades after the Nakba.

Regarding the first aim, in agreement with Kronfeld's criticism, I do not think that it is sufficient to regard Yahya Hassan's, Ahmad Mahmoud's, and Abdel Aziz Mahmoud's writings as exclusively immigrant in the Danish context—as Deleuze and Guattari's theory may imply. Also, Anton Shammas's and Sayed Kashua's (as well as Atallah Mansour's and Ayman Sikseck's) Hebrew novels cannot be regarded exclusively as minor literature within the local Israeli context—as most Israeli scholars tend to do.[28] This strategy ultimately suppresses the Palestinian identity of such works, as well as their relation to their multiple diasporic counterparts. That is to say, in the context of national displacement, these writings demonstrate localized developments of the Palestinian story in relation to one another and several other ongoing narratives. It is therefore pertinent to generate critical possibilities that challenge the widespread tendency to integrate Palestinian minority literatures exclusively into local canons without acknowledging their interconnectedness beyond political geographic borders.

In regard to the second aim, my contestation is that the development of a Palestinian polylingual literary category will allow for the generation of a critical multifaceted space whereby these linguistically distinct localized narrations sharing a cultural and national heritage are brought into dialogue. This space will simultaneously present Palestinian minority writings to variegated and larger audiences worldwide, as well as trigger a process of intertextuality that would yield a multifaceted narrative of intercommunal solidarity among Palestinians authors of distinct experiences of displacement. Whereas this space might seem to solidify the idea of national unity, it simultaneously foregrounds these writers' distinctive negotiations of their heritage. In this sense, the polylingual category accounts for the ongoing flow of the transcultural, multilingual proliferation of Palestinian writings, enabled by the variety of culturally diverse authors, readers, critics, and publishing presses around the globe. Whereas canonical Arabic writings have, since 1948, promoted specific political metaphors in narrations of experiences in political centers such as the refugee camps, diasporas in Arab nations, and the occupied territories, they (excepting Emile Habiby's *The Secret Life of Saeed the Pessoptimist* [1974]) rarely explore problems of assimilation and (dis)integration of the national identity as such in contexts of displacement—major processes framing Palestinians' realities in both Israel and the West.

Hence, to summarize my two aims in transcending the local value of Palestinian writings in the world, I argue that it is, first of all, critically insufficient to focus on Danish- and Hebrew-language works by Palestinians solely in local contexts. Rather, the densification of social relations in the global context suggests that the ongoing fragmentation of Palestinian reality has yielded a culturally nuanced space composed of various localities transcending the diasporic vernaculars and expressing the deterritorialization of a national center. In order to significantly account for the cultural proliferation of the Palestinian experience since the founding of the early diasporas, the polylingual category shows that Palestinian literature no longer subscribes to an exclusive national mode in terms of territory and language and, as a result, suggests a space for the transnational assembling of literary texts representative of various local contexts. My point is that in the study of these voices' distinct localities and their relation to the idea of a homeland, it is necessary to consider how literary production flows over local territorial borders into the global stream and generates critical possibilities for exploring the amalgamation of disparate literary units that constitute a single culturally heterogeneous Palestinian literary space. On the one hand, the transnational turn of Palestinian literature may mirror, as Anthony Giddens has it, "the intensification of worldwide social relations that link distant localities in such a way that local happenings are shaped by events occurring many miles away and vice versa."[29] On the other, it also reveals a vibrating literary process of "minoritizations," taking place on the margins of Palestinian consciousness in the fluid space between the local and global.

Françoise Lionnet and Shu-mei Shih offer a particularly effective theoretical concept to explain this process of global "minoritization"—"minor transnationalism." They contend that in the increasingly homogenizing global context, transnationalism—part and parcel of globalization—becomes culturally scattered and unscripted. I wish to quote this point at length, as they raise several interesting issues that I seek to pursue:

> Whereas the global is, in our understanding, defined *vis-à-vis* a homogeneous and dominant set of criteria, the transnational designates spaces and practices acted upon by border-crossing agents, be they dominant or marginal. The logic of globalization is centripetal and centrifugal at the same time and assumes a universal core, which spreads out across the world while pulling into its vortex other forms of culture to be tested by its norm. It produces a hierarchy of subjects between the so-called universal and particular, with all the attendant problems of Eurocentric universalism. The transnational, on the contrary, can be conceived as a space of exchange and participation wherever processes of hybridization occur and where it is still possible for cultures to be produced and performed without mediation by the center.[30]

The premise of Lionnet and Shih's argument emphasizes the potential of cultural "heterogeneity" under the auspices of corporate and imperial "homogeneity" of the global context, suggesting various ways of connecting between notions of an abstract universality and local particularities to the effect of arriving at momentums of "newness."[31] It may appear that in Lionnet and Shih's emphasis on the "homogenous and dominant set of criteria" as the basis of our global world, they prioritize "policy" over "process," echoing Edward Said's short argument in "Globalizing Literary Studies" that presents the globalizing world order as merely having replaced Eurocentric universalism—thus, moving the center from Europe to the United States.[32] However, although Said does not view globalization as an updated alternative to Eurocentric dominance in literature departments, Lionnet and Shih do. They address transnationalism as the site for processes of hybridization, wherefore the idea of the center seems all but irrelevant. In other words, rather than subject criticism to the perception of a unifying global world as such, it should be the aim of the transnational moment to study multiple margins in relation to one another instead of their respective relations to a center. In accordance with Lionnet and Shih's line of logic, Palestinian minorities and diasporas variedly participate in this moment, creating a literary network that defines the nuances of today's scattered Palestinian realities.

Certainly, a warning is warranted here, insofar as the global framework impacts the production of Palestinian literature in contradictory ways. As a literary critic, my aim to explore the potential of cultural heterogeneity of Palestinian writings under the auspices of corporate and imperial homogeneity is primarily in line with the arguments of the aforementioned theorists. Nonetheless, it is necessary to acknowledge that the occasionally vexed relation between local and global marketing of these minority writings both manipulates tastes and standardizes the idea of Palestinian literature, suggesting the homogenizing impact of globalization on cultural production. In other words, this same unified conception of the world presents a space whereby the proliferation of local texts both facilitates and resists cultural homogenization, suggesting that the distinct narratives of Palestinian displacement both manifest and challenge the centric national call. It is, therefore, necessary to point out that my study of the transnational turn of Palestinian literature is not entirely inseparable from materialist considerations regarding today's globalized world.[33]

Conclusion

I believe that global networks of minority communities—diasporic or indigenous—bring about creative critical interventions in the field of literary studies. Yahya Hassan's, Ahmad Mahmoud's, and Abdel Aziz Mahmoud's respective Danish writings, as well as Sayed

Kashua's and Anton Shammas's novels—representative of multiple margins—belong to and should be critically positioned in the growing list of literary works by Palestinian authors who write in languages other than Arabic, in order to renegotiate their cultural and political heritage from and in non-Arab contexts. In addition to the texts I refer to in this chapter, I wish to rotate the kaleidoscope and list Suheir Hammad's *Born Palestinian, Born Black* (1996); Mazen Maarouf's (Iceland) first poetry collection, *Our Grief Resembles Bread* (2000); Rula Jebreal's (Italy) *Miral* (2004); Randa Abdel-Fattah's (Australia) *Does My Head Look Big in This?* (2005); Randa Jarrar's (United States) *A Map of Home* (2008), *Him, Me, Muhammad Ali: Stories* (2016), and *Love Is an Ex-Country* (2021); Susan Abulhawa's (United States) *Mornings in Jenin* and *The Blue between Sky and Water* (2015); Selma Dabbagh's (United Kingdom) *Out of It* (2012); Susan Muaddi Darraj's *The Inheritance of Exile: Stories from South Philly* (2007) and *A Curious Land: Stories from Home* (2015); Ayman Sikseck's (Israel) *El Yaffo* (2010); Nathalie Handal's poetry collection (Haiti/United States) *La estrella invisible* (2012); Rodrigo Hasbún's (Bolivia) *El lugar del cuerpo* (2012) and *Los affectos* (2015); Lina Meruane's (Chile) *Volverse Palestina* (2014); Khulud Khamis's (Israel) *Haifa Fragments* (2015); Hala Alyan's (United States) *Salt Houses* (2017); Isabella Hammad's (United Kingdom) *The Parisian* (2019); Lena Mahmoud's (United States) *Amreekiya* (2018); and Etaf Rum's (United States) *A Woman Is No Man* (2019). These works, along with several others, also speak about distinct experiences and represent the problems, perspectives, and national imaginings of Palestinians belonging to minority communities in the Americas, Europe, and Israel.

2

The Anglophone Palestinian Novel

Between Orientalism and (Trans)nationalism

> We mustn't become just one story.
>
> —Elias Khoury, *Gate of the Sun*

Shifting the focus to the two Palestinian American women novelists Susan Abulhawa and Susan Muaddi Darraj, I wish to further expand my argument on the development of a polylingual literary category from the previous chapter. The purpose of this chapter is, thus, twofold. With a focus on Anglophone Palestinian writings, it primarily continues my discussion of the comprehensive polylingual framework that allows for the examination of the political and cultural characteristics of the various languages in which Palestinian narratives have been conceived since the Nakba. Second, anchoring my analysis in Abulhawa's novels *Mornings in Jenin* (2010) and *The Blue between Sky and Water* (2015) as well as Darraj's novel *The Inheritance of Exile: Stories from South Philly* (2007), this chapter also explores how Palestinian authors might variedly imagine the future of diasporic Palestinians against the backdrop of local cultural forces in the American context.

The specific development of Anglophone literary production (novels, memoirs, autobiographies, and poetry) has—nearly three decades following the publication of Jabra Ibrahim Jabra's *Hunters in a Narrow Street* (1960) and Isaak Dias's *A Bedouin Boyhood* (1967)—surged in numbers more than any other branch of Palestinian literature. The lingua franca of today's globalized world seems to have offered Palestinian and Palestinian-descended writers a sense of autonomy in telling their stories and the possibility for textual circulation on a global (Western) scale. However, this encounter between the unfulfilled national voice and the language of the former colonizer is not straightforward. The Anglophone context brings a burdensome historic cargo to the Palestinian text that, basically, can be located—among other Anglophone Arab productions—between, as Nouri Gana has it, "the legacy of British colonialism and the ascendance of American imperialism."[1] As stated at the outset, the instrumental roles played by the (territorial) British Empire and the (nonterritorial) US-led powers, in shaping the history (as well as today's circumstances) of the Israeli-Palestinian conflict according to deep-rooted Orientalist discourses, are insurmountable in a study of the ways whereby Palestinian narratives are formulated in the English language. These historic and contemporary forces are, as this chapter proposes to demonstrate, likely to steer the development of the Anglophone branch of Palestinian literature—vis-à-vis artistic and intellectual expectations (as well as market and critical reception)—in the distinct postcolonial and global contexts.

This particular literary branch marks a specific area of overlap between a contemporary transnational polylingual category of Palestinian literature that I propose and—to borrow a term coined by Edward Said and eventually further developed by Geoffrey Nash—"the Anglo-Arab encounter." That is to say, on the one hand, English-language writings by Palestinians configure, next to their counterparts composed in a number of other languages, connecting texts from "multiple margins" in relation to the idea of the "homeland"; on the other, they simultaneously partake in an Arab Anglophone tradition that encompasses writings by Arabs (and not only by Palestinians)—residing primarily in the United States and the United Kingdom but also in countries such as Australia, Canada, and South Africa—bringing together texts from a variety of locations that share a single language. It is worth mentioning that several scholars—such as Steven Salaita, Waïl Hassan, and Carol Fadda-Conrey, to name only a few—have, since Said's and Nash's founding commentaries, extensively worked to further expand the concept of Arab Anglophone literature.[2] My analysis of Anglophone representations of the Palestinian narrative and their critical reception is focused at this intersection of these two linguistically distinctive literary branches (the former polylingual, the latter monolingual).

This bilateral position of the Anglophone Palestinian writings adds a historical dimension that variedly influences how these authors portray their heritage. Compared to Palestinian writings in Danish and Hebrew that represent recent Palestinian itineraries of displacement, the English language represents a lingual milieu firmly based in powerful, long-standing Orientalist discourses. Anglophone authors such as Abulhawa and Darraj confront not only contemporary local and transnational axes in their works but also a historic axis that has eventually led to the creation of Palestinians' antagonistic status in the Western consciousness. My point is that both authors present distinct imaginings of the cross-generational implications of Palestinian displacement in the assimilative US context. My choice to focus on Abulhawa and Darraj is primarily based on the contention that their literary portrayals of the Palestinian-descended characters' idiosyncratic experiences variedly reinforce conventional nationalist and generate new challenging cosmopolitan dimensions to the Palestinian narrative. Abulhawa's invariable commitment to the national script in her writings facilitates an exclusive outlook that diametrically opposes Darraj's explorations of liminal diasporic identification in the US setting. It may seem that the historic and political circumstances framing Anglophone representations of today's Palestinian experiences ostensibly offer a legitimate basis whence to support the national script. However, the fixation on maintaining the idea of an immutable national core over a period of several decades might suppress meditations on these multiple developing narrations of localized Palestinian experiences in the various contexts of displacement.

Certainly, the relationship between Western Orientalist discourses and Zionist settler-colonialism cannot be overemphasized here, insofar as historic and contemporary Anglophone narrations of Palestine and the invention of Israeli "Hasbara" have ultimately transformed the Palestinian into the Caliban figure of today's globalized world. My aim is to demonstrate that whereas a literary text grounded in the national framework—such as Abulhawa's novels—might appear to resist these invasive foreign forces, it also presents the threat of trapping upcoming Palestinian generations in a script that does not comprehend the nuances of their idiosyncratic experiences. In bringing Abulhawa's and Darraj's novels together, I wish to point to this cross-generational conjuncture for Palestinians in the United States.

Between Orientalism and (Trans)nationalism

More than a decade ago, in an analysis of Ibrahim Fawal's and Shaw Dallal's respective English-language novels *On the Hills of God* and *Scattered Like Seeds*, Steven Salaita claimed that Palestinian prose was "going global." His argument presents Anglophone literary productions as "emblematic of a recent trend in Palestinian literature: writing rooted in diasporic countries but focused in theme and content on Palestine." Interestingly, rather than focusing on the global possibilities for the production and consumption of Anglophone Palestinian literature, Salaita anchors the identity of this branch in its loyalty to specific tropes that characterize the Arabic Palestinian novel in terms of style, setting, and thematic intention. Somewhat echoing Ghassan Kanafani's criteria in *'Adab 'al-Muqawama fi Filistin 'al-Muḥtalla, 1948–1966* (Literature of Resistance in Occupied Palestine, 1948–1966), Salaita states that this genre, first of all, presents Palestine as an object of desire by way of feminizing it; second, it typecasts other Arab nationalities as treacherous, in league with Israel and the United States; third, its plotline adheres to a conventional nationalistic script; last, it presents these themes through extensive dialogues among the characters. To Salaita, these poetic markers are the pillars of the thematic and stylistic correspondence between the Arabic- and the English-language Palestinian novels—a correspondence that offers legitimate grounds for establishing an exclusive Anglophone literary branch.[3]

On the one hand, Salaita's claim is legitimate only if we presuppose that the Arabic version of the Palestinian novel merely emulates a more or less fixed national narrative and that the Anglophone version mimics this idea of its older Arabic sibling. Salaita does not account for canonical Palestinian writers' vexed relationship to the national script. The Palestinian novel is not merely an artistic extension of the national narrative—to the contrary. As Bashir Abu Manneh has recently commented, "What we know as the Palestinian novel (the works of Kanafani, Jabra, Habiby, and Khalifeh) was written not only at a distance from mainstream Palestinian nationalism, but as a critique of its main political tropes, such as armed struggle and statehood. . . . The closer one comes to official Palestinian political ideology the more distorted and propagandistic the novel becomes." The aforementioned writers are far from being simply politically committed to "the cause." Their writings demonstrate a deep interest in philosophy, metaphysics, superstition, and Arabic literary tradition. Therefore, rather than assess the Arabic Palestinian text in the service of a single (national) discourse, as Salaita does, it is fruitful to consider it in reference to Nicolas Bourriaud's concept of "relational aesthetics" and recognize its multidimensional character as a facilitating space for the encounter of several discourses: history, philosophy, aesthetics, social criticism, auto-critique, and so forth.[4]

On the other hand, it would be only partly accurate to assume that the Anglophone Palestinian text is an offspring of the Arabic text. This encounter between the English language and the Palestinian text is generating a new dimension to the ongoing Palestinian story that is diasporic (and Western) rather than indigenous. Similar to Yahya Hassan's, Ahmad Mahmoud's, and Abdel Aziz Mahmoud's writings in Danish (as well as Anton Shammas's and Sayed Kashua's in Hebrew), English-language writings by Palestinians are primarily constituted by local flows. However, the colonial history and today's role of the English language suggest an encompassing global framework that determines the character of these writings. For (trans)national membership, this branch is bound to present narratives countering, in Western contexts, long-standing Orientalist and

Zionist narratives of Palestine. The inseparability of Zionism and Europe's colonial appetite for Palestine cannot be overemphasized here. This foundational relationship has basically drawn today's Palestinians into a biblical narrative, (falsely) connecting them to the ancient Philistines, who arrived in Israel-Palestine from Philistia, Crete, around the twelfth century BCE. Despite historical inadequacies of such comparisons, this is the place today's Palestinians have symbolically come to occupy in the Israeli and Western religious imagination. Eitan Bar Yosef traces the history of English biblical imaginings of Palestine in Victorian England. Focusing on Palestine as the "Holy Land," he supplements Edward Said's secular notion of Orientalism with a discourse of the Orient as based upon the Bible. Bar Yosef's argument adds a crucial dimension to the historic and current Anglophone framework of the Israeli-Palestinian conflict. In this context, contemporary English-language writings by Palestinians such as Abulhawa and Darraj not only counter the effects of the Zionist narrative but also unsettle the biblical pillars of the West's claim to the Holy Land.[5]

The Orientalization of the Israeli-Palestinian conflict is simultaneously anchored in secular discourses. Regardless of internal diversities among both Israelis and Palestinians, in the Anglophone context, the conflict symbolizes the clash between a progressive Westernized people and a backward Eastern native population. The portrayal of Israel as an "outpost of progress" in an untamed Middle East is among the earliest ideas in the West regarding the role of Zionism in Palestine. For example, during those crucial years in the aftermath of World War II, the pavilion of "Jewish Palestine" at the New York World's Fair of 1939 titled "Building the World of Tomorrow" showcased before an American audience, as James Gelvin has it, "the good works and the civilizing role taken on by Jews in Palestine." At the fair, jurist Louis Brandeis—who was closely affiliated with American Zionism—was among the leading advocates for presenting Zionism as a "mission in the wilderness" and Zionists as representatives of the "civilized" world bringing enlightenment to the dark reaches of the globe. The purpose of the pavilion, as stated on the planning board, was to present "visual evidence of how the Zionist work in Palestine has benefitted the Arabs."[6] The "benevolent" colonial tenor of Brandeis's narrative did, of course, not bypass his more uncompromising colleagues at the fair: the purpose of Zionism was not to improve the lot of Arabs but to realize Jewish national aspirations. Notwithstanding such internal divisions, the "Jewish Palestine" pavilion demonstrates how Zionism was promoted to American benefactors through a familiar Orientalist discourse.

Although Salaita's scheme of correspondence does not address these nuances, his argument nevertheless suggests an interesting point in regard to the Anglophone novel's relation to specific tropes in Palestinian literature. This critical position raises a number of questions not only relating to the novel but also in relation to Anglophone Palestinian narratives at large: Is it possible for Palestinian authors to write against—as Mara Naaman terms it—"nostalgia for a static homeland" without running the risk of losing national membership?[7] Compared to Palestinian writings conceived in other languages, the English language seemingly offers the Palestinian writer a sense of national autonomy. However, does the Anglophone Palestinian text ultimately need to pass through the politico-historic loopholes of the 1948 and 1967 wars, and so on, perhaps to meet the commodified expectations of the literary critic and the imagined English-language reader? Or is it possible to diverge from the script and head toward more experimental destinations?

It is reasonable to assume that against the backdrop of the biblical and secular processes of Orientalizing the conflict, Anglophone Palestinian narratives will continue to express a state of emergency (insofar as the nation-building project remains unrealized) and maintain the tenor of third-world discourses of anticolonialism to resist inveterate misrepresentations of the Arab by a powerful Orientalist tradition and to undo decades of Palestinians having been muted by the deafening black hole of the Holocaust. However, it is crucial to stay alert to the inhibiting consequences of writing or experiencing the Palestinian identity exclusively in a state of emergency. For example, Yasir Suleiman's collection of more than a hundred personal testimonies by diaspora Palestinians, *Being Palestinian: Personal Reflections on Palestinian Identity in the Diaspora* (2016), is only one among several texts that both voice and suffer the consequences of nationalist emergency. The narratives of the Palestinian contributors chosen by Suleiman eloquently express and represent hardworking, urbanized, successful individuals who have "made it" and whose national identity will continue to remain symbolically rooted in images of the olive groves of a lost homeland. Suleiman's book not only manifests some form of nationalist pride in showcasing to the Western world highly successful and creative individuals as the face of the Palestinian people but also resists the portrayals of the "exotic" and "backward" Arab infested in Western imaginings of the East.

It may seem that the historic and political circumstances framing Anglophone representations of today's Palestinian experiences, such as Suleiman's, ostensibly offer a legitimate basis whence to invariably buttress the national script. However, it is important to keep in mind that the ongoing displacement of Palestinians has created diverse geographical, cultural, and social settings for the proliferation of the Palestinian story on a global scale. While *Being Palestinian* may present stories of Palestinian endurance and success to undo historic misrepresentations of the Palestinian Arab in Western discourse, it also points to a central problem in the Palestinian (trans)national context. Its definitive portrayal of a successful diasporic group may not realistically represent the majority of Palestinians either in the various contexts of Israel-Palestine or in the diaspora. Suleiman's narratorial move breeds an exclusivist outlook that is becoming increasingly insensitive to the growing diversities among diasporic Palestinian *communitas* around the globe. Ibrahim Abu-Lughod warned against this type of compression of Palestinian space as one of the "pitfalls of Palestiniology"—to solely view Palestinians in contradistinction to British and Zionist representations of the Palestinian.[8] Such fixations have so far relatively suppressed meditations on the multiple developing narrations of localized Palestinian experiences in the various contexts of displacement.

When examined against the backdrop of these contemporary realities, Suleiman's *Being Palestinian*, by focusing on a specific group that partakes in Saidean features of exile, appears to assume an elitist tenor. That is to say, his straightforward qualification of the contributors is based not only on their status as exiles who have "made it," but also on their being more or less modeled after the image of Edward Said—the most prominent icon of the Palestinian diaspora, whose presence has effectively established a locus for exile whereby prestige and success meet the Palestinian tragedy. Appropriately, the collection is dedicated to the memory of Said and opens with a photography of Said and a young Suleiman standing together, garbed in ceremonial university graduation robes at Edinburgh University.

Conversely, it may be fruitful to consider the relationship between Anglophone Palestinian writings and the national script in reference to this tensional site. On the one hand, the Palestinians who currently reside in English-speaking countries at large have—through their idiosyncratic experiences—significantly expanded the definition of this identity that stems from more or less shared memories and narrations of a lost homeland. On the other, while the national script certainly stores passions of allegiance and delineates the sense of a distinct moral being across borders, its monolingual character does not adequately encompass the diversity and ambitions of literary productions in languages other than Arabic. The long-term implications of displacement running through several generations in the Anglophone world overflow the edges of this curricular national framework and necessitate the creation of new spaces to expand the scope of Palestinian writings. This may be easier said than done, since attempts at marginalizing or rewriting the national script in the English language for the purpose of assuming, perhaps, an individual and self-reflexive attitude may be inevitably exposed to censuring critical interpretations.

Certain myopic misconceptions regarding readership may add some insight to this extended compression of Palestinian space in the Anglophone context. It seems that to postcolonial critics such as Salaita and Suleiman, the imagined English-language reader is allegedly "white," "Anglo-Saxon," and immersed in an "imperialistic" outlook that is thoroughly permeated by Orientalist presumptions. However, as we may all attest, contemporary Anglophone readership is not homogeneous. Global mobility of the past century has led to the creation of a culturally diverse Anglophone readership that allows for the possibility of multiple receptions of the text. Decades of Palestinian displacement in today's global context intersecting with the ongoing implications of centuries of immigration and other forms of mobility make it reasonable to imagine contemporary ethnic generations residing in metropolitan centers such as London, New York, and Sydney, constituting a culturally heterogeneous readership. Having grown up within the frameworks of an immigrant or exilic family and Western educational institutions, they may both favorably view the national script as part of their cultural heritage and agree that it no longer conceptually comprehends the diverse experiences of upcoming Palestinian generations in the various contexts of displacement in the diaspora.

To exemplify this misconception of the Anglophone reader, I wish to comment on the contentious reception of Fawaz Turki's highly self-critical memoir *Exile's Return: The Making of a Palestinian-American* (1994). Turki's portrayal of the Palestinian exile's journey starts with the publication of the first memoir, *The Disinherited: Journal of a Palestinian Exile* (1972), and continues in the second memoir, *Soul in Exile: Lives of a Palestinian Revolutionary* (1988). *Exile's Return* describes Turki's visit to Israel-Palestine following the signing of the Oslo Agreement and his meditations on the permanent loss of home for the exile. The evolution from a "Palestinian exile" into a "Palestinian revolutionary" and then into this obscure creature—"Palestinian American"—eventually assumes a critical stance toward the cultures and politics of the Arab world. Turki does not persist in criticizing the shallowness of American political culture, as in his earlier memoirs. Alternately, a more or less Americanized Turki coins the term "neobackwardness" to direct his criticism toward today's Arab who, as he describes, despite appearing modern, educated, and "'normal' to the naked eye," will inevitably be infected by the incurable "germ of traditionalism." Turki explains that the mode of "neobackwardness" rules the contemporary Arab world. Instead of constituting a single secular Arab nation, the region is divided into disparate "authoritarian regimes that rely on coercion, violence, and terror and demand from their people unilateral submission, obedience, and conformity."[9]

Turki's evolution has not been favorably received by critics. For example, Ahmad Sa'di does not accept Turki's ability to move on as logical: "The picture that Turki paints is too neat, easy, and deceptive. The past is not a book placed on our shelf which we can summon at our own convenience and hold open, and put aside when we wish."[10] Waïl Hassan's commentary is particularly condemning. Hassan finds Turki's self-defining terms of "exile" and Fanonian "revolutionist," in the early memoirs, legitimate (and even admirable). However, the shift of tone in *Exile's Return* seems to diverge from Hassan's expectations of the "exiled revolutionist." Moreover, in Turki's meditations on the Arab world through his increasingly Americanized Palestinian experience, Hassan recognizes a kind of complicity with Western Orientalist assumptions:

> Because of that tempestuous life, not to mention his fiery temperament, the existential predicament of homelessness and exile is painfully and dramatically captured in Turki's three memoirs. They chronicle his wrestling with his sense of identity and his role in the Palestinian movement. Written in Paris and first published in New York and London in 1972, his acclaimed memoir, *The Disinherited: Journal of a Palestinian Exile*, powerfully attacked the myths surrounding Israel and the Palestinians. He came to the U.S. in 1973 and published *Soul in Exile: Lives of a Palestinian Revolutionary*, his second memoir, fifteen years later, in 1988. Despite the differences in time and location, those two books are more or less continuous with one another—the one retelling, amplifying, and updating the other. In both, he assumed the stance of a Palestinian revolutionary who is totally dedicated to the cause, and framed his discourse in Fanonian, Third-Worldist terms. However, in his third memoir, *Exile's Return: The Making*

> *of a Palestinian-American* (1994), Turki takes on the PLO, Palestinian society, and Arab culture in general in an all-out attack that falls back on Orientalist discourse.[11]

Although Turki's scrutiny of Arab culture seems reformist, as Hassan points out, he goes to great lengths to explain that it also relies too heavily upon Orientalist ideas that, at best, may generate only simplistic analyses of what Turki finds at fault with the cultures of the region. In comparing Turki's authorial activity to Edward Said's *Out of Place: A Memoir* (1999) and the earlier memoirs with his last, *Exile's Return*, Hassan creates a framework that undermines not only the value of Turki's writings but also the principle of any prospective criticism of the Arab world composed in the English language by an Arab writer. It seems that Turki's narrative of becoming a Palestinian American and his criticism of the Arab world cannot escape accusations of complicity, insofar as it is, first of all, construed in English and, second, to the extent that it diverges from the canonical national script, demonstrating—in light of the substantial body of auto-critical texts in Arabic—that writing in the native language is more liberating than writing in a historically charged language such as English.

While Hassan significantly broadens the theoretical framework for the study of Anglophone Arab writings and delivers fruitful analyses of Ameen Rihani's, Kahlil Gibran's, George Haddad's, and Mitrie Rihbany's respective careers and works (among several others), his reading of *Exile's Return* seems oddly inadequate. Hassan's critique falls short, insofar as he does not account for the changing character of readerships during the twentieth century. Although Arab authors may write in English, it should not be immediately assumed that their productions are solely read by certain groups of British, Americans, or Australians. As mentioned, global mobility of the past century has led to the creation of a culturally diverse readership in the West that allows for the possibility of multiple receptions of the texts. Whereas one reader may regard narratives of "backwardness" in the Arab world as confirmations of existing preconceptions regarding the other, another reader may assess them as narratives of introspection and dissent.

However, it is also pertinent to accept that such interpretations exist in tandem. As Samia Serageldin explains, the pitfalls of "external agendas" alert us to the constant risks that these texts might be "coopted in the service of agendas beyond" the authors' control. The problem in Hassan's scrutiny of Turki's self-reflexive criticism is that he does not offer parallel interpretive contexts and focuses solely on its Orientalist reception. Rather than highlighting the multidimensionality of a heterogeneous global readership and the multiple possible receptions of a highly critical text such as *Exile's Return*, Hassan merely trivializes the problems of the Arab world by way of casually pitting them against the problems of other random cultures: "The problem with *Exile's Return* is not that Turki criticizes Palestinian and Arab societies. No society is free of weaknesses and, like any other society, there is much to criticize in the Arab world—patriarchy, authoritarianism, sexism, conservatism, corruption, nepotism, sectarianism, limited personal freedoms, homophobia, and so on. The trouble is that he seems incapable of doing so without resorting to the most bigoted and simple-minded inanities found in anti-Arab propaganda, as though his new self-identification as a 'Palestinian American' required him to adopt racist views."[12] It would seem as though Hassan were telling his audience that narratives such as Turki's do not offer serious critique, insofar as they merely present simplistic, one-dimensional configurations of the Arab that accommodate racialized and Orientalist slurs in the American context rather than identify the "real" problems of the cultures in the Middle East that are not so different from those of "other" (?) cultures.

An example in point is Egyptian novelist Ezzedine Fishere's fictional character Professor Darwish in *'Inaq ind Jisr Bruklin* (*Embrace on Brooklyn Bridge*, 2011). Scornful of his former Egyptian peers and an avid admirer of real-life British Lebanese Oxford historian Albert Hourani, Darwish is an elitist intellectual who looks down on his fellow Arabs. His ongoing argument with past British girlfriend Jane regarding Egyptians and Egyptian culture presents a reversal of conventional positions. She is infatuated with Arab "warmth" and "good-naturedness," whereas he is critical of Arab "irrationality." Jane constantly justifies what Darwish refers to as "their backwardness," while he cannot accept that Arabs should be regarded as some "corrupt offshoot of the rest of humanity," abiding by different moral standards than the rest of the world.[13] Although elitist, in Arabic his criticism seems introspective rather than confirming to Orientalist slurs. However, reading those same words in John Peate's English translation, a change in interpretation may take place. As Ezzedine himself has it, "But when I saw the text emerge in English I could feel the red lines beaming beneath the words, and I am still unsure whether these lines are crossed."[14] Notwithstanding these interpretive possibilities of the English version, *Embrace on Brooklyn Bridge* is originally an Arabic novel and, therefore, not susceptible to critics' condemnations of confirming Orientalist misrepresentations that are generally reserved for Arab Anglophone authors who may present similar views as Ezzedine's Professor Darwish. Critics assume a more tolerant attitude toward translations, since it is, perhaps, understood that the words were not originally intended for Western eyes. The imagined English-language readers are merely voyeurs, anonymously watching a "private" argument between Arab authors and their Arab audiences. Within the Arab Anglophone context, critics are less forgiving, since the implied Anglophone readers are the intended audience, and it is assumed that they approach the text with certain prejudices.

To reiterate my point regarding the repercussions of the Anglophone Palestinian text—and to sum up this part—the English language offers both postcolonial critics and Arab Anglophone authors a lingual environment that is inseparable from the complexities of centuries-old Orientalist notions and their formative influence on the current Israeli-Palestinian conflict. As shown so far, the critic navigates a densely compressed space that exclusively accounts for the immediate rather than the long-term, cross-generational consequences of the Nakba. Consequently, it appears that narratorial configurations of the Palestinian plight necessarily need to pass through recognizable thematic and historic portholes to accommodate the national sentiments of one kind of readership while resisting the prejudices of another hypothetical homogeneous readership. However, in my view, the problem is that this strategy seeks to freeze history and solely comprehend the Palestinian plight through rather static concepts. Placing the Anglophone Palestinian branch of literature in a polylingual category presents a conceptual framework that allows the critic to consider the flaws of modernity and the injustices of history as ongoing processes that have basically framed the variegated manifestations of modern Palestinian literature. It is only reasonable to infer that since the early waves of immigration to Latin America and during seven decades of Palestinian displacement since the Nakba, the story of Palestine has developed into several stories, representing diverse experiences of distinct upcoming Palestinian generations growing up in various locations around the globe.

The Generational Conjuncture

The focus of this final section shifts from the critical to the literary dimension of the Anglophone branch. In accordance with my argument on the critics' commitment to the national script, the purpose here is to show how the prioritization or marginalization of this script in the novel respectively compresses or expands artistic space with regard to representations of upcoming Palestinian generations in diaspora. In their novels *Mornings in Jenin*, *The Blue between Sky and Water*, *The Inheritance of Exile: Stories from South Philly*, and *A Curious Land: Stories from Home*, both Abulhawa's and Darraj's depictions of exiles and immigrants of Palestinian descent represent distinct visions of the future of the Palestinian identity in the diaspora. Certainly, their works belong in the Arab American genre that is becoming an inextricable part of the ethnic landscape of literary America. Nonetheless, while it is not the aim of this chapter to bypass such a major context in the study of Anglophone Palestinian writings, my reading of Abulhawa's and Darraj's representations of the next generation as diasporic highlights the transnational dimension of their works.

My argument is that Abulhawa's artistic commitment to the national script facilitates an exclusive outlook—similar to Suleiman's in *Being Palestinian*—that presents Palestinian diasporas as a uniform static outcome of a historic injustice that needs to be undone in order for upcoming generations to be allowed to move on. Amal Abulhawa's Americanized daughter, Sara, in *Mornings in Jenin* and Nur Valdez upon her journey to Gaza in *The Blue between Sky and Water* remain deeply endeared by their parents' tragic heritage and are never allowed to break free. As second- and third-generation exiles and immigrants, both characters' respective relations to their Palestinians origins, nonetheless, appear uncharacteristically two-dimensional. The American and Palestinian cultural elements never seem mutually disruptive, but rather Sara's and Nur's respective experiences unselfishly ("re")connect them to their roots on account of relinquishing their more or less Americanized identities.

In *Mornings in Jenin*, Sara seems to be uncritically mirroring her mother's identity without addressing potentially disruptive elements of her American lifestyle. Rather, her identity appears balanced as a young Palestinian woman living in the United States. She favors Palestinian dishes (*makloobeh*) and merely reacts in awe and asks predictable questions regarding her family's both tragic and fantastic story, clear of the complexities of a second-generation exile burdened by a national heritage: "Although Sara was *stunned* to learn about David and *hurt* that her mother had kept so much from her for so many years, she was mostly *intrigued*. She was *grateful* to know, however belated" (260; emphasis added). "Sara gasped. She had never known" (280). "Sara's face opened like a wound. Disbelieving, intrigued, hungry for the full story" (280). "'Wow!' Sara said. 'It's beautiful'" (290). "'I can't wait to meet Huda and hear stories of you two.' Sara was visibly excited" (293). It seems that Sara exclusively functions as the constantly fascinated and positive recipient of her mother's stories when Amal decides to open up to her daughter. That is, Sara comes to life in the novel only through her reactions to Amal's heritage. Sara's sole initiative is manifested in her decision to go to Palestine in order to discover who she "really" is: "'Mom, I'm going to Palestine. I want you to come too.' . . . 'It isn't just because of these filthy politics and injustice, Mom,' Sara said, the rims of her eyes darkening into red and tears pooling over them. 'I want to know who I am'" (281). There is no room for details of Sara's American existence in Abulhawa's fictional universe. It is symbolically put on hold as she decides to (re)locate her "essential" Palestinian self by way of "returning" to Palestine with her mother.

Even at the request of following her request to travel to Palestine to find her roots, she is never allowed to develop an independent identity during their journey. Amal refers to Sara only as an extension of herself, as if her daughter might view Palestine only through the mother's eyes: "Sara and I" (see, for instance, 295, 296, and 299). Moreover, Sara's dependency on Amal's narration is further established insofar as Amal seems to finally discover that her daughter exists during a moment of shared trust that culminates in an intimate symbolic embrace, suggesting the melting together of two entities into one, or, more accurately, the subsuming of one into the other: "Sara lay her head in the nook of my shoulder wrapping her arms around me, as she had not done since she was too young to remember. And while the air outside was foreboding and pulsed with coming death, I burned with the love I had denied myself and this perfect child resting in my arms. It occurred to me then that I had found home. She had always been there" (297). Following this moment of intimacy, Amal begins to reveal, as if to herself, traumatic experiences from the past regarding her own displacement and her husband's (Sara's father's) death in Lebanon. Again, Sara's reactions are restricted to emotional outlets in relation to her mother's story: "Sara was crying. Guilt, because my behavior then had irritated her. "'Oh, Mom. I'm so sorry. I had no idea. I was so insensitive. I didn't understand'" (301), suggesting that now she understands and has taken yet another step toward foregrounding Amal's complexities rather than her own. Even during extended periods of terror, under an Israeli military siege, Sara does not express a longing to return to her relatively safe existence in Philadelphia. Although she is extremely terrified during moments of genuine danger, Amal's narration disallows her the right to claim a "home" in the United States, where she grew up as the daughter of a Palestinian exile.

In *The Blue between Sky and Water*, Nur Valdez is a third-generation immigrant born in the United States to a Palestinian father and a Mexican mother. Following her father's untimely death and later her grandfather's, Nur is left to fend for herself, daily targeted by her (non-Palestinian) mother's abuse and her American stepfather's sexual assaults until she is located by the authorities in a dire state. Nur is first hospitalized and then for several years pushed from pillar to post between a number of foster homes, suggesting that for the Palestinian there is no real home in the United States, merely a series of temporary lodgings. During Nur's excruciating childhood, which has led to her developing a deep sense of self-loathing and to eventually suffer from bulimia, she is checked up on by Nzinga, a Black social worker of South African origin. Her only happy childhood memories are of the time she spent with Jiddo Mamdouh ("grandfather" in Arabic) before she was left at the mercy of her mother. It is a feeling she rediscovers upon her journey to Gaza, where she joins her Palestinian family and, at long last, feels at home. In *The Blue between Sky and Water*, Abulhawa divides the world into two: the Palestinians and the rest. Nur feels happy and at home when among "her own" and miserable and self-loathing when she is not. Even her bulimia is framed by this equation. After having spent some time in Gaza, and now pregnant as a result of a short affair with a local doctor, during a brief reunion Nzinga points out that she always knew about her condition and is confident that Nur has now found her place in the world, since the signs of her eating disorder have disappeared: "'That's how I knew you were home when you went to Gaza. You didn't have those red marks anymore'" (267). Symbolically, Palestine is not only home but also a cure for the miseries of exile.

Nur's "homecoming" is, however, not merely expressed through the improvement of her psychological and physical state. In the magical realist narrative style of the novel, Nur's "return" to Gaza fulfills a secret family prophecy guarded by her great-aunt, the family's matriarch, Haje Nazmiyeh. The primary commentator on the

Baraka family's history is Khaled, who, uncommunicative to the other characters, speaks to the reader from his "comatose" (locked-in syndrome) state, suggesting the symbolic status of the Palestinians' general condition—alert and receptive, but unable to engage with the world. From the outset, Khaled's narratorial presence in the text is rendered supernatural. Several decades before his birth, Khaled already appears as a ghostlike figure in that magical place of "blue," whereby he speaks to Mariam (his great-aunt)—Haje Nazmiyeh's younger sister—and teaches her to read and write before she is killed in 1948 by Zionist forces. Returning from the dead, Mariam asks Nazmiyeh to name her daughter Alwan ("colors" in Arabic), who eventually names her son Khaled. In this magical realist setting, it is not clear if Khaled the narrator is named after Mariam's imaginary friend or if he, indeed, is the same boy. Notwithstanding the opaqueness of Khaled's origin and his own confusion regarding this point, Khaled's supernatural presence offers a master narrative framework for Nur's story of "return": lost and shattered in exile, her arrival "home" restores order to a fundamentally chaotic state. In Khaled's own words in the introduction to the novel:

> *Then Nur came, her mouth full of Arabic words that were sawed off and sanded at the edges with curly accent of a foreigner. She came with all that American do-gooder enthusiasm that thinks it can fix broken people like me and heal wounded places like Gaza. But she was more shattered than any of us.*
>
> *And every night, when Nur put my sister Rhet Shel to bed, Teta Nazmiyeh pulled the sky in place and Mama embroidered in it the stars and moon. And in the morning when Rhet Shel awoke, she hung the sun. That's how it was when Our came back.* (2–3)

In this opening monologue, Abulhawa expresses her strict adherence to the national script, countering a rich discourse on the problems of exile. Whereas exiles view their state as both a psychologically and an existentially everlasting predicament—as so many revered Palestinian figures such as Edward Said, Mahmoud Darwish, and

Mourid Barghouti have extensively elaborated—Abulhawa regards it as a temporary and curable condition once a reconnection to their Palestinian roots has been established. Everything will be as it once was, as if the Nakba had never come about, and, hence, its traumatic consequences will magically disappear.

In contradistinction to Abulhawa's unconditional loyalty to this fixed conception of the national script, in *The Inheritance of Exile*, Darraj presents a somewhat more complex portrayal of the intergenerational conflicts between unassimilable immigrant Palestinian mothers and their Americanized daughters. Darraj's novel is rather exceptional in the Anglophone Palestinian branch in that it presents the experiences of upcoming generations as part of an ongoing chapter in the contemporary unfolding of the Palestinian story. Nadia, Aliyah, Hanan, and Reema, the protagonists of Darraj's novel, are not hemmed in by their national and cultural heritage represented through their respective mothers' strong presences in the way Abulhawa's Sara is. Rather, they engage the local Philadelphia settings as young (Arab) American women, confronting both their Americanness and their Arabhood as they engage the realities inside and outside their parents' homes. Canonical Palestinian themes do not explicitly surface, but, in their implicit presence, they nonetheless frame the intergenerational conflicts between mothers and daughters. Rather than explicitly address the national script, as Darraj does in her second novel, *A Curious Land*, in *The Inheritance of Exile* she seems to be more interested in transferring the cultural nuances from back "home" into Philadelphia's apparently uniform settings of identical streets and row houses, determining the first-generation females' diverse immigrant experiences and their influences on their daughters' lives.

The novel goes back and forth between Philadelphia and Jerusalem settings, portrayed by first-generation immigrants who nostalgically reminisce about the "homeland," while exploring the foreign US context. It also presents stories about the second generation and their need to grapple with a national and cultural heritage while also having to cope with the complexities of growing up as daughters of

Arab immigrants. "Reading Coffee Cups" and "The Journey Home" are particularly revealing chapters in the context of these cultural aspects of the Palestinian story. In the first, Lamis, Aliyah's mother, falls back on Palestinian class consciousness in her relations with her Arab friends when Nader buys a dishwasher for his wife, Siham. Lamis is bothered by Nader's gesture because it somehow perpetuates Siham's privileged social status from back home, issuing from urban Jerusalem and daughter of the well-known Dr. Al-Medani. It is a distinction that, according to Lamis, should not apply to the Philadelphia settings whence they are equally estranged: "Here, in America, our water comes in from the same pipe and our sewage exits from the same pipe—here, we are all the same" (58). The dishwasher triggers a sense of resentment in Lamis toward Siham and toward what her status from back home represents, even in Philadelphia: "My father could have been wealthy also—he had owned half the farmland in the village! God knows what it was worth now, especially in a prime location like Jerusalem's outskirts. But now, in Philadelphia, we shared even our walls with our neighbors. I counted pennies painstakingly, because I had four children who eventually would need college money, and I rarely bought new dresses or fancy clothes—and here was Siham with a fancy, expensive new machine, to remind me of what had been lost" (64). Being from a village situated at the outskirts of Jerusalem positions Lamis a tip "below" Siham, who is a native Jerusalemite. Even her university education cannot make up for this gap, according to the class hierarchies from back home: "Siham was a lady, the closest thing to bourgeoisie we had in our South Philadelphia neighborhood. I wasn't one of them, because my family were villagers, though at least—I feel guilty when I think about this, because I know it is wrong—we are not from the refugee camps like poor Layla" (57). Of course, Lamis cannot escape these class distinctions, insofar as they may also work in her favor vis-à-vis Palestinians from the camps: "Why did I resent her [Siham]? Because she liked to show off? And I . . . I was no better than Samira and her mother, the way I still thought of Layla and even Reema, both of whom had grown up in the camps. Somewhere between Palestine and having children, I had developed a class conscience" (65). My point is that Darraj offers a rare look into how the Palestinian cultural heritage frames Lamis's, as well as her friends', immigrant experience in the United States. Certainly, Palestinian political history represents a fundamental aspect of this framework, but *The Inheritance of Exile*, rather than focusing on historic injustices, presents the stories of hardworking Palestinian Arab women counting pennies to get their daughters through college while struggling to protect them from the cultural "risks" of assimilation in American society.

The novel also explores the implications of this cultural heritage through the perspectives of the daughters. In the chapter "Preparing a Face," Hanan, a young, rebellious Arab American woman, maintains a constantly confrontational relationship with her mother, Layla, a hardened woman who grew up in a refugee camp. Hanan revolts against her mother's emotional extortion of not being sufficiently Arab, of not sufficiently understanding "our" ways, and of not having been able to sufficiently acquire Arabic. Following one of many cultural transgressions while having her uncle Ibrahim over, Hanan retires to her bedroom and makes a definitive decision that echoes throughout the narrations of her experiences: "She was not an Arab" (81). She distances herself from a heritage she does not comprehend and that constantly makes her feel "insufficient" (a concern, as we find out in the following chapter, "Sufficing," she has inherited from her mother). Even her mother's background seems to mean little to Hanan: "Her father was an American, born to Arab parents, but her mother hadn't been born here—she'd grown up in the hilly town of Ramallah, had fled a series of wars, had left behind camps strewn with shrapnel, legless corpses, wailing women, and eyes too weary to weep. But Hanan had been born right here, in Philadelphia, in St. Agnes Hospital on Broad Street, and she had lived here all her life" (81). Eventually, Hanan learns that such a definitive position does not save her from the complexities of the ethnic landscape in the US context, whereby her lineage continues to define her. To her American in-laws, she will always be "Hunan," who ate chicken with her fingers and wiped her plate clean with bread (129); to John, her husband, she is exotic; and to his colleagues at the University of Pennsylvania, she is "genuinely" Arab, qualified to assess the "authenticity" of the department chair's thesis on Arab and Muslim women's political education and careers in the Middle East (138). Hanan is constantly warding off these labels. However, she also seems unable to suppress certain cultural mannerisms during encounters with the middle-class WASP community in Philadelphia. She not only eats with her fingers and defensively condemns Hollywood Orientalist portrayals of the Arab, but also, following an awkward exchange about Israel-Palestine with two senior professors from John's department, makes—to John's horror—the fatal mistake of kissing one of them on the cheek as they part: "He leaned in—why, I wasn't sure, but my instinct took over, and I kissed his cheek, which was right next to my mouth. I did it because that was how I kissed all my uncles and cousins and relatives . . . a handshake and a kiss on the cheek. But I knew, even as my lips had made a slight indent on his soft, weathered cheek, that I was making a big, big mistake" (141). It is as though her heritage steered her toward further transgressions, to make things worse—in a cultural context in which Hanan has decided to exclusively belong. Professor Keriakis's telling response basically rejects Hanan's application for cultural citizenship and disallows her from escaping her heritage: "That was a pleasant surprise. I was only going to tell you that I spent a lot of time studying in the Middle East—and now I feel right at home. I guess you can take a girl out of Palestine, but . . . well you know the rest" (141). Hanan's definitive contention repeatedly fails as she marries and eventually divorces John, singlehandedly raises a child, and becomes economically independent, gradually discovering that she belongs in both worlds while belonging in neither.

Conclusion

The basic distinction between Darraj's and Abulhawa's novels in their representations of the second generation points to a larger thematic crux in Anglophone Palestinian writings. Whereas Darraj specifically portrays the complex experiences of four young Arab American–born women with passing references to historico-political events, Abulhawa anchors her characters' fates in the canonic national script, unwilling to move beyond and explore contemporary consequences of Palestinian displacement in the US context through characters such as Sara and Nur. As a Palestinian author of the Anglophone novel, Abulhawa belongs in the group of writers represented by authors such as Ibrahim Fawal and Shaw Dallal, whose novels, according to Salaita's classification, constitute an additional branch in the literary canon since they remain loyal to specific tropes in Palestinian fiction. In this sense, *The Inheritance of Exile* stands out in its capacity to tell stories about Palestinians while backgrounding the national script. I do not claim that this literary move makes the novel less Palestinian. To the contrary, it is precisely the prioritization of the cultural nuances in the transnational context through localized sentiments that I find significant in establishing a relevant collective script that may comprehend today's increasingly diverse Palestinian experiences across borders and generations.

The danger of further compressing Palestinian space is that it may become irrelevant to future generations. The idea of the peasant who thought it inconceivable to be separated from the land more than seven decades ago probably does not represent the experiences of today's Westernized and urbanized English-speaking Palestinian individual. Certainly, it may present a symbolic icon indispensable for maintaining the collective memory of a shared past—"in order not to forget." Nonetheless, the manifold stories of upcoming generations start elsewhere and probably stand in tension with their parents'. It may be helpful to look at what's going on in Arabic. I wish to refer you to a recent article in *Ha'aretz* by the talented journalist Janan Bsoul about the current state of Palestinian literature in Israel. During a string of interviews with Palestinian writers in Israel, both authors and scholars of Arabic letters converge on the point that following decades of a vibrant Arab cultural scene in Jaffa, Haifa, and Jerusalem, in 1948 the Nakba confined literature to a tragic national framework. I believe that while an upcoming generation of writers in Israel-Palestine is gradually turning to exploring "life itself," in English (aside from a few individual works), Anglophone writers and their critics seem to be fixated on this "cruel love" of our Palestinian tragedy. Of course, such discrepancies between Arabic and Anglophone Palestinian literary productions further prove that writing in the native language, indeed, allows for a sense of freedom that a foreign language, such as English, cannot offer. To conclude, I wish to quote Israeli-Palestinian author 'Alaa Hlehel's words from the same *Ha'aretz* article in order to rethink the perimeters of Palestinian literature in English: "A writer sometimes need to 'burn the flag.'"

3

(Tres)passings

The "No-Man's-Land" of Palestinian Imaginings

> If only you could see what I've seen with your eyes.
> —*Blade Runner*

Notwithstanding the distinct geographical and socioeconomic conditions of the various Palestinian contexts of displacement, the character of the European Jew has occupied a major position in the national imagination. It is even reasonable to assume that it has become an inextricable part of various Palestinian self-imaginings regardless of geographical location. Nonetheless, Palestinians from different contexts would still view their Israeli counterparts through different lenses and see different manifestations of this adversarial other. There are wide gaps between the soldier monitoring Palestinian movement at various checkpoints, the invasive settler disfiguring the Palestinian landscape, the soft-spoken Holocaust survivor praising the miracle of Israel, and the pleasant family arriving in the Galilee to enjoy authentic hummus in the Arab-populated countryside. These diverse manifestations of the Zionist subject variedly furnish Palestinian projections of the self. More significantly, they distinctively furnish Palestinian self-conceptions. Under occupation in the West Bank, resistance and steadfastness configure as virtuous qualities, determining the character of Palestinians' relationship with soldiers and settlers. In Israel, principles of civility and discourses of coexistence more or less frame how Arabs see themselves relating to their Jewish neighbors. Palestinians in the various diasporas—while preserving customs and ties to the homeland—rarely interact with Israelis in their host nations. They might, nonetheless, occasionally encounter security personnel at Ben Gurion Airport and soldiers at checkpoints upon visiting Israel-Palestine. However, the majority would, in their different locations of residence, sympathize with or actively engage in different forms of solidarity movements such as, among others, the Boycott, Divestment, and Sanctions movement.

To explore such distinctions through literature, this chapter seeks to explore the rare literary trope of passing in Susan Abulhawa's *Mornings in Jenin* and Sayed Kashua's (Israel) Hebrew-language novel *Goof Sheni' Yaheed* (*Second Person Singular*, 2010).[1] Both authors present Arab characters who, under unique circumstances, impersonate or literally acquire the identity of Israeli Jewish characters. Such (tres)passing in Palestinian literature—entering "enemy territory"—was first presented by Ghassan Kanafani during the late sixties. In *A'ed 'illa Haifa* (*Returning to Haifa*, 1969), Kanafani narrates the story of a Palestinian couple, Said and Safeyya, who fled their home in Haifa in 1948. Following the Six-Day War of 1967, they return to find out that their infant son, Khaldun, whom they had left behind, has been raised as an Israeli by a Jewish widow, Miriam, whose husband had died in the Suez War eleven years earlier. Khaldun, now Dov, an officer in the Israeli army, upon meeting Said and Safeyya and discovering the truth, blames and rejects his biological parents for their cowardice—how could they abandon their infant son? Said, first heartbroken and then furious, concludes that armed struggle against Israel is inevitable. As he and Safeyya return to the West Bank, Said wishes that Khaled, his other son, would have left home to join the fight.

More than four decades after the publication of Kanafani's novella, Abulhawa and Kashua, Palestinian authors of different political and cultural experiences, revisit this rare literary trope, each in her and his unique way. In their respective creations of Ismael/David and Amir/Yonatan, both writers construe fictional characters whose existence within the framework of Palestinian literature blurs the borderlines between various versions of today's Palestinian Arabs and mainstream projections of their Israeli counterpart. These characters represent, as I will demonstrate in this chapter, the respective authors' attempts at experimenting with the ongoing implications of the idea that, as a result of the historical events of the Israeli "Independence" and the resulting Palestinian Nakba, the collision of two national yearnings has created a liminal space in which both the Israeli and the Palestinian narratives gradually infiltrate one another, developing an inextricable and dynamic bond between various manifestations of Palestinian and Israeli identities. That is to say, projections of the adversarial other interrelatedly (without ignoring the power imbalances) invade both Israeli and Palestinian self-conceptions. It is not to naively preach that if somehow Palestinians get in touch with the Israelis inside them and vice versa, there will be regional peace. Also, I want to distance my argument from Frantz Fanon's psychoanalytically oriented theory in *Black Skin, White Masks* (1952) of the colonized people's appropriation and imitation of the colonizer's culture. Rather, Abulhawa's and Kashua's characters show how projections of the Israeli other variedly unsettle the concept of national identification as such for Palestinians in the diaspora and for those persons who remained in the homeland.

Abulhawa's and Kashua's lives and careers represent different stories of Palestinian displacement—one in exile and the other in Israel-Palestine as part of an underprivileged minority (although Kashua and his family today live, in their seventh year, in the United States). As a result of both authors' particular immersion in distinct local cultures, framing their respective Arab communities in the diaspora and in the homeland, they have chosen—or, as both authors have expressed on separate occasions, had no other choice—to write in languages other than Arabic.[2] Moving across borders, languages, and generations, the polylingual category produces a framework for bringing these novels together to examine them as Palestinian texts that represent literary portrayals of culturally diverse experiences in distinct localities of displacement. As described in earlier chapters, Abulhawa, daughter of refugees of the Six-Day War from at-Tur, Jerusalem, and author of the diaspora, resides in Yardley, Pennsylvania; Kashua, a citizen of Israel, originally from the village of Tira in the Triangle area, is a (former) Jerusalem resident in the homeland and belongs to a group composed of Palestinians who write in Hebrew. My aim in bringing these authors together is to explore the ways whereby they work out the implications of displacement through their relation to representations of the Israeli other, based on the authors' shared yet distinct feelings of homelessness, while searching for new ways of self-identity and their cultural heritage in local languages and contexts. I think it is necessary to recognize this duality in both Abulhawa's and Kashua's writings in order to examine their impact in both the Palestinian and respective local contexts. On the one hand, they tell a particular Palestinian story. On the other, since they are composed in English and Hebrew, they inject this story into local mainstreams vis-à-vis Deleuze and Guattari's theory of "minor literature."

Mornings in Jenin and *Second Person Singular* not only are linguistically different novels by authors of distinct Palestinian experiences but also set their stories in widely different settings. As previously described, Abulhawa thematically presents a broad overview of modern Palestinian history from 1941 until Israel's military invasion of the Jenin Refugee Camp in 2002 through the story of the Abulheja family's dispossession. Shifting the focus from how Abulhawa portrays upcoming Palestinian generations in *Mornings in Jenin*, this chapter centers on her portrayal of the complex Palestinian-Israeli character Ismael/David. Ismael/David is the long-lost son of the Abulhejas, abducted in infancy and raised by a childless Israeli Jewish couple, Moshe and Jolanta Aviram. In adulthood, he becomes both the Israeli doppelgänger, unwittingly punishing his Palestinian biological brother in a security facility at an Israeli checkpoint, and the paradoxical figure sitting at the kitchen table with his sister, Amal, the novel's protagonist, in Philadelphia, coming to terms with the truth as they, through dialogue, retroactively narrate the story of the Abulhejas. Abulhawa diverges from conventional literary projections of the Jew in the Palestinian imagination as the unknowing European immigrant who transforms into the oppressive Israeli soldier. She implants a Palestinian person into the identity of an Israeli

Jew and positions him at the table of narration as an observer, an inquirer, and an auditor.

Second Person Singular explores the problem of cultural and national identification for Israel's Arab minority—the Palestinians who remained. Kashua, similarly, but perhaps more disturbingly than Abulhawa, creates an Arab protagonist who willingly begins to impersonate an Israeli Jewish character. Whereas Ismael/David's unique experience is the outcome of an abduction motivated by Moshe and Jolanta's desire to have a child at any price, Amir, in Kashua's novel, intentionally transforms into Yonatan, impersonating him in public and assuming his position as Rachel's son at home. Amir Lahab is an Arab social worker who, rather than return to the Arab village of Jaljoulia in the Triangle area in Israel upon completing his university studies, decides to stay and work in Jerusalem. He is socially awkward, suffering the consequences of having been raised by a single mother in a ruthless patriarchal culture. In Jerusalem, owing to a minor traumatic experience of being ridiculed by his male colleagues while going to a party with his female coworker Leila, Amir not only leaves the party but also resigns from his position and his former life as an Arab in Israel, gradually entering the plot that transforms him into Yonatan Forschmidt.

In the following parts of this chapter, I intend to discuss how Ismael Abulheja's and Amir Lahab's unlikely transformations variedly challenge current authoritative notions of Palestinian and Israeli identities. Abulhawa's and Kashua's "invasive" literary engagements lead to diverse rewritings of "Palestinianhood" in contemporary contexts of displacement. This chapter has a three-part structure. In the first, I develop a conceptual framework for reading these characters in relation to various prominent Palestinian literary figures' (for example, Mahmoud Darwish's and Anton Shammas's) depictions of the Israeli Jew. My purpose is to employ these projections for distinguishing between Abulhawa's and Kashua's statuses as Palestinian writers and to show that they enter "enemy territory" through different Palestinian experiences. In the second part, I explain how Abulhawa's and Kashua's subversive representations of Palestinian and Israeli maternal figures guarantee the fulfillment of the authors' literary (tres)passing. The transformations of Ismael and Amir not only are framed by these representations but also reveal complementary historic and mythical burdens of Palestinian and Israeli motherhood. In the third, I present an overview of the critical consequences of Ismael's and Amir's respective transformations into David and Yonatan. As I demonstrate, both authors experimentally destabilize established orders of authority between Arabs and Jews in contemporary contexts of conflict.

(Tres)passing

The Israeli-Palestinian conflict has triggered processes of national intertextuality that yield unidentifiable cultural configurations incomprehensible in the contesting national discourses. The various contemporary sociopolitical and cultural Palestinian realities of displacement have pushed Palestinians (and Israelis) beyond their national narratives. This discrepancy has created a hostile yet inextricable bond between the various manifestations of both Palestinians and Israelis. My point is that, thematically, Abulhawa's and Kashua's experimental literary creations of Ismael/David and Amir/Yonatan should be positioned in this liminal gap between national narratives and the anxiety caused by transcending them. The improbability of their identities demarcates the limits of canonic historical frameworks and pushes us beyond contemporary conventions of national identification—toward uncharted spaces.

Near the end of a landmark interview in 1996 with Hilit Yeshurun for the Israeli literary journal *Hadarim*, Mahmoud Darwish, the renowned Palestinian national poet upon his return to Ramallah following the signing of the Oslo Agreement in 1993, points to a specific unsettling outcome of the historic collision between Israeli and Palestinian national yearnings: "It is impossible to evade the place that the Israeli has occupied in my identity. He exists, whatever I may think of him. He is a physical and psychological fact. The

Israelis changed the Palestinians and vice versa. The Israelis are not the same as they were when they came, and the Palestinians are not the same people they once were."[3] Darwish's observation primarily confirms that history has triggered processes of national intertextuality leading to unique cultural configurations that are unidentifiable in both Israeli and Palestinian historical frameworks. Also implied is that available conceptual frameworks cannot in return encompass these developing novel configurations since they have turned out differently from what was intended. For example, the fantasies of the Zionist settler who arrived in Palestine at the turn of the twentieth century with a pickax in one hand and a rifle in the other in order to determine his own destiny and the Palestinian peasant who loyally worked the land he thought inconceivable to be separated from have interrelatedly infiltrated each other. Such infiltrations of historic national stereotypes suggest the necessity for inventing contexts that may comprehend the production of new unusual cultural configurations. In other words, bringing together and reinterpreting contemporary Palestinian and Israeli identities is an inevitable and necessary phase in a conflict that seems insoluble, insofar as the contemporary contesting attitudes are still formulated firsthand and handed down by respective survivors of the Holocaust and the Nakba. In the vein of Darwish's statement, I think it is possible to trace a process whereby Abulhawa's and Kashua's literary (tres)passing—their experimentations of positioning Palestinian Arab characters within Israeli Jewish identities—intertwines current ideas of contesting national identities and produces new original ones that transcend contemporary political and cultural discourses.

However, the implications of Darwish's observation do not straightforwardly frame my argument. To the contrary, they complicate matters because I think it is also necessary to consider Darwish's personal evolution from a young persecuted Israeli Arab poet and newspaper editor during the 1960s to his subsequent status as the exiled national Palestinian poet. As Almog Behar adequately describes Darwish's complex personal history:

> Darwish represents the "state" of the Palestinian in the second half of the twentieth century—continuously in exile and under siege: exile from the Galilee to Lebanon in 1948, return to his destroyed village in the Galilee and life as a present absentee, life as a Palestinian citizen of Israel under the military government, departure for exile in the Palestinian diaspora, joining the PLO, the siege on Beirut and the exit from it, life in Tunis, the life of the exile in Paris, living in Ramallah after the establishment of the Palestinian Authority, and living in Amman. His broad personal experience and its connection to so many of his people's experiences have established him as a national poet.[4]

On account of Darwish's diverse personal history, my point is that when he refers to *his* ("my") identity as representative of all Palestinians—constantly "in exile and under siege"—this move should not overshadow the other personal dimensions of Darwish's self-reference. As Ibrahim Muhawi has it, in the foreword to the translation of Darwish's *Yawmiyyat 'al-Huzn 'al-Adi* (*Journal of an Ordinary Grief*, 1973), the poet's self-reference points both to himself as an individual and to his role as an extension of the entire Palestinian people.[5] Darwish's personal journey is unique, even in a Palestinian context. Unlike his compatriots, who respectively found themselves trapped in one of the various afflicted Palestinian realities following the wars of 1948 and 1967, he moved between different realities. Darwish's three major prosaic memoirs span his career as a poet and, more important, narrate the transition from being part of one particular community to belonging to all Palestinian communities. The first, *Journal of an Ordinary Grief*, describes Darwish's experiences of persecution in Israel: house arrest, encounters with Israeli interrogators, and periods spent in prison. Also, this memoir demonstrates his familiarity with Hebrew literature and Arab localities inside Israel. The second, *Dhakira lil-Nisyan* (*Memory for Forgetfulness*, 1987), describes the 1982 Israeli invasion of Lebanon, and the third, *Fi Hadrat 'al-Ghiyab* (*In the Presence of Absence*, 2006), appears following his "return" to Ramallah and two years before his death. Considering the extent of his career, it is only reasonable to presume that when Darwish refers to the Israeli as part of *his* Palestinian identity, the younger Israeli Arab poet's personal familiarity with Israeli persecution during the early years after the Nakba resonates in the words of the now older national poet who sits for the interview with the Israeli *Hadarim* upon his "return."[6]

Bringing Darwish's personal history into interpretations of his comment regarding Palestinians and Israelis connects it to Kashua's and Abulhawa's different Palestinian experiences. Manifestations of the Israeli other inevitably, yet distinctively, invade all attempts of self-definition in the various contemporary contexts of Palestinian displacement. Darwish sees this inevitability as a historic outcome that Palestinians cannot possibly avoid upon embracing their cultural roots. At an earlier stage during the interview with Yeshurun, Darwish describes a Jewish presence inside the genetic code of the Palestinian Arab identity. Whereas "the *Israeli* has changed the Palestinian and vice versa," *Jewish* culture is one among the various historical elements that brought about the emergence of a Palestinian consciousness long before the establishment of the State of Israel:

> The Jew won't be ashamed to find the Arab element within him, and the Arab won't be ashamed to acknowledge that he is also composed of Jewish elements. Especially when speaking about "Eretz Yisrael" in Hebrew and "Palestine" in Arabic. I am a son of all the cultures that have passed through the land—the Greek, the Roman, the Persian, the Jewish, the Ottoman. A presence that exists at the very core of my language. Every powerful culture passed through and left something. I am the son of all these fathers, but I belong to one mother. Does that mean that my mother is a prostitute? My mother is this earth; she received all of them. She was both a witness and a victim. I am also the son of the Jewish culture that was in Palestine. That's why I don't recoil from the comparison.[7]

Darwish's subversive descriptions of this intimate relationship between Arabs and Jews—and consequently Palestinians and Israelis—are unsettling in a zero-sum context where two competing national narratives seek the destruction of one another. My contention is that

Abulhawa's and Kashua's literary creations of Ismael/David and Amir/Yonatan demonstrate the necessity for recognizing alternative outcomes of the historic collision between Palestinians' and Israelis' national yearnings as Darwish's comments suggest, allowing for the development of conceptual frameworks that may comprehend these unusual divergences. Whereas Darwish refers to an intimate and inextricable bond between Palestinians and Israelis on a symbolic level, Abulhawa's and Kashua's literary (tres)passing presents experimental transformations that allow for unsettling explorations of "enemy territory" and, consequently, of whom they themselves have become in their respective contexts of displacement.

In other words, Abulhawa's and Kashua's creations of Ismael/David and Amir/Yonatan do not necessarily reveal nuances of, as I shall demonstrate shortly, how they imagine the Israeli Jewish other. Rather, leaving behind the familiar and heading into "enemy territory," both authors depict original manifestations of their Palestinian identity in this hostile environment. To theorize this space, I want to briefly turn to Lital Levy's *Poetic Trespass: Writing between Hebrew and Arabic in Israel/Palestine* (2014). Levy outlines a liminal linguistic zone between two languages outside the nationalist-monolingual cultural space that she dubs, based on the title of Anton Shammas's second Hebrew-language poetry collection, *Shetah Hefker*, "no-man's-land." As Levy has it, "In the literary context in question, the no-man's-land is at once a space *between* Hebrew and Arabic and a space *outside* the ethnocentric domain that equates Hebrew with 'Jewish,' and Arabic with 'Arab.'"[8] Despite describing this space as an abandoned zone between two alienated languages (exclusively Hebrew and Arabic), Levy does recognize its potential for allowing writers to transgress the boundaries of language and identity inscribed in available sociopolitical codes and explore alternative poetic visions and cultural possibilities. I do not want to employ Levy's concept of liminality in a strictly linguistic sense to demarcate a no-man's-land between Hebrew and Arabic. Rather, I highlight Levy's latter point to refer to a kind of no-man's-land of Palestinian imaginings that both Abulhawa and Kashua engage when they transcend familiar discourses in their creations of Ismael/David and Amir/Yonatan—fertile ground for Darwish's subversive visions of identity.

I think it is pertinent to further add a few points to the apparent differences between Abulhawa's and Kashua's positions as Palestinian authors in order to show that they enter "hostile territory"—the no-man's-land of Palestinian imaginings—from different points of departure. Critically, scholars such as Steven Salaita position Abulhawa's writings in the Arab American canon that is being, as previously mentioned, further established by distinguished scholars of postcolonial theory and cultural translation such as Waïl S. Hassan and, more recently, Carol Fadda-Conrey and Nouri Gana.[9] She belongs to a particular branch within this canon that Salaita, in his analysis of Shaw Dallal's *Scattered Like Seeds* (1998) and Ibrahim Fawal's *On the Hills of God* (1998), categorizes as a potential fourth branch (referring to Jayyussi's distinction of literary productions in Arabic from Israel, the occupied Palestinian territories, and the diaspora in the Arab world as being the other three) of the Palestinian literary canon.[10] This unanimous recognition of Abulhawa as a Palestinian writer is rooted in her status as a Palestinian exile—a position she shares with, among others, Edward Said, who along with more or less contemporary compatriots such as Ghassan Kanafani and Mahmoud Darwish (after 1973) effectively established a narrative space for the exiled in the Palestinian consciousness.[11] Abulhawa's Palestinian identity, similarly to other exiles, is identifiable and unconditionally "authentic." Ironically, Palestinian exiles, who do not possess official citizenship for the potential nation-state they claim to belong to, view the Palestinians in Israel, who continue to live in the village or town where their families lived before 1948, as chained by their citizenship and basically existing as strangers in a homeland that has been rendered unrecognizable by Israeli political and social configurations.

To distinguish between these two areas of identification—"outside" and "inside"—literary critic Karen Grumberg borrows the concept of "tied up" from Israeli author David Grossman's interview with a Palestinian youth from the West Bank in *Ha-Zman Ha-Tsahov* (*The Yellow Wind*, 1987): "Yet Judat, the Palestinian interviewed by David Grossman, insists that it is *he* who is truly free and not the Israeli Palestinian, who is 'too tied up' with Israeli Jews." According to Grumberg, the notion of being "tied up" is a powerful reference to Shammas's liminal "no-man's-land" that seems to be the habitat of Arabs writing in Hebrew. It positions the Israeli Arab between "authentic" Israelis and equally "authentic" Palestinian exiles, demarcating, to employ Homi Bhabba's concept, a "third space" to account for processes of cultural hybridization. However, Grumberg points out—basing her view on interpretations of Shammas's and Kashua's literary works—that, in the case of Palestinians in Israel, this in-betweenness does not offer a fertile space for identity formation to escape the politics of polarization.[12] To the contrary, she turns to Said who, in the vein of Judat's comment (Grossman's interviewee), explains, "Being inside is a privilege that is an affliction, like feeling hemmed in by the house you own."[13] Said, all too familiar with the exile's habitat "outside" Israel-Palestine, presents a speculative conception for Grumberg's observation of the infertility of the Israeli-Palestinian landscape "inside."

It may be unreasonable to impose such restrictive generalizations—"feeling hemmed in" or "too tied up"—on the entire Palestinian minority in Israel, particularly since Grumberg bases her observation exclusively on Shammas's and Kashua's careers and works. I do not claim that Israeli Arabs' Palestinian identity is not constantly framed and simultaneously disrupted by their Israeli citizenship. Nonetheless, it is necessary to point out that Shammas's no-man's-land—which Kashua subsequently enters as a third-generation Israeli Arab through his Hebrew-language writings—emerges in the Israeli urban environment. Both Shammas and Kashua left their respective Arab villages at a relatively early age and moved to Israeli cities where they also attended schools with a mixed or an entirely Jewish student population. Both authors have on different occasions and through different media described the agonies they went through encountering the Israeli Jewish reality for the first time.[14] Rather than returning to their villages, both eventually settled down in Jerusalem at different periods before moving to the United States. My point is that their experiences as Arab citizens in Israel are not conventional. It is not to claim that other Arabs have not followed similar paths—from the village to the city via Israeli Jewish schools. Still, it is interesting to hypothetically ponder in which languages Shammas and Kashua would have written and what experiences they would have portrayed had they stayed in or at some point returned to the village where things more or less remained recognizably Palestinian, notwithstanding the constant cultural and economic influences of the Israeli reality. It is safe to assume that Shammas's and Kashua's literary identities have to a large extent been formed through their engagement with the Israeli urban landscape, whereas the majority of their fellow Arab citizens occasionally visit there—mostly during periods of university studies—before returning to the familiar rural environment of the village.

As a result, both authors—urbanized in Israeli cities—when they revisit the village in their respective works, express a kind of estranged familiarity with the place. For example, the first half of Shammas's acclaimed *Arabesques* is largely a narrative about Fassuta—the author's hometown, located in the upper parts of the Galilee—and his family's history there. This celebrated novel reveals Shammas's intimate relationship with the place but also his complex meditations on identity between Israeli and Palestinian realms that culturally position him at a distance from the village. Such a perspective that could only have developed as a result of existing in the urban no-man's-land for years becomes even more evident in Shammas's later nonfictional articles such as "Kitsch 22" (1987), where he describes a visit to Fassuta for the purpose of condoling a bereaved acquaintance. Going through the rituals of such occasions, Shammas turns his attention to the stone wall in the house of the widowed husband and engages in a discourse on how recent architectural transformations of the wall in Arab homes mirror generational changes to the Palestinian identity in Israel. Rather than merely accepting the functions of the wall like the bereaved owner of the house, Shammas's momentary return from the city enables him to scrutinize its symbolic value in relation to problems of national identification outside the village. Similarly, Kashua develops the outsider's perspective of the familiar through the protagonist-narrator in *We Yehye Boker* (*Let It Be Morning*, 2006). The novel opens with the protagonist and his family's return to his childhood home, Tira, following a ten-year absence, mostly spent in Tel Aviv. He searches for a quiet and safe life among his own, away from the discriminating and threatening climate of Tel Aviv. However, owing to his estranged familiarity with the place—the result of years spent in a major Israeli city—the larger part of the narrative critically foregrounds the nuances of the Palestinian village. Like Shammas, the protagonist's liminal existence in a largely Israeli Jewish space enables him to distance himself from the familiar workings of Arab life back home. Perhaps because of this outsider position, cultivated in the Israeli urban environment and expressed in both Shammas's and Kashua's works, critics such as Grumberg as well as Hannan Hever, Batya Shimony, Gil Hochberg, and Rachel Feldhay Brenner, among several others, have adamantly pursued, in their respective analyses of Shammas's and Kashua's novels, the tradition of positioning Hebrew-language writings by Arab authors exclusively within the Israeli canon while relatively eschewing their problematic position in the context of Palestinian deterritorialization.

These writings interrelatedly belong in both the Israeli and the Palestinian canons. Therefore, although Abulhawa's and Kashua's statuses as Palestinian authors differ—one in exile, while the other is a citizen of Israel (but today also in self-imposed exile)—they, nonetheless, represent quintessential Palestinian positions. From these positions, both authors respectively revisit a Palestinian, though rare, literary trope first presented by Kanafani and speculatively work out the implications of the historic collision of two contesting national narratives through the fantastic transformations of Ismael and Amir. As explained earlier, such literary experimentations not only produce unique cultural configurations but also necessitate the invention of conceptual frameworks for comprehending these configurations. It is in this sense that I refer to Levy's concept of trespass and Shammas's no-man's-land. Ismael/David and Amir Lahab are products of the authors' literary trespasses in the sense that Abulhawa and Kashua leave behind familiar discourses of identity and enter a kind of no-man's-land of Palestinian imaginings through different languages and cultural experiences. Both authors trigger processes for rethinking the Palestinian identity, in different contexts of displacement, by way of inventing Palestinian characters that pass as Israeli Jews. Abulhawa's and Kashua's distinct points of departure may seem relatively comprehensible since they belong to more or less recognizable communities in the larger Palestinian context. However, significant questions, which I will discuss in the following sections, arise: Where do Abulhawa and Kashua posit this no-man's-land of Palestinian imagination in the narrative plot? And how do they engage it?

Between Fertile and Barren Motherhoods

The unusual transformations of Ismael and Amir seem rather implausible. Nonetheless, both Abulhawa's and Kashua's realistic writing styles enable readers to suspend disbelief in regard to these characters' metamorphoses. Abulhawa and Kashua may engage "enemy territory" through different cultural experiences, as explained earlier. However, thematically, both authors similarly view this area—where Ismael and Amir successfully transform into the other—between representations of Palestinian and Israeli mothers. This maternal juxtaposition frames the intertwining of Palestinian narrations and perspectives with those experiences of their Israeli counterparts. The figurative movement from the pain of the fertile Palestinian Arab mother toward the desire of the childless Israeli Jewish mother demarcates the no-man's-land of Abulhawa's and Kashua's Palestinian imaginings regarding the other. Whereas the former literary configuration is the product of both the historic injustice repeatedly committed against her people before and after 1948 and her community's suppressing confinement of female figures to spousal and maternal roles, the latter is the product of a long history of persecution and in a certain way modeled after barren biblical matriarchs—a mother longing for a son. I argue that the portrayals of the respective Palestinian and Israeli maternal figures in Abulhawa's and Kashua's novels serve peculiarly similar purposes in that they present untold stories of injustice and social suppression of Arab female strength that infiltrate the desires of Jewish female characters through Ismael's and Amir's transformations.

In *Mornings in Jenin*, Dalia, a wild young Bedouin girl, grows into a stoic mother, following traumas of war and the kidnapping of her infant son Ismael. She rarely expresses affection for her other children, Yousef and Amal, and raises them to emulate her resilience: "*Whatever you feel, keep it inside*" (56). Following in her mother-in-law's footsteps, Dalia becomes the midwife of the Jenin Refugee Camp. Calm and skilled in her profession, she mentors her daughter to follow suit. Dalia is aware of her maternal shortcomings: "Dalia knew she had neglected Yousef since Ismael had disappeared" (50). She seems emotionally detached, and, nonetheless, her cool and efficient performance of midwifery becomes a means of communication to forward coded signs of affection to her daughter—"imparting skills and forestalling weakness were the ways Dalia loved" (56). During the later part of Dalia's life, as her children enter their teens, she starts to show signs of dementia and gradually ceases to communicate with the outer world altogether: "I [Amal] could at last see through the gaunt shell of my mother to the colorful, daring, and vivacious Bedouin girl whose fire had been tamped with a hot iron and whose wits had been doused with the ashes of too much death and too many wars" (119). Old, senile, and profoundly traumatized by experiences of war, social injustice, and an unbearable personal tragedy, she quietly passes away—harboring an untold story representing the predicament of many Palestinian women.

In *Second Person Singular*, Amir abandons his real mother, a widowed schoolteacher in Jaljoulia—a single mother, exposed to the abuse of a fundamentally patriarchal society. Amir's father dies when he is a year old, and when the mourning period ends, his mother escapes the village of Tira, abandoning her parents and in-laws who demand that she marry her late husband's younger brother to preserve her honor. Both families cut her off and leave her vulnerable to society's discriminating attitude. Amir grows up while suffering the consequences of his mother's pariah status. Society's abuse continues to haunt him in adulthood. During a rare visit to his village after he begins to impersonate Yonatan, Amir reminisces about the viscous attacks:

> My mother's honor all the kids knew, was free for the taking. That's how I learned that mother used to show her tits to all the kids in the class; that my mother wore red bras and short skirts; that my mother was ousted from her village for whoring; that at night, after I went to sleep, my mother hosted all sorts of men in her bed; that she smoked cigarettes and drank alcohol; that she collaborated with the authorities; that she slept with policemen; that she slept with the principal; that they did it in the school library; that she'd been seen dancing at nightclubs in Petach Tikva; that she was sleeping with the math teacher, the history teacher, and the supervisor; that on the class trip she'd been seen peeing in the bushes and she, for a fact, wore no underwear. (272–73)

Kashua creates a disturbing collage of society's abuse. There are no male figures to hide behind and ward off the attacks. Instead, Amir's mother and her son silently accept society's targeting and suffer the traumatic consequences. She grows detached and emotionally distant as she endures the crushing pressure of patriarchal suppression: "When I finally got home for the Festival of the Sacrifice, I squeezed my mother's hand and she squeezed mine. I could see in her face that she wanted to hug me, but she knew it was best to resist that urge. Instead her eyes glazed over. Me and my mother did not hug or kiss" (100). Like Dalia, Amir's mother is a stoic woman who seems unable to communicate affection: Dalia's attitude—"*Whatever you feel, keep it inside*"—resonates in hers, rendering Amir socially isolated, upon succumbing to her emotionally dysfunctional behavior.

There are several ways to interpret the figure of the afflicted Palestinian mother, unable to maintain a healthy, affectionate relationship with her children. Her maternal dysfunctionality symbolizes the historical gap between exiled subjects (children) and homeland (mother). But her personal suffering is also an indictment against gender discrimination within Arab society. Palestinian mothers' resilience forces them to radically retreat from society's predetermined female roles and consequently transforms them into absences. My point is that Dalia and Amir's mother transcend hegemonic social contexts. Nonetheless, they cannot exist outside the perimeters of society and, as a result, are destroyed by a coercive framework that negates the validity of their need for independence and fulfillment of desires. The wild Bedouin girl and the single mother who refuses to remarry must be eliminated, cast off, if society fails at taming and subjugating them under patriarchal control. Deeply scarred by the consequences of their positions outside the conventional, they retreat from the public and transform into severely dysfunctional individuals. Dalia and Amir's mother become unavailable to their children. They do not offer gestures of affection; their emotions should be hidden away, buried within, until they altogether wither and decay.

Whether willingly or unwillingly leaving behind their Palestinian mothers, Ismael and Amir transform into the other and fulfill the craving of the Jewish woman to mother a son. In *Mornings in Jenin*, Ismael is kidnapped in infancy and raised as David Aviram by Moshe and his wife, Jolanta, a young physically and emotionally scarred woman, unable to conceive as a result of the rape and torture she went through under Nazi confinement at an undisclosed concentration camp in Europe. In *Second Person Singular*, upon completing his studies and later quitting his position as a social worker, Amir begins to work for Rachel Forschmidt, a single mother and a professor at the Hebrew University of Jerusalem who has grown emotionally detached from her comatose son, Yonatan. Jolanta zealously grows into the role of motherhood as she raises David. However, whereas she becomes overprotective and increasingly anxious that her son's secret will someday be revealed, Rachel does not express maternal affection toward either Yonatan or Amir, who is gradually transforming into Yonatan. Her complicity is rooted in a philanthropic desire to offer the underprivileged other an opportunity for life: "And what you have here . . . is an organ donation that could very well save your life" (291), she repeatedly tells Amir. Both Jolanta and Rachel become symbols of hope, drawing Ismael and Amir away from their Palestinian Arab mothers and their respective tragic national destinies as a refugee or a member of the disadvantaged Arab minority in Israel.

It is difficult to ignore the biblical allusions in Abulhawa's and Kashua's portrayals of Israeli Jewish maternal characters. The craving for a son is an ancient Jewish theme that refers to the infertility motif related to three of the four matriarchs: Sarah, Rachel, and Rebecca. The relationship between the Jewish mother and the absent son, as in the cases of Jolanta and Rachel, becomes a literary window for Abulhawa and Kashua to inscribe the Israeli narrative into the Palestinian identity. Or, in another vein, these authorial choices might suggest Islamic rewritings of Jewish texts to intertwine history and the prospects of a common future. Ismael, in allusion to Abraham's exiled first born, the son of Hagar (whose name translates into both Arabic and Hebrew as "emigrate" or "going into exile"), and ancestor of the Prophet Muhammad, the founder of Islam, becomes David—an allusion to the ruler of the Jewish kingdom—as a result of Jolanta's plight and desire to overcome her barrenness by having a son at any price. Amir, "prince" in Arabic, becomes Yonatan, alluding to King Saul's son who defies his father in an attempt to save his best friend, the future King David. Amir, the "prince" from Jaljoulia, assumes the position of son for Rachel and her former (absent) husband, Yakov, alluding to the parents of Joseph, destined to lead the tribes of Israel between exile and nationhood. The religious overtones in Jolanta's and Rachel's complicity in Ismael's and Amir's transformations are intriguing, and they ultimately suggest an Arab Islamic infiltration of Jewish biblical themes, respectively, through English and Hebrew. However, Abulhawa's and Kashua's literary experimentations with identity should not be interpreted as expressions of some form of suppressed Palestinian desire to become Israelites. These modern allusions to ancient Jewish texts serve as conceptual frameworks for creating new versions of identity that are neither Palestinian nor Israeli as such—that is, the longed-for Jewish son is Arab, and the Arab abandons his heritage in order to perform a radical metamorphosis and fulfill the symbolic desire of Jewish motherhood.

At the end of *Mornings in Jenin*, during David and Amal's first encounter, they compare Jolanta and Dalia. David wants to know the woman who had given birth to him, and Amal wants to know more about the Jewish woman who raised her brother. David paints a portrait of Jolanta as a warm, colorful person who raised her son lovingly and attentively. However, he admits with some bitterness that his mother zealously protected him not only from the world but also from his true origins. Recognizing the ironic similarities between Jolanta's past of persecution in Germany and Dalia's tragic loss of her family and then her son in Palestine, Amal turns defensive to match David's portrayal: "It was Dalia and me against Jolanta and David. Dalia and me against the world. And I laid bare the fundamental truth of Mama's heart, which I had found in the endless early-morning reflections of exile, peeling back the layers, the personal fortress that she and destiny had conspired to construct. 'She loved beyond measure,' I said" (273). Amal's description of their mother to David transforms Dalia's retreat from the world into signs of profound tenderness that cannot survive in the hard world of the Israeli-Palestinian conflict. Within the silent, isolated woman who mercifully sinks into dementia to escape the horrors of her loss, Amal, in her conversation with David, discovers Dalia's boundless love for her children. Amal's descriptions may seem to be based on imagination more than on fact. Nonetheless, she finds comfort in an image that replaces memory as she sits across from David. Amal and David are siblings, but whereas one searches for her mother in a figure that had retreated from the world when she was alive, the other discovers, at his father's deathbed, as David recalls to Amal, that his mother's love could not atone for the colossal deception regarding his identity: "I loved Jolanta. She was the only mother I ever knew. But she allowed me to live a profound lie that came to much personal harm, for the sake of uncontested motherhood" (275). Figuratively, the absence of one mother and the deception of the other give birth to tragic identities that may not survive in contemporary national contexts. Nonetheless, they offer hope in that their children, who suffer the consequences of their maternal shortcomings, will identify not only with their own tragedy but also with that of the other.

Entering Enemy Territory

Upon symbolically suppressing the domain of Palestinian motherhood and moving toward the domain of the Jewish mother's desire, Abulhawa and Kashua explore "enemy territory" by way of entering the "no-man's-land" of Palestinian imaginings. Both authors' present unsettling visions of identity, variedly mixing together, as mentioned, two contesting national narratives. *Mornings in Jenin* presents the adversarial counterpart on both diegetic and extradiegetic levels in the fashioning of modern Palestinian identity. On the diegetic level, the novel, opening in 1941, presents various Jewish characters, introducing, initially, young Ari Perlstein, the son of a German professor who has recently fled Nazism. Ari befriends young Hasan Abulheja when they meet for the first time at the Damascus Gate in Jerusalem. It is a friendship that lasts despite the decades of ongoing conflict between Arabs and Jews. Later on, in 1948, during the Arab-Israeli War, Moshe Aviram, a Holocaust survivor turned Israeli soldier, not only participates in the fighting that leads to the surrender of Ein Hod—the Abulheja family's village—but is also a tormented antagonist who commits the fateful crime of kidnapping Dalia Abulheja's infant son Ismael. Finally, in 1967, we meet Ismael/David for the first time in the novel. Because of his secret, David is a rather complex character, diverging from the other two depictions of the Jew. He constantly grows throughout the novel, and, eventually, the reader discovers that he also partakes in the narration through the dialogue with his sister, Amal Abulheja. Transcending relatively familiar projections of the adversarial Israeli Jew in the Palestinian imagination, Abulhawa creates Ismael/David, a narrator-character who is essentially neither the Israeli Jew he has been brought up to believe he is nor the Palestinian Arab he can no longer return to become. His identity is liminal in terms of the contemporary Israeli and Palestinian discourses.

After Amal hangs up the phone, following her first conversation with David, she reveals the story of Ismael to her daughter, Sara. She tells her how her other brother Yousef may have once met Ismael, but as enemies in an Israeli prison. These exchanges between mother and daughter not only lead to both fascinating and disturbing realizations regarding their family history as previously described but also raise a critical question: "Who and what is Ismael/David?" When Sara asks Amal if "Ismael" had tortured Uncle Yousef, Amal replies, "I don't know. And I think we should call him David" (261), justifying her decision with the rationale that it would be less unbearable to imagine David—rather than Ismael—torturing Yousef. At Amal and Ismael/David's first encounter outside her home in Philadelphia, with some hesitation, she finally calls him "David": "He had not been Ismael for fifty-three years" (262). However, Amal's choice does not prioritize her brother's Israeli identity over his Palestinian origins. She recognizes the political gambit in her brother's situation: "He knew the improvised history of modern Israel was not really his. The heritage that ran through his blood was vintage, yet somehow that, too, was not his. Fate had placed him somewhere between, where he belonged to neither" (264). Ismael/David metaphorically mirrors the irreversible changes that history has inflicted on both Palestinians and Israelis. Enveloping David's Arab roots there is an Israeli culture, and within his Jewish existence there lies a Palestinian selfhood. Abulhawa captures this confusion in Amal's mixed feelings toward her brother: "I wanted to hate him, because I loved Yousef. But in David's melancholy face, I could see the shadows of Mama's eyes, Baba's nose, and David's own mistaken identity" (265).

Facing her brother, Amal searches for answers and starts to inquire into Yousef and Ismael's encounter decades earlier. She asks if he was the Israeli soldier who had beaten Yousef at the Barta'aa checkpoint, rendering him impotent. David admits to having done so and is unable to rationally explain his motives: "There is no reason or logic. I was twenty years old and they gave me total power over other human beings, Amal. I was angry. Somehow I knew he was connected to the secret I knew my parents harbored. And somewhere inside, I feared I might be an Arab. Rage and impunity I knew I had throbbed in my arms when I was holding the rifle" (266). Abulhawa creates an unusual political situation: she positions an Israeli character across from his Palestinian sibling, thus providing the grounds for highlighting the irrationality of an Israeli individual's personal aggression toward Palestinians. To rephrase David's reply, "What I did was illogical. I abused my power to ward off suspicions of who I essentially am." Within the framework of Darwish's observation of Israeli and Palestinian identities, David's explanation echoes a deep-seated anxiety regarding the problem of national identification in the context of the Palestinian-Israeli conflict. This constantly increasing distance between conceptions of the self and the narratives that hitherto allowed for the emergence of these very conceptions has developed deep anxieties regarding processes of identification, insofar as both Palestinians and Israelis may be rendered unrecognizable to themselves, since they are no longer who they imagine themselves to be. In this context, Ismael/David is a literary experiment whose outcome transcends contemporary and conventional frameworks and, more incisively, yields a character whose fate remains uncertain in the novel.

At the end of their conversation, as David asks Amal if she still conceives of him as an abstraction, her reply sums up the insoluble problem posed in his existence:

> *No, she thought. Of course not. You and I are the remains of an unfulfilled legacy, heirs to a kingdom of stolen identities and ragged confusion.* In the complicity of siblinghood, of aloneness and uprootedness, Amal loved David instinctively, despite herself and despite what he had done or who he had become. She ached

> to gather him in an embrace and absolve the pangs of conscience that tormented him. She wanted to fill a seat at his table and share in his loneliness. But all that left on her lips was an arid, "I don't know." (270)

The existence of Ismael as David sets in motion contradictory feelings in Amal that remain unresolved. She is even unable to decide if he, as a person, a brother, and a cultural divergence, is an abstraction. She does not know; even her brother is also uncertain: "At least you knew who you were and where you came from," (276), implicitly referring to his own undecipherable existence. To complicate things even further, and perhaps alluding to the kind of hybrid discourses developing in both the Israeli and the Palestinian consciousness, the narration of their first encounter ends with Amal's irrational sentence upon introducing "Ismael" to her daughter, Sara—uttered from Palestinian lips in English, "Habibti, I want you to meet my brother David" (278).

Whereas Abulhawa's poignant literary experimentations regarding the adversarial other unsettle projections of fixed stereotypes in Palestinian mainstream, turning to Kashua, *Second Person Singular* offers an "inside" view of Israeli culture from an Arab perspective. That is, unlike Abulhawa's *Mornings in Jenin* that may be defined as a strictly Palestinian novel (although written in English) since its story line progresses within a conventional Palestinian narrative framework, Kashua positions his story in contemporary Israeli settings, in the complex space between the Arab East and the Jewish West Jerusalem areas. As explained, because of his lifelong residency in Jerusalem and daily engagement in relations with Israeli Jewish compatriots, Kashua is able to trespass social borders and navigate the dense minefield of cultural prejudices.

In *Second Person Singular*, looking away from Yonatan and his mother, Rachel Forschmidt, other Israeli Jewish characters of various backgrounds emerge sporadically in the novel as part of the urban landscape of Jerusalem, but they are merely static presences that do not evolve. For example, in the chapters following the successful Arab lawyer, one of the novel's two protagonists, who becomes trapped in an evil cycle of jealousy and paranoia—having found a short suspicious note with his wife's handwriting in a recently purchased copy of Leo Tolstoy's *The Kreutzer Sonata*—the reader briefly encounters Mr. Yehezkel, the old polite guard "with a black *kippah* on his head" (17), the "helpful and polite" Meirav in the used bookstore (28), and Oved, owner of Oved's Cafe and "the last of the socialists in the center of town or . . . the one and only communist Kurd in Jerusalem" (19). In the chapters following Amir Lahab's gradual transformation, the reader briefly encounters Osnat, Yonatan's other and more seasoned caretaker (82), and the ethnically discriminating owner of the café in Ben Yehuda Street (202). None of these characters develop in the way Abulhawa's characters do. They remain marginal as Kashua explores the Arab identity within the contexts of the Israeli domain.

Unlike the other Jewish characters in the novel, Yonatan, although in a coma following a failed suicide attempt, is multifaceted and passively enters into a complex relationship with Kashua's Arab protagonist.[15] Yonatan is a living but inert body. Osnat and Amir daily move, turn, and clean him. However, for Amir, Yonatan's life and belongings become a window unto the Israeli reality. Amir, who at some point starts to sporadically impersonate Yonatan, decides to apply for the Bezalel Academy of Arts and Design at the Hebrew University under his new identity. As the novel progresses, Amir feels increasingly secure in the role of Yonatan, and becomes reluctant to give up this privileged position, until he entirely transforms into the other: "I was in my fourth and final year at Bezalel, one of thirty photography majors. Nothing special. Nothing out of the ordinary. A classic Bezalel student, the kind the school was for. I was Yonatan Forschmidt: Israeli, white, Ashkenazi, a consumer of Western culture. I was not Sephardic and I was not the token Arab" (283). I think that it is important to point out that, like Abulhawa's Ismael, Kashua's Amir does not transform into the Israeli "Mizrahi" Jew who is ethnically closer to both authors' Arab protagonists. In both novels, it is projections of the "white, Ashkenazi, a consumer of Western culture" that resonate in the Palestinian imaginings of the Israeli other. The fictional David and Yonatan both belong to this category in the Israeli society. Considering Abulhawa's and Kashua's distinct backgrounds and that they enter "enemy territory" from different positions, it would seem an extraordinary coincidence that both Ismael and Amir (and even Kanafani's Khaldun) transform into Israeli Ashkenazi Jews. Nonetheless, the reason for this fortuity may be found in exploring the question of who the Israeli Jewish other is in the Palestinian consciousness. It is not the early "Sabra" in Palestine or the Arab Jew who resided in the neighboring countries and arrived in Israel during the fifties. The other is rather the European Zionist who allegedly disrupted the "fine balance" among Muslims, Christians, and Jews prior to the establishment of Israel. Only recently did Israeli-Palestinian member of Knesset, and head of the Arab nationalist party Balad, Jamal Zahalka remind his Jewish colleagues and the Israeli public, in an outburst of rage, that it is the (Ashkenazi) Labor Party, and not its opponents, that represents other strata of the Jewish society in Israel, which is responsible for the Palestinian Nakba:

> The Labor Party expelled the Palestinians from their land; it dispossessed us far more than the right, killed tens of thousands of Palestinians, and they come to preach morals to us. . . . [T]he Labor Party is the father and mother of racism. . . . Those who took away our land, who expelled us, are not those who chant "death to the Arabs," but those who told us "we come in peace." . . . Who hurt us most—the Likud or the Labor Party? Of course, the Labor Party. The Likud built settlements next to Arab localities. You built your kibbutzim, your socialism, on the ruins of our villages.[16]

Zahalka, of course, refers to the left-wing Mapai Party, acronym for Mifleget Poalei Eretz Yisrael (Workers' Party of the Land of Israel). It was a dominant force in Israeli history that, in 1968, merged with other smaller factions and became the modern-day Labor Party. Mapai was headed by the historical figure and Israel's first prime minister, David Ben Gurion, and it was mostly identified with the

Zionist settlement movement arriving from Europe. To this day—in its increasingly deteriorating role against the backdrop of an Israeli society that is moving further and further to the right—the Labor Party mostly serves as the political home for Ashkenazi Israelis. Zahalka's speech shows that owing to the Mapai Party's historic role in the founding of the State of Israel, it is still (today) the figure of the European Jew that is most identified with the anxieties associated with the Nakba in the Palestinian consciousness.[17]

This notion has also entered Anglophone Palestinian literary works such as *On the Hills of God*, a novel composed in English by Palestinian American author Ibrahim Fawal. Set in 1948, shortly before the Nakba, the novel presents the story of Yousif Safi (a Christian), Amin (a Muslim), and Isaac Sha'lan (a Jew) in the fictional resort town of Ardallah (God's Land). Representative of conventional Palestinian imaginings, Fawal portrays a community that historically privileges cultural nuances over national aspirations. Arabs and Jews live peacefully together, sometime before the emergence of the prospective vacuum awaiting at the end of Britain's mandatory rule. In this context—as Steven Salaita points to in his reading of the novel—Zionism is conceived not as a Jewish project but rather as an alien European one that destroys the idyllic character of Palestine and creates the Israeli enemy—"white, Ashkenazi, a consumer of Western culture."[18] My point is that the concept of "other" refers to the stereotypical portrayal that causes the deepest anxiety. Or, as Homi Bhabba has it, the other is the outcome of cultural attempts at homogenizing the image of the oppressor or the enemy that has caused the greatest damage to the self.[19] Similarly, in the Israeli consciousness, Palestinians are conceived not as multifaceted but rather as one-dimensional. Ignoring existing nuanced realities, in the Israeli mainstream, the Palestinian is the Muslim terrorist who is out to destroy Israel or the (cheap) unskilled laborer whose services we are better off without. In this sense, Abulhawa's and Kashua's, as well as Kanafani's, choices represent Palestinians' confrontations with a particular other that has assumed the most painful position in the national consciousness regardless of local experiences, excluding the possibility for other facets of the Jew to emerge. That is, although Abulhawa and Kashua are authors of distinct Palestinian experiences and concomitantly rely on different sources for the creation of Ismael/David and Amir/Yonatan (Abulhawa seemingly borrows this trope from Kanafani, whereas Kashua relies on personal experiences as an Arab living in Israel), they similarly fall back on a recognizable stereotypical projection of the other in the national narrative.

Amir's transformation into the Israeli Ashkenazi Jew may imply that Kashua aims to metaphorically invade the other. Conversely, it may also suggest that he aims to conquer Palestinian anxieties toward this particular other. However, these lines of interpretation are not mutually exclusive; I believe they are inseparable and work effectively in unison. Yonatan's pastime of photography becomes a particularly important medium to convey Kashua's ambiguous gesture. Amir initially sets out to meticulously study Yonatan's photographs and become familiar with his fifty-millimeter Russian Pentax. Through the snapshots he begins to take of people in the Old City and of workers in a Ben Yehuda Street café, he visually explores Jerusalem's complex reality. Kashua presents Amir's/Yonatan's interest in capturing images as a vent for appropriating the identity and perspective of the privileged other. That is, Amir not only overcomes his personal anxieties by impersonating the other, as argued by Batya Shimoni, but also attempts to conquer Yonatan's Israeli Jewish perspective through photography.[20]

There are several ways to theorize this invasion. Susan Sontag's *On Photography* (1979) presents an interesting perspective in this context, explaining the connection between the photographer and the object photographed: "To photograph is to appropriate the thing photographed. It means putting oneself into a certain relation to the world that feels like knowledge—and, therefore, like power."[21] Like Yonatan before him, Amir wants to photograph people. He wants to acquire some form of authority over others by way of invading their private worlds through the camera lens in order to assume control over his own existence. The knowledge of others' inner worlds makes Amir feel confident, unlike the insecurity he had experienced in his earlier Arab life. He not only steals Yonatan's identity but also seeks to possess his perspective: "I wanted to see if I could be as precise and knowing as Yonatan, if I could also take the kind of sharp, detailed pictures that revealed the entire world of the stranger on the other end of the lens" (197). Sontag explains that not only does photography allow people to enter a space in which they otherwise feel insecure, but the camera itself acts as the ideal extension of consciousness in its acquisitive mood.[22] The activity of photography becomes particularly aggressive when it is directed toward other people: "To photograph people is to violate them, by seeing them as they never see themselves, by having knowledge of them they can never have; it turns people into objects that can be symbolically possessed."[23] My point is that the medium of photography in *Second Person Singular* becomes a symbolic political tool for reversing the power relations between Israeli Jews and the state's Arab minority. Amir does not merely physically invade the other in becoming Yonatan; he also seizes control of his vantage perspective, creating multilayered conceptualizations of the Israeli reality compared to a less sophisticated version that may exist in Arabic literature in general. Behind the camera, inside Yonatan's Jewish identity, there is an Arab viewing the world through Israeli eyes. Conceiving reality through the eyes of the privileged other is a kind of assumption of authority that is not dissimilar to the one involved in processes of narration in *Mornings in Jenin*. Whereas Abulhawa invites the Israeli Jewish character to partake in narration of the Palestinian voice, Kashua allows for the Arab to take absolute control of reality by taking over the lens privileged exclusively for Israeli Jewish eyes.

To conclude, Abulhawa and Kashua revisit a rare literary concept in Palestinian literature first presented by Kanafani. However, rather than inferring that the conflict may be resolved only through armed struggle, as Said does in *Returning to Haifa*, both Abulhawa and Kashua experiment with other more complex possibilities that recall Mahmoud Darwish's observation of processes of hybridization in both Palestinian and Israeli identities. Ismael/David in *Mornings in Jenin* and Amir/Yonatan in *Second Person Singular* represent the authors' respective attempts at intertwining contesting national narratives to work out the implications of Palestinians' and Israelis' intersecting histories. As a result, both characters transcend contemporary discourses, and their existence calls for the creation of new frameworks that may relatively allay the anxieties caused by the widening gap erected between who Palestinians historically think they are and who they have variedly become since 1948.

4

Sexual Politics and Nationhood between Exile and the Homeland

> My father was a statesman, I am a political woman. My father was a saint, I am not.
>
> —Indira Gandhi

Focusing on Randa Jarrar's novel *A Map of Home* (United States, 2008) and Maysaloun Hammoud's film *Bar Bahar* (Israel, translated into English as *In Between*, 2017), this chapter explores how the sexualization of the female body in fictional representations of Palestinian women unsettles conventional discourses and opens new venues for rethinking gender politics in the national framework. As previously explained, the continued absence of a chronotopic nation-state and the ongoing displacement of Palestinians generate a complex interpretive space for the analysis of the multifaceted development of the Palestinian story. On the one hand, the national script continues to express a state of constant urgency, prioritizing the call for national liberation at the expense of marginalizing other discourses of liberation, such as specific feminist discourses relating to representations of the female body. On the other, as argued from the outset of this book, experiences of Palestinian displacement can no longer be explained by the study of a single itinerary of deterritorialization. Narrations of Palestinian experiences of displacement are proliferating into multiple directions across borders, generations, and languages. Rather than concentrate on a single isolated Palestinian context—Palestinian women in Israel, Palestinian women in the occupied territories during the First Intifada, or women in the refugee camps[1]—I wish, in this chapter, to present, through Jarrar's and Hammoud's works, a relational analysis of the topic of sexual politics and the arts in the various contexts "inside" and "outside" Israel-Palestine.

Jarrar's and Hammoud's respective lives and careers represent distinct Palestinian experiences and grapple with different social and cultural conditions in their creative work. Jarrar was born in Chicago to a Greek Egyptian mother and a Palestinian father. She grew up in Egypt and Kuwait, but following the First Gulf War in 1991, Jarrar and her family moved back to the States, settling down in the New York area. A relatively controversial figure in some US circles for having eulogized Barbara Bush on Twitter as a "magnificent racist," Jarrar nowadays teaches creative writing at Fresno State University in California. Hammoud was born in Hungary to Palestinian parents from Israel. She grew up in the Israeli city of Beersheba and now lives in Jaffa. Following a short teaching career after graduating from the Hebrew University of Jerusalem in Middle Eastern studies, she went on to study film at the Minshar School of Art in Tel Aviv. Although Jarrar's and Hammoud's personal and professional experiences represent distinctive trajectories, as Palestinian women bearing hyphens of displacement (vis-à-vis Palestinian-American and Israeli-Palestinian), they would, nonetheless, be intimately familiar with the boundaries of Arab traditions and the "safe zones" of female sexuality. As I shall demonstrate in the following, both Jarrar and Hammoud, sharing a cultural heritage, present fictional creations that challenge conventional body and sexual politics that have determined the progressive and less progressive roles prescribed to the Palestinian woman according to the national script.

Jarrar's *A Map of Home* presents the semiautobiographical coming-of-age story of Nidali Ammar. The novel opens in Boston and then takes the reader to Kuwait and Egypt before returning to the United States—this time to Texas. Born to Waheed from Jenin and Fairuza, of Greek and Egyptian descent, Nidali grows from a Persian Gulf schoolgirl into a young, sassy Arab Texan adolescent. The impermanence of home for a Palestinian family constantly relocating owing to wars and politics in the Middle East is an overarching theme that frames the early years of Nidali's life. In this recognizable Palestinian context, *A Map of Home* is not unique, insofar as it traverses the thematic thresholds of displacement, movement, wars, the search for home, and so forth, unmistakably positioning the novel under the developing category of Anglophone Palestinian literature. Nonetheless, demonstrating an extraordinary talent for storytelling, Jarrar punctuates this all too familiar itinerary with intimate details about Nidali's explorations and thoughts on sex and sexual relations. Jarrar's portrayal of Nidali's sexual maturation certainly resists—as Nancy El Gendy, among others, has commented—"the ideological manufacture of the Muslim female body propounded by US Orientalism, Islamist orthodoxy and secular Arab patriarchy."[2]

Bar Bahar tells the story of three Palestinian women living together in the Yemenite Quarter of Tel Aviv. They hail from different social backgrounds and seem to have little in common, if anything at all. Laila (Mouna Hawa), from the city of Haifa, is a sexually active, big-haired, leather-jacketed, chain-smoking lawyer. Her seductiveness transcends ethnic borders, as she is constantly approached by both Arab and Jewish men. Salma (Sana Jammelieh) is a rebellious DJ who quits her kitchen day job when her Jewish boss scolds her for speaking Arabic at the workplace. Salma is also gay, but the force of her defiant attitude repeatedly wanes upon arriving in Tarshiha—her hometown—where she repeatedly fails to confront her Christian family regarding her sexual orientation. In contradistinction to these unconventional Arab women, Nur (Shaden Kanboura)—who arrives in Tel Aviv as their new roommate—is a quiet hijab- and jilbaab-wearing computer science student from the Muslim town of Umm al-Fahem. She is out of sync with Laila's and Salma's carefree lifestyles but, nonetheless, endures their wild exertions and sticks around. Nur is also engaged (by arrangement) to Wissam (Henry Andrawes)—a religious young man and a social worker, also from Umm al-Fahem—who repeatedly expresses his dismay vis-à-vis Nur's current living arrangement. *Bar Bahar* portrays how the three young women, navigating the minefield between political discrimination, tradition, and modernity, gradually learn to accept one another's religious, cultural, and temperamental differences and develop a bond based on womanhood.

Jarrar and Hammoud confront the mutually exclusive challenges of liberation and traditionalism, while harboring conflictual sentiments regarding cultural and social practices in the homeland. In sexualizing the Palestinian woman through their respective fictional works, they alter her assigned role as "the birther of the nation"—in Rhoda Ann Kanaaneh's terms—and grant her the privileges of choice, enjoyment, and empowerment. In order to highlight the challenges posed by Jarrar's and Hammoud's respective works to the national framework, I wish, in the following part, to present an account of the ways whereby womanhood has been construed in the national narrative during different periods. My aim is to present a historical overview of how representations of Palestinian women have been edited, censored, and revised to accommodate a monolithic, male-centered national framework over the past century.

Sexuality and Nationhood

I wish to begin with a fictional if iconic exchange between a Palestinian activist and his cynical counterpart at some undisclosed political event. The cynic is watching the activist protest against the Israeli establishment and is infuriated by what he discerns as the activist's hypocrisy. He mockingly proposes: "You want to liberate the homeland? Go liberate your sister's vagina first." The cynic presumes that while the activist poses as a militant protester against the Israeli occupation, calling for freedom and independence, he will probably not grant his sister those same rights. Rather, he regards the activist's national struggle as a longing to go back to tradition and preserve patriarchal social structures. This exchange has most probably transpired in real life on different occasions. Nonetheless, because of the universal recognizability of the cynic's statement in Arabic ("Badak itharer watan? Harer kos okhtak bil-awal"), it has been elevated to the status of an anecdote. It is noteworthy, however, that while the exchange between the cynic and the activist jocularly points to the vexed relationship between conceptions of the female body and nationhood in the Palestinian struggle for liberation, the absence of a female voice renders the anecdote problematic. The symbolic cry for the liberation of the "vagina" is addressed from one male to another, keeping the fate of the Palestinian woman's sexual liberation subject to the wills of two disagreeing Arab males.

Notwithstanding the third-world anticolonialist tenor of the Palestinian call for liberation, it is safe to assert that the national vision is rooted in sexual politics of censorship. It is conceived as a narrative construed exclusively by and for the male protagonist, whereby women are portrayed to participate through their body, "honorably" reproducing the nation biologically, culturally, and symbolically.[3] This gendered division highlights the contradiction between the progressive character of the nationalist call for liberation and the tradition it purports to possess, revealing that the national discourse simultaneously moves in opposite directions: on the one hand, it presents promises of advancement toward modern values such as liberty and social equality; on the other, it moves backward in its claim to fend traditions and culture against the unsettling effects of modernity. The paradoxical character of Palestinian national ambition is certainly not exceptional. National ideologies claim, in general, to offer a modern political framework for its subjects to enjoy specific configurations of their "original" culture, thus addressing both progressive and conservative political sentiments and embracing the constantly changing tension between narrations of the past and the future. However, while subjects of sovereign democratic nation-states participate in this ongoing tension through governmental and nongovernmental institutions, the majority of today's thirteen million Palestinians lack such institutions. And, as we know only too well, the world has yet to see the creation of a Palestinian state.

The Palestinian national call continues to primarily address the current scattered state of Palestinians and is rooted in nostalgic sentiments over a lost pastoral past. This reality of multiple conditions of displacement has, somewhat, foregrounded socially conservative agendas, supporting the male-centered tenor of the national script, while marginalizing progressive ones, particularly in relation to women. I do not imply that the prospective nation explicitly and straightforwardly calls for its women to remain subjected to patriarchal social structures. Rather, narrations of the "modern" Palestinian woman are sophisticatedly appropriated to accommodate these structures.[4] As Ipshita Chanda has it, "The struggles between 'tradition' and 'modernity,' 'progress' and 'backwardness,' 'bondage' and 'emancipation' have been variously articulated and have impinged upon hegemonic gender ideology in ways that keep different patriarchal formations in operation."[5]

Historically, patriarchal tradition has unconditionally framed the official Palestinian political discourse. Following the overwhelming defeat of the Arab armies in 1967 and the Palestinian guerrilla groups' takeover of the PLO—led by the young, ambitious Yasser Arafat—the original Palestinian Nationalist Charter (Al-Mithaq al-Qawmi al-Filastini, 1964), composed by Ahmad Shuqairy, founding head of the PLO, was amended and published under the title of the Palestinian National Charter (Al-Mithaq al-Watani al-Filastini, 1968). The former document had already described, in the introduction, the Zionist conquest of Palestine through metaphors of gender, by way of portraying the native population as children of a raped maternal land. Although such language was removed from the latter modified version, it is noteworthy that Articles 4 and 5 were preserved and defined the Palestinian identity as a patrilineal heritage: "The Palestinian character is an essential and undying feature that is passed from fathers to son" (Article 4); "Palestinians are those Arab residents who were living in Palestine until 1947 . . . [and][a]nyone born, after that date, to a Palestinian father—whether inside Palestine or outside it—is also a Palestinian" (Article 5).

This identification through paternal lineage outweighs the universal principles of "justice, freedom, sovereignty, self-determination, and human pride" in Article 21. For example, the addition of Article 9—calling for an armed struggle against Israel—which marked the transition from Shuqairy's Arab government-sponsored leadership of the PLO to the declaration of an autonomous Palestinian leadership under Arafat—also appeared to express ambitions for mobilizing the largest number of the population, both men and women. Nonetheless, the national movement was—as Rabab Abdulhadi specifies—faced with a paradox: "how to define and conceptualize women's roles without disturbing the delicate gendered balance in Palestinian society."[6]

Abdulhadi's observation shows that, regardless of the necessity of mobilizing women, there was a general concern over the buttressing of the existing patriarchal structures—thus rendering the revolution anticolonial but not necessarily social. Julie Peteet presents a revealing example of this stasis in her description of sexual relations among unmarried men and women during the early period of Palestinian nationalist activity. She explains that these exceptional instances remained confined to small groups of intimates—hailing from the university-educated middle class—who began to daily meet and work together in new contexts, far from the censoring eyes of family and society. Such relations, however, did not alter gender structures in Palestinian societies or ideas on sex in any meaningful way. Women activists had to move back and forth between two worlds, dressing, behaving, and talking differently at home than they did with their fellow male activists.[7]

Palestinian poetry written by men played a major role in conceptualizing this gender imbalance. The works of prominent Palestinian literary figures such as Abu Salma, Ibrahim Touqan, and Mahmoud Darwish initially feminized the nation in their writings. These poets were committed to the nationalist struggle during different periods, and their respective writings metaphorized Palestine as the mother/daughter/sister/woman, groomed, defended, abandoned, mourned, desired, and loved by the Palestinian male, rendering the Zionist colonization of Palestine inseparable from the colonization of the female body in the national script.[8] Abu Salma's poem "I Love You More" and Darwish's "A Lover from Palestine" are among the most famous texts to describe the loss of Palestine in terms of the male's longing for his lost lover, and, by and large, they set the tone in contemporary Palestinian poetry. As a side note, we only need to recall the conclusive fictional report of the Zionist delegates who arrived in Palestine to assess the sustainability of founding a Jewish state: "The bride is beautiful, but married to another man."[9] Palestine, figuratively, becomes the woman patiently waiting for the men to resolve their argument. Firmly grounded in conventional conceptions of gender, the national narrative construes the woman as an ideological marker that keeps upholding a masculine discourse. Amal Amireh explains that given the male-centered national script, the feminization of the lost homeland renders the narrative of the Palestinian defeat as the "male loss of virility"—expressing, more than anything else, the Palestinian men's sense of humiliation vis-à-vis their ineptitude to defend their home. It is not uncommon, in Palestinian and Arab national discourses in general, to describe the loss of Palestine in sexual terms—as, for example, in the early version of the Palestinian National Charter—representing the idea of the feminized land that has been possessed by other, more virile, actors than Palestinian men.[10] Sheila Katz sums up this point on men's pervasive control of women in the national framework, in that "reverence for land could be opposed to love for woman, transcendent of it, or just like it. Both land and women were represented as objects of desire and inspiration. . . . [F]or male nationalists the end of political suppression did not mean the end of sexual repression. In fact, it was the opposite: nationalism depended on continued control of women's sexuality."[11] This line of argument might seem to contradict the historic roles played by Palestinian women in the national struggle. The objectification of the Palestinian woman in male discourse does not mean that women in Palestine were altogether passive during the tumultuous decades preceding and following 1948. According to Ghazi al-Khalili, female activism may be traced back to the early 1920s, to the foundation of the Palestinian Women's Union, which spearheaded demonstrations against the Balfour Declaration and later organized the General Palestinian Women's Congress in Jerusalem in 1929.[12] Ellen Fleischmann turns our attention to headlines of the Arab press between 1929 and 1947, revealing the nationalist direction of female activism: "We Women Are Not Less Nationalistic than Men," "The Arab Woman—Always in the Vanguard and the Forefront of Ranks," and "Demonstrations of the Ladies of Jaffa Yesterday—Magnificence, Organization, and the Recitations of Nationalist Fervent Speeches."[13] During the 1936–39 revolt, Palestinian women continued to play active roles, taking up arms, hiding rebels, signing petitions, and caring for the injured.[14] Moreover, between 1948 and 1967, women's presence was evident in various political movements, such as Fatah, led by Yasser Arafat, and the Arab National Movement, led by Dr. George Habash and Dr. Wadea Haddad. However, even though Palestinian women were publicly active from early on and their activism was primarily nationalist, their presence does not seem to have swayed the gender structures predicating the national struggle.

This exclusive dominance of the androcentric national script also influenced the development of early Palestinian women literature. Powerful literary figures, such as the renowned poet Fadwa Touqan—among several others—was bound to, time and again, prioritize her commitment to the national struggle, paying the price of suspending her ambitions for women's liberation. Touqan's literary experience, as she describes it in her autobiography, *Rihla Jabaliyya Rihla Sa'ba* (*A Mountainous Journey*, 1985), explicitly renders this conflictual relation between the national and the feminist struggles. Her earliest poetry, to her father's great dismay, was self-centered and emotional rather than national. Although Touqan's poetry eventually made a radical turn toward the national in the wake of the Six-Day War of 1967, in the early phase of her career, she defends her artistic choices against her father's pressure by way of pitting national politics against social justice: "*How and with what right or logic does Father ask me to compose political poetry, when I am shut up inside these walls? I don't sit with the men, I don't listen to their heated discussions, nor do I participate in the turmoil of life on the outside. I'm still not even acquainted with the face of my own country, since I am not allowed to travel*" (107). Owing to the struggles of pioneering figures such as Touqan, Arabic letters have come to feature a multifaceted and nuanced female presence that constantly challenges the dominant male hegemony. Contemporary Palestinians novelists such as Sahar Khalifeh and Liana Badr—not to mention the strikingly talented Adania Shibli—living and writing during different periods under the Israeli military occupation have, in their respective works, focalized the national story through female perspectives in ways that both call for maintaining the idea of a national collective and challenge the masculine tone of the national script. Expectedly, these writers' artistic endeavors to create a dynamic space for the female voice and the female protagonist have and continue to constitute a merciless uphill struggle, insofar as the national script perseveres at resisting progressive representations of the body and sexual politics that might unsettle its foundations.

Nationalist politics of censorship became—as Amal Amireh demonstrates—particularly explicit during the First Intifada. Amireh explains that the women of the intifada posed a serious threat to the national narrative, insofar as they "played a visible role in this resistance, in the streets, in neighborhood committees, and in leadership." Their visibility—reminiscent of Palestinian women's activism in the '30s—unsettled conventional gender roles, and, this time during the late '80s, the consequent anxiety among conservatives was expressed "in sexual terms as male fear of the female body." Stories about Palestinian women seducing Palestinian men to recruit them as collaborators with Israel began to circulate, capsizing interpretations of social spaces in the occupied territories: the streets were regarded as safe zones—spaces of fraternity and solidarity, keeping men safe—while interiors, such as "homes, seamstresses' shops, and hair salons," posed grave danger to men as spaces of seduction.[15] Drawing on Edward Said's and Lila Abu-Lughod's works, Amireh suggests that in a culture in which masculinity is synonymous with self-discipline and bodily control, there did not seem to be room for the emerging activist Palestinian woman in the Gaza Strip and the West Bank during the First Intifada.[16]

In order to present literary voices of social resistance in reaction to the radicalization of conservatism during the First Intifada,

Amireh turns our attention to the protagonist of Khalifeh's *Bab 'el-Saha* ("The Door of the Courtyard," 1994), Nazha ("honest" or "honorable" in English)—a twenty-seven-year-old Palestinian prostitute who represents the decadent sexuality that, during the intifada, became a national threat. At the beginning of the novel, Nazha is persecuted by her brother, who is suspected of having publicly stabbed his mother to death (also a prostitute and allegedly an informant for Israel). Rather than vow herself to the nation, Nazha speaks of a "monstrous" Palestine, "constantly devouring and never satisfied." However, toward the end, she joins the intifada. Nazha ignites a Molotov cocktail and prepares to burn the Israeli flag, stating that she is doing it not for the sake of "monster Palestine" but for her brother who was recently killed by Israeli soldiers. Khalifeh's artistic choice is, indeed, subversive in its presentation of the female scapegoat–outcast narrative. In Amireh's words, "She tells a story that is not usually told by the dominant national narrative: a story of a divided, cruel, hypocritical, patriarchal society that exploits poor women like her."[17] Khalifeh ultimately enlists the prostitute in the struggle, presenting an alternative Palestinian reality that questions the entrenched precepts of female sexuality and honor and comes to terms with the "decadent" sexualized Arab woman. It is, of course, problematic to cast a prostitute as the proponent of progressive sexual politics, since her profession and social status represent the commodification of the female body rather than its liberation. Nonetheless, in *Bab 'el-Saha*, Khalifeh poses female sexuality as a serious challenge to the national framework.

Conversely, when analyzing sexual politics and Palestinian nationalism, it is necessary to keep in mind that—contrary to popular opinion—there is no archetypal Palestinian woman. As Valentine Moghadam argued several decades ago, the Middle East is not a uniform and homogeneous region. Women and men live in cities, provincial towns, and rural villages "inserted in quite diverse socioeconomic and cultural arrangements."[18] Moghadam's argument explicitly targets the Orientalist homogenization of the Arab woman as a faceless member of the isolated, erotic harem or the suppressed veiled Muslim woman, and so forth, but, in the context of this chapter, it might also afford an insightful perspective on the homogenization of the Palestinian woman in the national narrative.

If we look back into the Palestinian women who actively participated in the struggle against the British and the Zionists during the first half of the twentieth century and, after 1967, to iconic figures such as Leila Khaled and today's young Palestinian activist Ahed Tamimi, it may seem that all Palestinian women share an identical temperament and unanimously prioritize national ambition. However, in agreement with Moghadam's initial point on the socioeconomic and cultural diversities in the Arab world, this book also highlights that not all Palestinians live in autonomous Arab societies. Palestinians in Israel, Europe, and the Americas are economically and culturally engaged in local social frameworks, unsettling the idea of a homogeneous Palestinian womanhood and a single overarching collective ambition inscribed in the national script. For example, Gil Hochberg's interview with leading Palestinian figures of queer activism in Israel and the occupied territories is particularly revealing of potent, unconventional female voices that are challenging the patriarchal infrastructure of Arab communities.[19]

Contemporary Palestinian arts and letters certainly offer valuable frameworks for the presentation of progressive, even unconventional, discourses. They are, however, solely available in specific contexts and to specific social classes and not necessarily relevant or suited for what many Palestinians would view as real-life conditions in the various current contexts of displacement. Although the Palestinian woman has been the object of numerous such literary portrayals and critical discussions, the topic of sexual politics remains sensitive and is still weighed down by Arab societies' cautiousness with regard to the "dangers" inherent in the female body. Artistic imaginings or critical discussions of the nation continue, in substance, to ossify convention with regard to expressions of female sexuality. This sexual politics of censorship is, I wish to point out, not an exclusively local issue. Regardless of location and social context, it appears that despite the variegated social formations (under occupation, as an indigenous minority in Israel, as an immigrant community in Europe or the United States, or as a refugee in an Arab country), both local and diasporic Palestinian communities roughly share in the idea of controlling women's sexual activity, insofar as sexual freedom is commonly regarded as posing a direct threat to (trans)cultural views on family control and continuity.

Whereas one group of writers and critics (affiliated with different Palestinian social groups) has, by and large, pointed to condemning patriarchal and misogynistic attitudes in their respective communities, another (seemingly progressive and feminist) has set up its literary and critical output in ways that accommodate the national framework, muting representations of female sexuality. Lisa Suhair Majaj's argument on diasporic Palestinian women's longing to return to the homeland in "On Writing and Return: Palestinian American Reflections" is a case in point. Describing the connotations of both physical and figurative conceptions of Palestinians' ambition to "return," Majaj focuses on the notion of a homeland rooted in history and memory, but re-created through imagination, in the writings of Palestinian American poets Suhair Hammad and Nathalie Handal. Majaj contends—in reference to the obvious political (Israel) and social barriers (patriarchy) facing Palestinian women—that "returning" to the homeland is not merely a going back but also a moving forward "to create a new future from the fragments of a reclaimed past."[20] This single symbolic move not only realizes the national desire of Palestinians to return to their homeland but also deconstructs the social structures of patriarchy manifested in many parts of contemporary Palestinian communities. To account for this move, Majaj references Hammad's plea for a new Palestinian future for women in the poem "Broken and Beirut" from her collection *Born Palestinian, Born Black* (1996):

> These and other lines of Hammad's make clear the extent to which return—to history, to an imagined future, and ultimately, to the self, whether personal or communal—lies at the heart of both memory and transformation. In her work, return to Palestine is

> not a return to patriarchal structures, but to a homeland created anew. The journey may be difficult, even impossible: the past lies irretrievably behind us; homelands lie unreachable beyond borders marked by barbed wire and guns. But it is through return, Hammad suggests—to the past, to memory, to the homelands that exist in reality and the ones we create—that we ground the self and hence provide the means to move forward into the future.[21]

Majaj's reading of Hammad's vision straightforwardly connects Palestinians' national desire to feminist aspirations. Majaj is, of course, not unaware of the basic tensions between the conservative masculine tenor of the nationalist discourse and the unsettling character of feminist discourse. In response, she argues that Palestinian women "can no more be expected to 'choose' between their national and gender identities than U.S. women can expect to 'choose' between being American and being feminist."[22] In its inextricable linking of the national call for a Palestinian return with feminist discourses, Majaj's reading of Hammad's poem seems to set a relatively uncomplicated perspective that suggests that progressive diasporic Palestinian women's poetic return to Palestine will fulfill the national desire and eventually change the social texture in the homeland.

However, whereas American-born Palestinian women, such as Hammad and Handal, call for social liberation through the national script, local Palestinian women are conspicuously absent from Majaj's reading. Her argument does not reveal the complex reality in the different parts of the homeland. Majaj obscures the diversity among Palestinian women in Israel-Palestine and the different roles they have assumed in relation to local patriarchal social structures. Whereas some groups might variedly voice their dissatisfaction with the current state of womanhood in the nation, others may defend the patriarchy as an inextricable part of the tradition they aspire to facilitate through nation building. However, being there—part of the Palestinian diaspora—Majaj and her literary compatriots Hammad and Handal regard national and social liberation as mutually inclusive. Khalifeh's "monster Palestine" is merely a figment of a fictional prostitute's imagination, and the dream of a nation entails dreams of—among others—sexual liberation.

My reading of Jarrar's and Hammoud's respective works, in the following section, diametrically counters Majaj's critical point of departure. The national script definitively cancels out ideas of sexual liberation; "monster Palestine" cannot tolerate the sexualized Palestinian woman. As explained earlier, Jarrar and Hammoud confront the mutually exclusive challenges of liberation and traditionalism, while nourishing conflictual sentiments regarding cultural and social practices in the homeland. By sexualizing the Palestinian woman through their respective fictional works, they alter the roles assigned to her in the national script and confer her the privileges of choice, enjoyment, and empowerment. Jarrar and Hammoud respectively show that—whether the protagonist grows up as a Palestinian girl constantly on the move or lives in Tel Aviv as a young Palestinian woman—narrations of displacement cannot continue to keep on muffling expressions of sexuality and female autonomy.

Uncharted Spaces

It is clear, from the outset, that in *A Map of Home*, Randa Jarrar seeks to tell us a Palestinian story in a slightly unusual tone. The creation of Nidali, as well as the acerbic tenor of the narrative, poses serious challenges to traditional conceptions of Arab womanhood and to the Palestinian story at large, in both Arabic and English. Jarrar situates Nidali at the intersection between several contesting traditions in relation to the representation of the Palestinian Arab woman. On the one hand, the unredacted descriptions of Nidali's sexual maturation run counter to the censorship of female sexuality in societal and national Arab contexts. On the other, they also challenge the stereotypical, homogeneous representations of the suppressed Muslim woman in the Anglophone context—partly rooted in a long-standing Orientalist tradition and partly in a contemporary post–9/11 Islamophobic climate.

Jarrar sets the tone in the opening chapter, which tells the story of Nidali's birth. Nidali's father—Waheed Ammar—is standing at the nurses' station of St. Elizabeth's Medical Center of Boston, following a difficult birth whereby Nidali had been revived several times. As soon as the doctor assures him that the baby is fine, he rushes to fill out the birth certificate, unaware of his daughter's sex. However, an adult Nidali describes her father's callousness in retrospect: "That didn't matter; he'd always known I [Nidali] was a boy, had spoken to me as a boy while I was tucked safely in Mama's uterus amid floating amniotic debris"—caricaturing an Arab father's trenchant patriarchal desire for a son. He writes the name Nidal ("struggle" in Arabic) into the box to be filled with "Name of Child," completes the entire form, and relays it to the nurse. He rushes back to the maternity ward and enters the birthing room as his wife is nursing their newborn daughter. Upon asking "How is my queen?" and caressing his wife's face, he realizes his mistake when she replies that "she [their daughter] is fine" (4). He abruptly runs off again, rushes back to the station, and screams for the nurse to whom he had relayed the birth certificate. The nurse returns with the form, and, with a heavy heart, he adds the possessive, feminizing *i* to the end of the name "Nidal." To explain the commotion surrounding her birth, Nidali describes how her father had grown up as the youngest and only male among his six sisters, whose births had all gone "uncelebrated" and whom he had watched "grow up and go away, each one more miserable than the last" (5). Waheed, of course, did not want to bring into the world a daughter who might go through a similar experience. His predilection for a male child leaves the question of whose struggle his newborn daughter's name refers to. It remains ambiguous whether Nidali—meaning "my struggle"—refers to *his* struggle in raising a daughter or, rather, to *hers*, growing up as an Arab girl. In foregrounding the chaotic circumstances of Nidali's birth—oscillating between life and death and in between genders—Jarrar takes aim at Arab patriarchy.

This opening scene adds yet another dimension to the unusual tone of the novel. Nidali's mother, Fairuza—"Ruzz"—Waheed's

Egyptian-born wife, is a forceful presence, effectively countering her husband's stormy character. Their momentous clashes are rendered in an acerbic discourse that defines the language of Nidali's narration throughout. Her mother is not merely a wife who talks back at her husband; she is also profane, relentlessly referencing sexual organs in her retaliations. Upon settling the confusion over Nidali's gender, Waheed returns to the birthing room to see to his wife, and a heated face-off immediately takes place:

> Moments later, Mama, who had just been informed of my *nom de guerre*, and who was still torn up in the nether regions, got out of bed, flung me into a glass crib, and walked us to the elevator, the entire time ignoring my baba, who was screaming, "Nidali is a beautiful name, so unique, come on Ruz, don't be so rash, you mustn't be walking, your, your . . . *pussy*"—this in a whispered hush, and in Arabic, kussik . . . "needs to rest!"
>
> "*Kussy? Kussy ya ibn ilsharmoota?*"—My pussy, you son of a whore? "Don't concern yourself with my pussy, you hear? No more of this pussy for you, you . . . ass!"

Critics such as Dina Jadallah have held Jarrar's bawdy language against her, maintaining that it undermines the believability of Nidali's narrative. Her parents' "abundant use of obscenities," Jadallah states, "is not very common"—probably referring to the rareness of such expressions among Arab couples.[23] I agree with Jadallah, but I do not think that Jarrar is unaware that the risqué language employed by her characters is unusual. Yet she goes for it, introducing a discourse whereby Ruzz and subsequently Nidali use obscene references not only for the sole purpose of being obscene. On the one hand, they respectively strip off the role of the "good" submissive Arab wife and daughter; on the other, they assume ownership over their bodies. In Jarrar's fictional universe, blatant references to female body parts are no longer circumscribed to a derogatory male discourse but bespeak an autonomous female one. The possessive-pronoun transition from "your . . . pussy" ("kussik") to "my pussy" ("kussy") suggests the transference from male to female ownership of the woman's body in Nidali's narrative. She repeatedly makes references to her "breasts," her "hard nipples," and her "clit," transforming the woman from an objectified sexual figure in male discourses into an autonomous sexual organism that constantly explores, enjoys, and satisfies itself. More significantly, the autonomous Palestinian female body also resists. It simultaneously resists multiple intersecting discourses, such as Arab and Muslim patriarchy as well as Western Orientalism that, for too long, have narrated the dispossession of the Arab woman's body.

Ruzz's staunch defiance both strengthens the mother-daughter bond and inspires Nidali's relationship with her own body. On the way to Jenin in the West Bank, the members of the Ammar family are subject to invasive security checks at Israeli checkpoints. Men are separated from the women, and Nidali sits with her mother and a group of other "suspect" half-naked women waiting for their turn to be searched by female soldiers. Upon Ruzz's turn, she lets out a "a huge silent fart," to the embarrassment and discomfort of everyone except Nidali, who high-fives her mother as the soldiers leave the room. From the door they are told to put on their clothes and move on—the body resists the invasiveness of the Israeli occupation. Earlier in the novel, Jarrar explores the power of the farting female body in a context different from that of the Israeli occupation. Nidali goes through the rituals of ablutions to desperately pray against kissing when she grows up:

> I got up and did my ablutions as quietly as possible so as not to wake up Baba. I slipped a towel on my head for veil and faced the direction Baba faces when he prays once a week, on Fridays. I thought about Esam, who I hadn't thought of in a while. I wondered if he was back on the West Bank now, married, happy . . . kissing. I shook my head; I had to stop thinking about that! I wondered if I should perform my ablutions again since I'd had an impure thought but I decided I didn't have to, so I began my prayers for Mama. The entire time I was worried whether my prayers counted or not, and just as I was about to finish, I inadvertently let out a long fart. I knew I'd have to repeat both the ablutions and the prayers now but

> I didn't because I was too lazy, and I hoped God hadn't heard my fart, even though I know he smelled it. (70)

The playfulness of young Nidali's uncertainties delivers a profane message against religion, on par with the many discourses that Jarrar takes aim at through the female body. Ruzz liberates Nidali and herself from subjection to further humiliation by Israeli soldiers, and Nidali unknowingly undermines all decorum as well as the sacrosanctity of religious prayer. In Jarrar's fictional universe, liberation and heresy do not amount to historic acts, but are (humbly) performed by the female body, intentionally or unintentionally, passing gas. She jocularly makes this natural function of the body part of the discourse of the defiant woman. Its offensive smell becomes a mocking expression of female defiance and sabotages the sexual objectification of women.

This significant rewriting of the female body is aptly weaved into the overriding Palestinian theme of the temporariness of home for a Palestinian family constantly relocating owing to wars and politics in the Middle East. Palestinian wandering frames the early years of Nidali's life. Born in Boston, growing up in Kuwait and Egypt, and then moving back to the United States—this time to Texas—Nidali matures from a Persian Gulf schoolgirl into a sassy Arab Texan *chica*, whose main concern is to explore her own sexuality. However, her sexual initiation does not take place in Texas. Nidali goes through her first sexual experiences in Kuwait and later in Egypt. Jarrar seems to eschew the narrative plot of the "good," chaste Arab girl, who is then corrupted by the "decadent" American society. As Nidali reaches puberty, her sexual explorations are revealed to the reader through humor and narratorial ingenuity against the backdrop of major historical events that have determined many Palestinians' unfortunate itineraries: "Four weeks into the [Iraqi] invasion [of Kuwait], Gamal discovered a black cat licking itself in the bidet and screamed at the top of his lungs. We all ran to the bathroom, and Baba yelled, 'all that for a cat, you son of a bitch, you scared me!' Mama was already beginning her histrionic attempts at capture. As for me, I was completely relieved that for once, there was someone other than myself masturbating on the bidet" (131). The Iraqi invasion of Kuwait, which eventually led to the First Gulf War, becomes the backdrop for the comic scene leading up to Nidali's casual confession of her using the bidet for sexual stimulation. It is the contrast between the devastation of war and Nidali's concerns with her sexual explorations that renders Jarrar's novel unprecedented. Nidali is not the conventional victim we have encountered in previous Palestinian novels. The main focus of her constant displacement is not explicitly expressed through the sense of "homelessness" and an overriding national desire to return. Rather, Jarrar foregrounds Nidali's frustrations about missed opportunities for further sexual exploration.

As Nidali is escaping from Kuwait with her family (along with hundreds of thousands of her Palestinian compatriots), she writes a letter to Saddam Hussein that explains these personal frustrations:

> *Dear Mr. Saddam Hussein,*
>
> *I am in my parents' falling-apart car, and we are crossing your beautiful country, fleeing from your ugly army. My father has thus far distributed four bottles of Johnny Walker and three silk ties to checkpoint personnel; my mother has pinched my leg approximately 13 times in the past forty kilometers alone, and my cousin, who is now riding in my uncle's van after my aunt's Firebird caught on fire and was abandoned in Karbala, has been giving me the arm roughly every 45 seconds. And I, you may wonder, what I am doing while these boring goings-on surround me? I am bleeding in my panties and too embarrassed to make the caravan pull over, and I am writing you this letter to humbly inform you that, although I admire your sense of fashion, green is so last season. Also, when you decided to invade the country where I grew up (and when you decided this, sir, were you on some seriously strong hashish?) did you, at any point, stop and consider the teenage population? Did you stop and consider how many of them were dying, just dying for summer to be over and school to restart, for classes*

> *to resume and crushes to pick up where they left off in June? For your information, I was anxiously awaiting to see a certain Fakhr el-Din, a very handsome, sarcastic, 9th year student. I had kissed him a couple of times by the dry-freeze animals in the school entrance, and I've since been making out with my left hand, but it's not the same. He was supposed to be my boyfriend this year, but that's scrapped now, thanks to you. I hate your fucking guts. I wish you nothing less than violent anus-expansion via rocket ships launched from close proximity, and I hope that you too will be expelled from your home and forever cut off from your crush and sentenced by almighty Allah to eternity in the final circle of hell where you will forever make out with your left hand, the skin of which will burn off and re-grow for all of eternity.*
>
> *Yours sincerely,*
> *N.A.* (155–56)

Nidali's uprooting (and the historic exodus of two hundred thousand Palestinians from Kuwait in 1990–91)—transpiring under the uncomfortable circumstances of her mother's pinches, her cousin's provocations, and her father's briberies of border officials while she menstruates—is linked to frustrations about not seeing Fakhr el-Din, her prospective boyfriend, again. She had kissed him "a couple of times," an experience that had furnished her sexual fantasies during masturbation. Nidali expresses her belonging not to a—yet again—displaced Palestinian population, but rather to a teenage population that was looking forward to escaping the summer heat and returning to school. Surely, the larger implicit affiliation reverberates in the reader's mind owing to historic contextualization and Nidali's reference to Kuwait as "the country where I grew up." Nonetheless, Nidali reacts to Saddam's transgression in relation to her and her age group's concerns, wishing him eternal physical pain in a sexless afterlife after he also "will be expelled from his home."

Jarrar's sexualization of Nidali challenges not only the fashioning of the timid Palestinian woman in the national script but also conceptions of female heterosexuality. Nidali fantasizes about Fakhr el-Din and eventually loses her virginity with Medina, but she is also sexually drawn to other girls. While still in Kuwait during the Iraqi invasion, Ruzz allows Nidali to pay her friend Rama a visit after having been locked up in their home for several weeks. At Rama's parents' villa in Jabriyya, the girls go to Rama's room and lock the door. Listening to Indian music and reading old fashion magazines, they begin to chat about Nidali and Fakhr el-Din. Rama unexpectedly pinches Nidali's breast, and they playfully begin to wrestle on her bed. Play soon turns erotic:

> Soon we were tickling each other and she stuck her knee right in between my legs. A moan escaped from my mouth; it felt good, her knee there, and she moved it over me in a circle. I grabbed her thigh and guided the circle until I felt the way I felt whenever I sat over the bidet for too long. I turned away from Rama and jumped off the bed. I had no idea what had just happened and Rama seemed just as confused as I was. She turned on her music and we read magazines until Mama called to me from downstairs. (142)

Both girls are caught by surprise. Their bodies act out latent desires that run counter to the cultural principles that Rama and Nidali have been brought up on regarding sexual orientation. Ruzz interrupts the awkward silence following their sexual encounter and Nidali is rushed home before it gets dark outside. On the way home, Nidali quietly cries at her bewilderment—living under siege, unable to comprehend her secret experiences, and vulnerable to the risk of hers and her family's displacement. Shortly after, they escape from Kuwait.

Nidali's relationship with Jiji in Egypt presents another opportunity for further exploring her bisexuality. Unlike her onetime accidental experience with Rama, Nidali appears to be more conscious of her attraction to other girls with Jiji. She reflects on her desire to kiss Jiji and later carefully seizes the opportunity to do so: "I wanted to tell Jiji that I'd give her her first kiss. I hadn't thought of it before but just then, when I saw the slimy frog, I thought, *I* should give her

her first kiss. I'll go to hell, I thought. I liked boys, I assured myself, because I did. I wanted to kiss them. But I wanted to be the first one Jiji kissed instead of some slimy toad of a guy" (170). Against the backdrop of Palestinian exile following the First Gulf War, Nidali ponders her homosexual attraction through a conceptual framework that arbitrarily casts her on the wrong side of religion and culture. She likes boys as she should; she will go to hell for wanting to kiss another girl—a punishment she seems to accept. On the eve before the beginning of winter break, upon meeting Nidali at the library, Jiji asks Nidali to join her for lunch at her parents' home. Despite the usual and strong objections of Waheed, Nidali defiantly takes Jiji up on her offer. After lunch, they go to Jiji's room, where Nidali, at some point, cunningly offers Jiji to practice kissing on her. Jiji is immediately taken aback by the offer for fear of participating in—as she sees it—lesbian activity. When Nidali, then, explains that she could imagine her as a "pillow, but with real lips" rather than a girl, Jiji hesitantly agrees and locks the door. Jarrar describes their kiss in great detail:

> Our lips touched and I parted hers until I found her tongue. I was licking a gelato on the beach at summer; Fakhr's tongue hadn't felt this smooth or slippery or cold. She laughed, then moved her tongue around in rapid circles. I slowed it down and then brought it to a halt and sucked on it. She made a whimpering sound. I opened my eyes and saw that hers were open too. I reached up and closed them with my thumbs, then caressed the side of her face, stuck my fingers in her thick knotty hair. I kissed her lips, quick pecks that she returned, and I tugged at her bottom lip with both of mine. I felt dampness in my panties, as though I'd left them out on the humid balcony overnight, and a hard pain between my legs, which I tried to ignore. We kissed until my lips felt electrocuted, until someone knocked on the door and asked if we wanted dessert. (176)

Replaying the kiss in her mind afterward, Nidali struggles to understand her bisexuality. Available religious and cultural conceptual frameworks do not offer reasonable explanations but afford only the prospects of punishment for her fallen state. Nidali recognizes that it is "bad enough to like boys," but her attraction to girls must lead toward inevitable punishment that she, then, endures at the hands of her increasingly violent father, who beats her up for having returned home late. Nidali willingly submits to Waheed's violence, for she believes she deserves to be punished. However, during the beating, Nidali's pain also vanishes as she remembers her and Jiji's kiss. Again, rather than relinquish her desires, she accepts the punishment for realizing them.

Foregrounding the sexual explorations and frustrations of the adolescent Nidali against the backdrop of Palestinian displacement, Jarrar alters the typology of the national script. Rather than sacrifice the female voice at the altar of Khalifeh's "monster Palestine," Jarrar creates a subversive text that, in its representation of a young woman's tumultuous sexual experiences while constantly moving about, disrupts the concept of the fertile Palestinian woman as the "birther of the nation." That is, the state of displacement does not solely frame Nidali's pervasive sense of homelessness; it also breeds disappointment while creating novel opportunities for further exploring her body. Jarrar focalizes landmark historical moments—such as the First Gulf War—through Nidali's perspective and, rather than spark national sentiments, narrates the frustrations of a teenage girl in leaving people behind and the anxieties entailed in meeting new ones while her body develops sexual needs—thus, transforming the male creation of the national superwoman into an autonomous, basically more humane figure.

Like Jarrar, Maysaloun Hammoud's *Bar Bahar* also redraws the image of Palestinian women. However, while Nidali's experiences develop through the trajectory of Palestinian exile, the intertwining story lines of *Bar Bahar* unfold in Palestinian contexts inside Israel. Sharing an apartment in Tel Aviv, Laila, Salma, and Nur move about between the seemingly liberal Israeli urban landscape and the conservative Arab inland communities in the Galilee and the Triangle. Much like Jarrar, Hammoud alters the typology of the national narrative. However, in contradistinction to the exilic context, the events of *Bar Bahar* take place in the Israeli setting of ethnic discrimination, social inequality, and compromised forms of citizenship, as Hammoud takes aim at sexual politics of censorship in local Arab communities.

Hammoud confronts this topic head-on in the opening scene. The film starts with the repeated sound of the tearing of human flesh against the backdrop of women's distant singing of a traditional Palestinian wedding song. The viewer then is exposed to a scene whereby the experienced hands of a veiled elderly woman sugar wax a young woman's body in preparation for her wedding. As the elderly woman meticulously goes about her work, she also initiates the young woman into the secrets of married life, describing how a wife should behave to meet her husband's expectations: "Don't raise your voice; men don't like women who raise their voices. Remember to always say a kind word and cook him good food. Don't forget to put on perfume and keep your body smooth so that when he desires you, he'll always know where to find you. In bed, do what he tells you. Don't let on that you know what you're doing." From the outset, Hammoud zeroes in on the Palestinian woman's body and its functions in the androcentric Arab social discourse. The young woman's smooth skin is juxtaposed to the wrinkled face of the elderly woman who—ages ago—had experienced sex only to satisfy her husband's appetites. The intertwining stories of Laila, Salma, and Nur depart from Rafifeh's (Nur's cousin), who, by marrying and moving to Kfar Yassif (an Arab town in the Northern District), abruptly vanishes from the Tel Aviv party scene. Their stories also diverge from the conventional itinerary of young Arab women who leave their villages and move to the city to pursue a university education before returning home—or, perhaps, to the villages of their new husbands.

Sassy Laila is the main character of the first story line. She is drawn to the mysterious Ziad Hamdi, who has recently returned from New York. The seemingly open-minded Ziad from the city of Taybeh and the strong-willed Laila from Nazareth engage in a romantic relationship that runs counter to local Arab conventions.

They begin sleeping together, and Laila does not feel pressured by social norms or expect that her relationship with Ziad should inevitably lead to marriage. She is open about her sexual activity and seems content with the choices she has made as a young professional Arab woman, living far away from the constraints of having to preserve her reputation to the satisfaction to meet the demands of a scrutinizing Arab society. Ziad seems the perfect match—a young Arab man who accepts Laila's temperament and choices. To the local spectator, it is clear that such a relationship might survive only in a distant urban environment, but Hammoud aims to show that even a city such as Tel Aviv cannot protect Arabs from the imposing presence of inland Arab conservatism. Ziad's open-mindedness is put to the test when Laila, instead of meeting him at the restaurant where they are supposed to have dinner, shows up at his place unannounced and meets his older sister, whose son was arrested the previous night for possession of hashish. Despite Ziad's reluctance to allow Laila into the apartment, he gives in and tells his sister to brief Laila on her son's predicament. Laila immediately assumes her professional pose and lights a cigarette. She tenderly asks Ziad to bring his sister a glass of water as she details the case in her notebook. Ziad's sister is taken aback by Laila's unconventional posture and immediately understands that her brother is involved with this woman.

Later, on the way to the restaurant for their planned dinner, Laila notices Ziad's awkward silence and asks what is bothering him. Ziad angrily expresses that he was troubled by Laila and his sister's encounter earlier. He proceeds to accuse Laila of not behaving properly and blames her for smoking in front of his sister. Their ensuing argument touches on all the social problems Laila had so far decided to turn her back on: How might a woman such as Laila return to an Arab community? How long does she think she might go on living in Tel Aviv? How much longer might she continue partying and doing drugs? Ziad insists that at some point Laila will need to calm down so that she can realistically find her way back to the Arab town. Laila refuses to apologize for her lifestyle, nor does she see it as a transitional period she is going through before calming down and preparing for going back. She calls out Ziad's hypocrisy and asserts that he is like everyone else—an Arab man who spends a few years sleeping around, pretending to be progressive but at some point longs only to return to his village. Laila breaks up with Ziad and later rejects his attempts at reconciliation. She goes on partying, but, in the final scene, rather than get high smoking weed, she snorts what seems to be heroin—suggesting the deteriorating state of a liberal Arab woman caught in the cramped space between tradition and modernity.

The story of Salma—Laila's roommate and best friend—also presents a challenging situation, whereby the pillars of local traditionalism are unsettled. A kitchen worker by day and DJ by night, Salma struggles with her sexual identity while coping with her parents' massive pressure to arrange her marriage. She defiantly quits her day job after being scolded by her Jewish superior for speaking in Arabic with her colleague in the kitchen. She goes on to find work as a bartender and meets Dunya—a medical student from Haifa—who becomes her lover. Like Salma and Ziad's unusual relationship, theirs can survive only in a place like Tel Aviv. Salma occasionally returns to Tarshiha and attends the compulsory dinners at her parents' home, where they attempt to set her up with "good" local men.

Hammoud shows that for a young unmarried woman in her mid- to late twenties, the intrusiveness of the village society is relentless. Salma's Christian identity does not protect her from family and neighbors' scrutiny—to the contrary. Rather than stereotypically contrast Christian progressiveness with Muslim conservatism, Hammoud presents inland Arab towns as the seat of conservatism, in contradistinction to coastal metropolitans such as Tel Aviv or Haifa. During one of those visits home, Salma brings Dunya and introduces her as a friend. Salma's parents are having George and his parents over for dinner in the hope that Salma will finally commit, and Dunya is privy to the ritual. As the dinner draws to a close, Dunya offers to prepare coffee, and Salma soon follows her to the kitchen, where they start to make out. They are caught in flagrante delicto by Salma's mother, who waits for her guests to leave before she reveals her daughter's secret to her husband. Dunya is asked to leave and never return to their home. Salma's father violently confronts Salma and forbids her to leave the house until she sorts out this "thing" she has contracted. During the night, Salma packs her things and runs away back to Tel Aviv, where she looks up Dunya to tell her that she is moving to Berlin. In the homophobic Israeli Palestinian reality of *Bar Bahar*, there seems to be no room for a lesbian Arab, even in Tel Aviv. Salma feels that she needs to cut ties with her uncompromising parents, who cannot fathom a female identity beyond conventional lines. Berlin is not another city for Salma to start over. Rather, it represents a different planet, whereby she will join an alien population that dresses in black, parties, and accepts homosexual orientations.

Nur's story is no less tragic than the experiences of her newfound sisters. Hers might even represent the most severe situation, insofar as Nur will not be able to permanently stay in Tel Aviv, nor is Berlin a realistic option. She is an observant Muslim woman and engaged to Wisam, a social worker from Umm el-Fahem and also religious. She moves in with Laila and Salma to complete her final year of studies at the Tel Aviv University and endures her roommates' unconventional lifestyles. Wisam appears to come from an esteemed family in Umm el-Fahem and is highly respected by Nur's parents. Upon his first visit to Nur's new place, he expresses his dissatisfaction with her living arrangements and decides to find her a new (more respectable) place. Nur silently complies, abiding by the obedient manners of a stereotypical Muslim woman. Gradually, however, she becomes fond of Laila and Salma and is increasingly reluctant to give up this relationship. Wisam senses this change in Nur and becomes increasingly aggressive toward her, until one evening when he turns physically violent and rapes her. Laila and Salma return late and find Nur broken and crying in the bathroom. Realizing what has befallen her, they carefully undress her and wash her body under the shower. The scene ends with Laila and Salma holding Nur in a sisterly embrace.

Following the explicit rape scene, Nur continues to endure Wisam's presence before her family in Umm el-Fahem. While Wisam goes about as if nothing has happened, Nur turns cold and avoids meeting his gestures. She is trapped in a relationship with her rapist, and there does not seem to be a way of breaking it off without causing a scandal for herself and her family. Nur turns to Laila and Salma for help, and they plot to set him up. Laila dresses up as a religious Muslim woman and reaches out to Wisam for help. At his office, she reveals that she has been repeatedly battered by her husband and uncovers herself to show him the marks on her body. Wisam is easily drawn in by Laila's web and is photographed in this compromising position. Laila, along with Salma and Nur, eventually confronts him with the pictures and demands that he go to Nur's father to call off the wedding. At first, Wisam attempts to shame Nur, calling her a "whore" who has been "polluted" by her "prostitute" friends, but he quickly understands that he is no match for this group of women. He unwillingly gives in to their demands. When Wisam and Nur go to see her father, Hammoud adds yet another twist to the restless plot of *Bar Bahar.* Nur's father immediately understands that his daughter has been violated, and, rather than consider the social repercussions of Nur's situation as might have been expected from a conservative Arab Muslim man, he defends her and tells Wisam to leave their lives for good. In juxtaposing the conservative Muslim father with the Christian father, Hammoud again breaks from Arab stereotypes. Whereas Salma's father from the mixed Galilean village of Tarshiha cannot accept who his daughter is, Nur's father embraces his, regardless of how the local community will expectedly twist things in Wisam's favor. The film ends with the three women back at their apartment in Tel Aviv, getting ready for tonight's party. The music is gloomy, and the camera works in slow motion as people dance, in a haze of drugs and alcohol. In the final scene, Laila, Salma, and Nur are standing on the rooftop, silently looking out at the city, scarred by society.

On the surface, it might appear critically convenient to regard the protagonists as trapped between Israeli modernity and Arab tradition, as several reviewers have done. Hammoud's choice of settings—Nazareth, Umm el-Fahem, and Tarshiha versus Tel Aviv in 2016—and her statements have certainly supported this interpretation: "My film is about liberation in many senses, but especially in the feminist sense. It's a political film in the sense that it places women in the center; it's a sharp and clear statement. The Palestinian women in the Tel Aviv urban space, through the city's view—that's political."[24] However, although Tel Aviv connotes Zionist conquest in the Palestinian context, it is important to point out that the Palestinian women's conflictual position between modernity and tradition did not come about with the establishment of Israel. Rather, their chastity has always been interwoven with the economic and cultural changes that took place after the 1930s in Palestine. The Arabic title of the film *Bar Bahar* (literally "land sea") captures the Palestinian geography of cultural conflict more accurately than its English translation, *In Between*.

The construction of the Jerusalem–Jaffa railroad line (later the Jerusalem–Haifa line) at the turn of the twentieth century probably configures as the most visible symbol of modernity in Palestine. However, this new line was only one among several major changes that irreversibly transformed Palestinian society before 1948. The growth of citriculture and its European market, the proliferation of wage labor related to the British war efforts, the employment of Palestinians in the government bureaucracy, as well as the transference of wealth from the agricultural industry to import-export trade and light industries all changed the social balance in Palestine, triggering a large-scale migration from the mountains to the coast during the 1930s, which gave rise to a new class of merchants and manufacturers in the cities of Gaza, Jaffa, Haifa, and Acre—the four cities that constituted Palestine's Mediterranean outlet to Europe. These changes, along with the emergence of an urban intelligentsia that founded newspaper and literary magazine presses, established the coast as the emerging seat of authority in Palestine. In other words, the growth of power in coastal cities posed a serious challenge to the authority of inner mountain cities, such as Nablus, Nazareth, Safad, and Hebron—the seats of conservatism and traditional leadership.[25]

The old system—based on clan alliances and relations of patronage with landlords and notables (some of them absentees, living in Lebanon or Syria)—was threatened, insofar as some of these landlords and notables, along with tax farmers, government functionaries, artisans, and merchants relocated in urban centers, constituted a privileged elite that facilitated its hegemony over Palestine. This decline of rural authority left the mountain communities to fend for themselves facing not only the economic force of the growing coastal industries, but also the imminent threat of the developing cosmopolitan coastal culture. That is to say, in a society that is persistently culturally bent on upholding female chastity through terms such as "honor," "virginity," and "*bint assel*" ("a daughter whose origins are known")—and I point to these terms at the risk of sounding like the classical European Orientalist—coastal culture became the locus that targeted female morality.

Viewing Laila's, Salma's, and Nur's experiences in light of this historico-geographical perspective dismantles the Orientalist dichotomy of Israeli progressiveness versus Palestinian backwardness. Jaffa—once the seat of Palestinian cosmopolitanism—has been overrun by Tel Aviv, Israel's contemporary coastal metropolis. These young women are caught in between inland conservatism and coastal cosmopolitanism, with a pungent Israeli twist. More significantly, the subversive power of *Bar Bahar* is not exclusively rooted in Hammoud's ability to tell a story of these three young Palestinian women caught between—to borrow Salim Tamari's coining—the mountain and the sea. This setting is also not merely a fictional device exclusively aimed at lending verisimilitude to the story; the actors behind the characters do themselves inhabit this polarized Arab Israeli reality. The risk they are faced with in playing these roles should also be acknowledged.

Mouna Hawa, Sana Jammelieh, Shaden Kanboura, Henry Andrawes, Mahmud Shalaby, and Ahlam Canaan engage in various sexually suggestive scenes that challenge their audiences' preconceptions of how a proper Arab woman should behave, even if she is performing a fictional role. It is important to keep in mind that this upcoming generation of artists is made up members of a tiny Arab minority in Israel, who are still somewhat expected to abide by social conventions.[26] To think of Hawa's explicit kissing and suggestive sexual scenes with Shalaby as Laila and Ziad, Jammelieh and Canaan's homosexual love scenes as Salma and Dunya, and Kanboura and Andrawes's graphic rape scene as Nur and Wisam, these actors seem to have personally transgressed major cultural barriers for the purpose of professional and artistic fulfillment.

Local audiences were divided. Whereas some groups and critics expressed their admiration for *Bar Bahar*, others condemned it altogether. We need to consider only how groups of young local Arab men were offended upon watching *Bar Bahar* and vandalized local theaters in response or the number of death threats Hammoud has received since her film came out. It seems that portrayals of female sexuality beyond the cultural "safe zones" continue to provoke violent reactions and disrupt national sentiments with regard to the position of Palestinian women. According to conservative views of large segments of the local Arab population, voices such as Hammoud's and performances such as the ones delivered by Hawa, Shalaby, Jammelieh, Canaan, Kanboura, and Andrawes should be banned from the public sphere to prevent their "corrupting" upcoming generations.

It does not seem that the nostalgic craving for a pastoral past could possibly comprehend the kind of social liberation that Jarrar and Hammoud have in mind. How does Lisa Suhair Majaj account for the conservative forces that refuse to move forward? It does not seem likely that were Suheir Hammad and Nathalie Handal given the chance to "return" to the homeland and express their socially progressive stances, they would be accepted with open arms by the local population. Their ideas—like those of Jarrar and Hammoud—would probably be censored as foreign (or Israeli, as in the case of Hammoud) cultural implants whose purpose is to pollute local "origins." Moreover, these voices would, of course, never be exempted from accusations of accommodating certain ideological conceptions regarding Arab patriarchy. Nonetheless, this critical gambit should not undermine Jarrar's and Hammoud's powerful introspective critiques against a traditionalism that not only characterize large segments of today's Arab communities but also constitutes the basic tenor of a worldwide nationalist ideology at large.

5

When the Exile Brings a Key

The Poetics of Palestinian "Homecomings"

> Confusion arises between the tourist's curiosity, the visitor's sadness, and the returnee's joy, diverting you from what you are feeling.
>
> —Mahmoud Darwish, *In the Presence of Absence*

The Palestinian Nakba is, among others, conventionally identifiable with the image of the old patriarch who while bringing little of his family's belongings into exile zealously holds onto the key for his home. He stands at the other side of the fence and looks into Palestine (now the State of Israel) at the Jewish settlers as they meticulously weave the ruins of his former reality into the construction of their future one. It is a tragic figure who dies in exile, eventually bequeathing his sons the key in order that they reclaim what rightfully belongs to them. In 2008 Palestinian refugees in the Aida camp near Bethlehem collaboratively produced a monument in the shape of a key. Weighing nearly a ton and measuring nine meters in length, it is made of steel and installed at the entrance of the camp. This symbol remains relevant in the Palestinian national consciousness insofar as the issue of the "Right of Return," enshrined in the United Nations General Assembly Resolution 194, Article 11, passed on December 11, 1948, has yet to be realized to this day. While still safely hidden away even though the lock has been replaced and the house itself may well no longer exist, artists and literary writers have variedly configured the item of the key in their works, turning it into an essential symbol of the ongoing Palestinian story. Along with Naji

Ali's iconic *Handala*, it continues to remind generations of exiled Palestinians of the duty to claim their right to return.[1]

During the spring and summer of 2015, it seemed as if dozens of descendants of Palestinian refugees from the Arab village of Tarshiha, located in the western part of the Galilee in Israel, temporarily realized this claim. They visited their location of origin, and their arrivals were heavily charged with symbolic references of "returning to the homeland."[2] Ironically, it was the first time any of them had set foot in Tarshiha; it was the first time they saw the remnants of or entered their parents' or grandparents' homes that were now occupied by remaining Arab residents or refugees from destroyed neighboring villages; it was also the first time some of them met close and distant relatives who were now citizens of Israel. The Facebook page entitled "Tarchiha Flstan" at the time, operated by a Palestinian refugee and activist in Lebanon (also a descendant of former inhabitants of Tarshiha), posted pictures of these events and encounters to the enthusiastic online responses of thousands of "Tarshihean" followers scattered around the globe. The local inhabitants welcomed and warmly hosted their exiled compatriots, allowing for the fulfillment of these personal journeys and simultaneously making sure that their guests visited local attractions. Sixty-seven years after the Nakba, such nationally motivated pilgrimages had become possible since these travelers—belonging to different diasporic Palestinian communities from around the world and now naturalized citizens in their host countries—were able to enter Israel on their acquired passports as tourists.

Online posts of Sanaa's (false name) journey became particularly popular. A young single mother arriving from Denmark with her two children, she immediately befriended the locals. Sanaa was greeted by the majority of the inhabitants as one of the village's long-lost daughters. They invited her to their homes and saw to it that she took part in public events during her stay in Tarshiha. They also brought Sanaa to her grandparents' former house and recorded how she effortlessly walked up a tiny path, leading to the front door. She entered and passed through a modern-looking living room before arriving at a stone wall at the center of the house, revealing its original Palestinian structure. She laid her hand on the white stones, and during a private conversation afterward, Sanaa described the moment she touched the wall, saying she was overwhelmed by the sensation of having finally arrived home. Sanaa realized that her father had played on these floors among these walls as a young child before becoming a Palestinian refugee, and *she* had successfully returned—although only temporarily. Two weeks later, she was on her way back to Denmark, bringing with her firsthand memories of the "homeland" into diaspora.

In the framework of this seemingly straightforward Palestinian narrative such as the one realized by Sanaa, the symbolic Palestinian "key of return" represents both a telos and a point of departure—an *arche*—in relation to a historical mission and a certain territory for its subjects. Today's Palestinian situation may appear relatively simple on the surface: first, the century-long process of realizing a European colonial project to facilitate Jewish nationalism in Palestine eventually displaced and dispossessed a local indigenous population that had inhabited the land for several centuries (*arche*); second, this population, while in exile, dutifully continues to claim its right to return to the homeland someday (telos); and third, "when" the Palestinians return, the symbolic key will fit the imagined lock and Palestinians will unconditionally feel at home upon arriving in Palestine—as if they had never left.[3] Sanaa's experience mirrors this latter assumption because her journey seems undisrupted by years of having cultivated a diasporic identity in Lebanon, the Gulf states, and Denmark. She was a young Palestinian woman feeling at home in the homeland.

However, comparing Sanaa's experience to textual portrayals that I focus on in the following parts of this chapter—memoirs by Palestinians (or authors of Palestinian descent) such as Fawaz Turki's *Exile's Return: The Making of a Palestinian-American* (1994), Mourid Barghouti's *Ra'aytu Ramallah* (*I Saw Ramallah*, 1997), and Lina Meruane's *Volverse Palestina* (*Becoming Palestine*, 2014)—her uncomplicated commitment to Palestinian imaginings of *al-awdah* is exceptional.[4] Whereas Sanaa's exilic background rather than disrupting her experience of "return" renders it fulfilling, these diasporic authors in their respective narrations of "homecoming" create venues that challenge the prospects of the national telos: exile does not anticipate a sense of ultimate fulfillment upon arriving in the "homeland"; rather, it serves as a window for reassessing the trajectories of belonging to the location they have imaginatively and conceptually cultivated a connection to from afar. These authors see their experiences as vehicles for exploring who and what they have become in exile as they encounter realities "inside" Israel-Palestine that have not only "naturally" evolved but also been rendered unrecognizable by Israeli military occupation in the West Bank and processes of Israeli "culturalization" inside the Green Line. Personal memories and the stories they grew up with may frame, but do not entirely comprehend, the paradoxical experiences of foreignness and familiarity Turki, Barghouti, and Meruane express during their sojourns—not only with the Israeli reality but also with locals and relatives.

I want here to bring up Alfred Schütz's foundational article "The Homecomer" (1945) to briefly theorize the multiple distinctions of the concept of "home" for its various inhabitants. Schütz contends, "Home means one thing to the man who never has left it, another thing to the man who dwells far from it, and still another to him who returns." He refers here to the various forms of "home" diasporic individuals may experience regarding their location of origin. Their intimate knowledge of the place is relatively lost, insofar as its details and inhabitants have changed during the immigrants' absence. As Schütz has it, "The homecomer is not the same man who left. He is neither the same for himself nor for those who await his return." The irreversibility of time frames the returnees' ambivalent sense of loss as well as their sense of estrangement, foregrounding who they have become in their current location of residence. Although Schütz's bases his observations on the immigrant's transnational relation to "home," I think they are also relevant to the circumstances of the exiled's relations. However, it is important to note that whereas the disruption of intimate knowledge and the sense of loss for the immigrant may surface on an individual level upon, more or less voluntarily, leaving the "homeland," the exiled share these predicaments with other displaced individuals who together formulate their desire for returning as a collective political call. The conflict between the personal and the political occurs in that the exile adheres to the apparently uninterrupted collective desire on the account of marginalizing the complexities of his or her individual relationship to the "homeland." Such tension inevitably grows, since the political realm continues to suppress the dynamics of distance and time, while, as Pnina Werbner puts it, "seen in the *longue durée*, history and memory are made elsewhere, whether at home or in the diaspora." Werbner challenges not only this political conception but also "the unproblematic assumption in transnational theory of uninterrupted, continuing, intimate, taken-for-granted sociality across homeland and diaspora." According to Werbner, such an assumption "misrecognizes the critical phenomenological question of how intimate knowledge is sustained over discontinuous space and time."[5]

As Schütz's article shows, the theoretical discussion about the distinct conceptions of home to the returnee began in the 1940s, and it certainly preceded the birth of the Palestinian exile. Nonetheless, whereas the sense of permanent loss is a universal characteristic for Schütz's "homecomer," in the Palestinian context, it has political consequences that unsettle how we might think about the basic tenet of the "Right of Return" in the national script. The discrepancy between diasporic narratives of yearnings for "return" and narrations of their virtual realizations show that between the historical *arche* and national telos, different contexts of Palestinian displacement similarly frame an abstract desire for a collective "return," but distinctively disrupt sensations of fulfillment during occasional simulated realizations of this desire. As a result, I think there is an increasing necessity for highlighting the consequences of the widening gaps between narratives of prospective returns constructed in diaspora and the ones constructed upon arriving in the homeland. Whereas the former maintains a coherent national narrative that present a framework that most Palestinians may more or less identify with regardless of location, the latter are rooted in experiences of displacement that have called for the construction of parallel narratives, representing the local story of each among the various diasporic communities. Historically, these diversities represent the ongoing consequences of the severe political changes that befell Palestinians during the twentieth century—primarily the cultural fragmentation that, rather than anticipating a desired conclusion to the Palestinian story, frames the continuing development of subplots, creating multiple story lines connecting the historical *arche* and the prospective national telos.

The purpose of this chapter is to configure a poetics of the Palestinian *awdah*. The aforementioned linguistically diverse memoirs mutually explore the conceptual tensions between national imaginings of *al-awdah* and their disruptive impact on virtual realizations of this desire, while simultaneously revealing the authors' culturally distinct experiences of exile. Their points of departure may appear identical since they share conceptions of "home" that are deeply rooted in a unified national configuration of more or less similar memories or narrations, depending on generation. However, the logic behind highlighting mutual thematic elements is based on the assumption that their journeys to the "homeland" reveal distinct diasporic experiences, representing both the ongoing cultural proliferations of the various displaced Palestinian communities and their ramifications in processes of identification. In this context, my argument both engages and diverges from the national template. The identifiable symbolic key handed down by the patriarch not only refers to a common collective desire, but, in my view, has also come to represent a token for past and current cultural diversities among Palestinians.

Poetics of Displacement

As explained at the outset, seventy years after the Palestinian Nakba and three generations later, against the backdrop of the national unified call for the "Right of Return," recent temporary reunions among family and compatriots in the homeland are revealing the ongoing outcomes of Palestinians' distinct experiences of displacement. To explore the implications of these diversities through the site of "return," further explication of the three terms brought together in the title of this chapter is warranted: "poetics," "Palestinian," and "homecoming." In my opinion, Turki's, Barghouti's, and Meruane's texts delineate a poetics of "return," insofar as their (artistic) narratives both aesthetically and thematically expand and complicate the Palestinian identity. They variedly unsettle conventional venues for identification by way of envisaging their experiences of arriving in their respective locations of origin against narratives and images of "home" preconceived in diaspora.

First of all, I want to distance my employment of the term "poetics" from the traditional Greek interpretation. Turki's, Barghouti's, and Meruane's narrations neither establish nor facilitate grand (national) narratives in the way Herodotus accredits the term to Homer's and Hesiod's poetry. Whereas ancient Greek poiesis involves depictions of the origins and ordering of the world—turning chaos into cosmos while explaining contemporarily unexplainable phenomena[6]—the poetic resonances of these memoirs, rather than narrating the desired definitive conclusion to the Palestinian story, render such a prospect ambiguous. My interpretation of poetics is influenced by Linda Hutcheon's definition in *A Poetics of Postmodernism* (1988). She describes it as "an open, ever-changing theoretical structure by which to order both our cultural knowledge and our critical procedures. This would not be a poetics in the structuralist sense of the word, but would go beyond the study of literary discourse to the study of cultural practice and theory."[7] In other words, instead of merely focusing on aesthetics and thematics in a study of literary poetics, Hutcheon suggests we expand the scope and explore their implications on theoretical and cultural practices. In this vein, I do not want to argue that these memoirs are literarily valuable in and by themselves. Alternatively, I think they necessitate a critical reexamination of the relationship between national imaginings and experiences of "return" for Palestinians from around the globe, insofar as their authors, upon arrival, discover that the reality of the homeland is far from what they have imagined in diaspora through memory and narration. They realize that the geographical location of Palestine may no longer serve as the proper habitat for their distinct exilic identities and leave the reader with the unarticulated question "Where to, from here?"—pointing to the acute uncertainties involved in pondering the prospects of Palestinian identities in diaspora.

The PLO's historic compromise in the nineteenth session of the Palestine National Council meeting held in Algiers in 1988 that, in hindsight, anticipated the signing of the Oslo Agreement in 1993 particularly complicated the issue of diversity in the Palestinian context.[8] Although the "Right of Return" dominated Palestinian political discourse between 1967 and 1987 (the eruption of the First Intifada), it was always only tangibly relevant to the refugee and immigrant communities. After 1993, as the center of gravity for the Palestinian nationalist struggle moved from the diaspora to the occupied territories that later became destined to house the prospective Palestinian State as part of the infamously controversial two-state solution, the claim for return was all but completely marginalized. Instead of continuing to symbolize the essence of Palestinian displacement or vanishing from the agenda of diplomacy altogether, it has become a disruptive point, constantly halting the proceedings of any negotiations between the Israel government and the Palestinian Authorities.[9]

Hence, that same Palestinian Declaration of Independence sealed the fate of millions of refugees who historically originated from locations inside the Green Line that the PLO now conceded any claim to. To them, even if a Palestinian State would be established and the issue of the "Right of Return" should be resolved, the occupied territories do not represent the "homeland" for the majority of exiles and refugees as well as the Arab citizens of Israel. Both Palestinian-Israeli poet, novelist, and translator Anton Shammas and the renowned national poet Mahmoud Darwish problematize this point. In the mid-1980s, during a friendly meeting with Israeli novelists A. B. Yehoshua and David Grossman, Shammas belatedly responds to

Yehoshua's suggestion—of some years earlier—for him to pack and move a hundred meters east if he needs to practice his Palestinian national identity. Shammas describes how he once temporarily went to live in the Palestinian town of Beit Jala in 1978 owing to the surge in Jerusalem rents and explains why he would never repeat this experience again:

> Not that I have a trace of feeling superior to the people in the territories. It's only a sense that it's not my geography there. Not my cognitive, spiritual, or mental map. I work according to other codes, my head, my imagination, my emotions . . . What bothered me more than anything else in Beit Jala was the gradual discovery was the gradual discovery that my neighbor spoke Arabic but not the same Arabic I did. An invisible but most palpable green line ran between us. I suppose it's as if a Hebrew Macintosh program were fed into your IBM word processor. I would guess that the neighboring had the same feeling—that there was a 1948 Arab speaking, really, a foreign language. (263)

Shammas's reply refers to the "Green Line" that the events of 1948 drew between the Palestinians who became legal citizens in Israel and those individuals who have since endured two consecutive military occupations in the Gaza Strip and the West Bank. Moreover, the distinctions between Shammas and his neighbor not only stem from the existence of Israel but also refer to nuances of historic local loyalties among Palestinians. Shammas, a Christian Arab, hails from the western Galilean Arab village of Fassuta that he immortalizes in *Arabesques.* Located more than two hundred kilometers north of Beit Jala and Jerusalem, Fassuta historically belonged to the Acre district, and its inhabitants speak a distinct Palestinian dialect of Arabic, different from what is spoken in the Jerusalem area. That is to say that Shammas's sense of alienation in Beit Jala is not merely the outcome of the Israeli citizenship disrupting his Palestinian identity. Rather, it may also be rooted in Palestinian localism that played an overriding role for self-identification during the nineteenth and early twentieth centuries and probably contested the emergence of a successful national framework.[10]

Similarly, Darwish repeatedly expresses the sense of estrangement upon his "return" to Ramallah in 1996. In a landmark interview with Hillit Yeshurun for the Israeli literary journal *Hadarim*, he explicitly distinguishes between "returning" and "coming" to live in the territories—the prospective homeland:

> Hesitance is the way in which I read what is happening. I am not returning. I am coming. No one can return to an imaginary place or to the person he once was. Al-Birweh does not exist anymore. Also, the Right of Return is not guaranteed. I am coming but not returning. I am coming but not arriving. And, this is not merely a poetic issue. It is realistic. I have visited parts of my homeland. I felt very alien in Gaza, since the land is only beautiful when it is whole. You cannot say she is beautiful based on one clove. Its entire geography is what gives beauty to our country. I went without illusions. I was prepared for disappointment and found it. But to return to the person who once was and to the place that once was—is impossible.[11]

Darwish does not see his arrival in the territories as a return, but as the title for Yeshurun's interview indicates—"Exile Is So Strong within, I May Bring It to the Homeland"—going "home" is yet another phase in Darwish's exilic journey, although he does, as he states elsewhere, feel more at home in the Arab world. Nonetheless, Gaza felt strange to him, and, as he tells Adam Shatz from the *New York Times*, so does Ramallah: "I had never been in the West Bank before. . . . It's not my private homeland. Without memories you have no real relationship to a place."[12] Al-Birweh is permanently gone, and so is the child Mahmoud Darwish, who along with his family and the other inhabitants of the village all became "present absentees." Consequently, Darwish does not think he will ever be able to return, insofar as the person who could have returned and the place he could have returned to have both long ceased to exist.

Such constant deferral of the exile's successful return also takes up a major part in the second half of Darwish's last prosaic work *Fi Hadrat 'al-Ghiyab* (*In the Presence of Absence*, 2006). In a form of premature self-eulogy, Darwish prepares for a two-day journey home in western Galilee to meet with family and friends for one last time.[13] His meditations on the conceptual and emotional significance of "return" brings up the fears of the "returnee" should he not feel at "home" in the "homeland": "But I, you tell yourself, prefer being a stranger in exile to being a stranger at home, because in exile it is required." Darwish anticipates his prospective foreignness upon "returning" and recognizes the difference between the "homeland" the exiles have constructed in their absence and the place that he is now preparing to return to: "You bid your farewell to Tunisia and to those returning to the back corner of the homeland. The ones leaving the realm of myth for the narrow confines of reality." A few pages later, Darwish continues to ponder this distinction between myth and reality:

> Has the journey ended or begun? Has he come closer to the place, or has the place departed from his imagination? The older returnee is prone to making comparisons, perplexed as to whether he should prefer the imagined over the real. As for the one born in exile and reared on the beautiful attributes of exile's antithesis, he might be let down by a paradise created especially for him, composed of words he soaked up and reduced to stereotypes that would guide him to difference. He inherited memory from a family that feared forgetfulness, upon which the others had wagered. He inherited memory from the steady refrain of anthems glorifying folklore and the rifle, which eventually became an identity when the "homeland" was born away from its land, the homeland was born in exile. Paradise was born from the hell of absence.[14]

Darwish not only distinguishes between the mythic homeland that Darwish himself—perhaps more than any other poet—effectively helped to create while in exile and to the Palestine where he is now going but also imagines this distinction from the perspective of second-generation exiles who possess no personal memories of the place as home, only their parents' narrations. To them, the poetic version of the "homeland" is the only available one, and the one that constantly pushes the real Palestine further away from the exile's reach, always disrupting the sensation of a genuine return. As Darwish puts it to the Yeshurun, "I was prepared for disappointment and I found it."

Like Shammas and Darwish, for millions of refugees from and current inhabitants of the Galilee area, the establishment of a Palestinian state in the occupied Palestinian territories does not serve, even if the Israeli government would allow it, as a space for practicing their Palestinian identity, as A. B. Yehoshua suggests. This version of a Palestinian state would solve only one among several problems: the occupation. For the majority of refugees both inside and outside Israel, Palestine refers to the village or the city from which they originate. In this sense, the tangible local identity still overrides the abstract national one. Palestine is not merely Palestine for the majority of the authors I refer to here. Rather, it refers to a particular location in Palestine—Jerusalem, Ramallah, Beit Jala, Haifa, Acre, and so forth. My contention is that although the national narrative seemingly continues to frame different experiences of Palestinian exile regardless of generation, it has become less dominant in relation to the distinct local narratives of displacement in the formation of the different versions of the Palestinian identity. These discrepancies between narrative and experience raise a difficult but necessary question: Insofar as both the idea of Palestine and available multiple processes of identification for Palestinians are no longer easily compatible, how may it be possible to conceptually establish a "new" Palestine that would be able to house these "new" Palestinians?

To clarify my question, I want to make a, perhaps flimsy, comparison with the long-term impact of the Jewish diasporas on the eventual realization of the Zionist project in Palestine. Rather than viewing Israel as the outcome of Jews' successful return to carry on a historic legacy that was cut short two thousand years ago (as the Zionist story goes), is it not, today, sound to assume that remnants of diaspora identities determine cultural and social class status in Israeli society?[15] An Israeli is not merely Israeli, but diasporic origins delineate if a citizen is "Ashkenazi" (European), "Mizrahi" (Oriental), Ethiopian, or distinctively Sephardic or Russian. These categories explicitly divide the Jewish Israeli society and more or less determine political representation in the Knesset, showing that the making of Israeli culture is an ongoing process of collisions, negotiations, and interrelations among the various diasporic narratives. In this historically exceptional context, experiences of displacement not only have not evaporated but also determine the making of Israel's social and political structure.

Would a similar process not also be the case in the Palestinian context even though its history of displacement is only a few decades old? May Palestinians return—if even for a short period of time—without feeling the pressing call of their distinct diasporic identities? Would it be possible to extract the camp from the refugee, the occupation from the occupied, the diaspora from the exiled, or the consequences of Israeli citizenship from the Arabs in Israel? Would these decades-long experiences of displacement not determine identity politics and social class in case Israelis decide that this nation-state gig is not a Jewish thing and return to their respective diasporas and these, by now diverse, Palestinian communities hypothetically reunite in their own independent state? For decades following the uprooting of the Palestinian people, several of these newly created displaced communities developed in total isolation from one another, and only recently have they started to interact and as a result created processes of transnational intertextuality that take place, among others, at the site of Palestinians' ubiquitous national aspiration: *al-awdah*. These questions may, of course, not be viewed through a single lens, nor can their complexities be resolved in a single magical stroke.

The following parts of this chapter will examine how, at this site, Turki, Barghouti, and Meruane present both the problems and the necessity for creating a conceptual space that may comprehend the various ongoing outcomes of historic Palestinian experiences of displacement. To begin, Palestinian director Annemarie Jacir's film

Salt of This Sea (2008), starring Palestinian American poet Suheir Hammad as Soraya and Israeli Arab actor Saleh Bakri as Emad, offers a comprehensive pretext for my argument in its caption of the ambivalence between the Palestinian "returnee's" claim of belonging and a simultaneous sense of estrangement toward his or her origin. Soraya, a Palestinian woman born in Brooklyn, travels to Ramallah to claim her grandfather's inheritance, stored in a local bank since his expulsion in 1948. Denied access to the savings since an impinging bureaucracy, mainly configured by Israeli law, does not acknowledge claims of ownership by descendants of Palestinian refugees, Soraya senses her frustration mounting to indignation, and, aided by Emad, a handsome waiter who hopes to win a fellowship to study abroad and is an easygoing filmmaker, she devises a plan to rob the bank and recover the money.

Following the robbery, Jacir turns away from the "heist" plot and transforms the film into a modern odyssey of the past and present through a rendering of contemporary Palestinian and Israeli realities. On the run, Soraya and her crew succeed in entering Israel disguised as Jewish settlers. They arrive in Jerusalem before heading to the coast of the port city Jaffa to visit her family home. Shortly after their arrival, she finds her grandfather's house and is warmly invited in by the Israeli Jewish woman who now lives there—a young artist about the same age as Soraya (the Israeli doppelgänger). Although the original architecture of the house is still visible, it is neatly worked into the current occupant's Israeli interpretation of Mediterranean space, symbolically representing the ways whereby the Palestinian past, if not destroyed, has been reckoned unrecognizable by weaving its remnants into the texture of Israeli reality. At first, Soraya warily accepts the invitation, but her indignation over the injustice that has befallen Palestinians eventually resurfaces, and she confronts the current occupant of her grandparents' house. During an altercation, the young artist dismisses Soraya's claims for ownership and asks her and her friends to leave. They arrive in other parts of the country, exploring the ruins of old homes and Palestinian villages buried underneath the Israeli landscape. Locating the ruins of Emad's family's destroyed Palestinian village of Dawayma, they decide to occupy one of the few seemingly habitable ruins, far from the tensions of everyday politics, imaginarily resurrecting the place from the dead to establish a life together. After a few days, their fantasy world is interrupted by a Jewish schoolteacher who is on a field trip with his students. He asks them what they are doing, and, upon receiving an answer from Soraya in fluent American English, he relaxes and introduces the "American tourists" to his students. Approaching the "idealized" ending of the film, despite the embittered Soraya's increasingly alienating experience, she does find love and a sense of home among the ruins, interlacing her relationship with a fragile reality and the stories handed down to her by former generations. However, it is a sensation that may be only temporarily facilitated in the world of make-believe and that will repeatedly and inevitably be disrupted by the Israeli reality. The film ends with Soraya's expulsion and her sitting in the airport—in "no-man's-land" where people arrive and depart seemingly unattached.

Although Jacir's film heavily invests in maintaining the Palestinian national narrative to frame Soraya's odyssey (even on the account of character development), it also unsettles the symbols and myths cultivated through memories and narrations of the "homeland" in the diaspora. Rather than presenting Soraya's journey as an experience of a successful fulfillment of a national desire, Jacir foregrounds her estrangement and the consequences of Soraya's refusing to give up on establishing a bond to the land despite its foreignness to her. Insofar as contemporary Israeli and Palestinian realities do not offer Soraya (and her real-life kindred compatriots in exile, as I shall demonstrate shortly) a genuine home, she, along with Emad, invests in establishing one in a dimension of make-believe—a fictional space that represents neither exile nor the homeland but rather a kind of liminality that negates Soraya's identity as a diasporic Palestinian and Emad's as a Palestinian living under Israeli military occupation. Among the ruins, they metaphorically return to a state of innocence, untainted by exile and occupation, suggesting that the Palestinian *awdah* as imagined in the national narrative belongs in the land of make-believe. In the real world, the contexts of exile, occupation, the refugee camps, and Israeli citizenship for those persons who remained have inscribed their realities into today's Palestinian identities, rendering any authentic attempt at returning impossible, insofar as the idea of the "homeland" exists now as a polyphonic possibility composed of memories and narrations in various Palestinian contexts of displacement.

Exemplary of this latter point is Fawaz Turki's deterritorialization, in *Exile's Return*, of the idea of "home" and his birthplace upon visiting there. Turki, born in the city of Haifa in 1940, is a first-generation refugee who, as a child, grew up in the Burj al-Barajneh camp, located in the southern suburbs of Beirut in Lebanon. The location of Haifa inside the Green Line as an inextricable part of Israel presents a dark context to Palestinian "homecomings," insofar as politicians and diplomats continue to consider the two-state solution. Haifa is forever lost to the Palestinian, and from the outset Turki disclaims an emotional bond to his city of birth as he stands on Mount Carmel four decades after he and his family were forced to leave:

> I am home.
>
> Yet as I say that to myself, I know how facile and illusory that outcry is. It is tawdry, I tell myself, for me to be saying that. I cannot return here, after forty years in exile, with my alternative order of meaning, my comfortable notions about homelessness being my only homeland, and say that I am home. The house is no longer as habitable as when I left it. The toys are no longer in the attic. An awry force in history has changed the place, and my own sense of otherness has changed me. This place could not be lived in by anyone other than its new inhabitants, and they have already stripped it clean of everything but themselves. From time to time I come across something here and there, inherited from nature—the view of the Mediterranean below, the cloudless sky above, the richly green trees around—that had always independently declared their own form of being, but apart from that, Haifa no longer speaks to me.[16]

Turki has returned, but Haifa is no longer home. These remnants of the past that are carefully woven into the texture of Israeli reality cannot coexist with conceptualizations of exile that Turki identifies as his "order of meaning." He heretically declares—countering his national heritage—that this place, as such, belongs not to him but to its new occupants. His estrangement highlights the tension between two basic concepts in the Palestinian narrative: "exile" and "home." Turki does express a sporadic familiarity with the natural landscape surrounding Haifa, but the city itself no longer speaks to the person he has become in the past decades. Following a similar itinerary as that of Soraya's, Turki goes to visit his parents' house—his childhood home. Turki's tone remains impassive (or perhaps deliberately restrained): "There is the house, as nondescript as ever, standing at the corner of Miknass and Talal streets. These names, like everything else in this city, have been changed. Three steps lead up to the front door. I climb them and knock." The longed-for return to his parents' house does not summon a mental process of reimagining the place in its former state—in a similar manner to the one described by Palestinian sociologist Reema Hammami during a visit to Jaffa, following her thwarted attempt to recognize her parents' house under its new Israeli guise. Whereas Turki does not find anything unique about the complex—being a stranger in a strange place—Hammami expresses familiarity with the minutest details upon her return: "The gate was open so I walked in. I found myself in the large *liwan*, the womb of the house, which still had its columns and original italianate tile floor. It was full of people who somehow didn't enter my field of vision: I was mapping the *liwan's* former reality, a process that excluded objects and people not part of that earlier moment."[17] Turki also enters, but, rather than relate to the space around him, he gets caught up in awkward dialogue with the current Jewish tenant:

> "Do you speak English, sir?" I ask the old man.
>
> He tells me, in a heavy East European accent, that he does. And I ask him if I could just look around the house a bit. He has

wrinkled eyebrows and a pouting underlip that expresses his puzzlement at my request.

"I was born here," I offer, in the way of explanation.

He lets me into the hallway without saying another word.

"You want that I show you the house?" he asks.

"That'll be very kind of you."

"You do not speak Hebrew?"

"I'm afraid not."

"And you were born here?"

He obviously thinks I'm Jewish, but I don't want to deceive him, so I say: "I am not a Jew. I am an Arab."

He looks at me uncomprehendingly. I can see the man has arthritis and his hands are shaking.

"I mean I'm Palestinian. I'm not an Israeli," I add redundantly, but this only excites the language of his wrinkled eyebrows and pouting underlip, and he looks at me as if I had smacked him. His hands begin to shake more visibly.

"I mean, like, you know, I'm actually American," I blurt out defensively. But the man wants me out of his house. His house. My house. Our house.

I leave without either of us saying another word.

I should have told him I wasn't there to reclaim the place, just the passions it once housed. I think he would have understood. He too was once in exile after all.[18]

Turki does not mention any details about the house or the "passions" it may arouse. He returns into exile and leaves "his house, my house, our house" to its current occupant—ironically, history's "eternal" exile, the Jew. Turki's *awdah* is rather awkward in relation to Hammami's, who, during her imaginative journey into the past, is interrupted by a woman in a white medical uniform. When Hammami identifies herself and the purpose of her visit, she is nervously ushered into the director's office of the day care for retarded children. She is warmly received and asked to sit, as the director painstakingly explains to her about the return of the Jewish people to the land of Israel and the historic success of the Zionist dream. Rendered speechless owing to what she takes to be a form of sadism in the director's gesture, Hammami excuses herself and continues to look around for another few moments.[19]

Meditating on Turki's astonishing impassivity and Hammami's emotional encounter, Palestinian sociologist Salim Tamari's visit to the "homeland" (also in Jaffa, and in the company of Rema Hammami) captures the sad irony entailed in these "returns." At the center of Old Jaffa, now Kedumim Square, Tamari and his friends enter an archaeological museum displaying Hellenic and Roman artifacts. At the entrance, they read the history of Jaffa on placards decorating the walls—an entirely Israeli narrative that excludes any mentioning of past or present Arab inhabitants of the city, unlike the biased descriptions in the brochures in Arabic stacked at the museum's entrance about Arabs' pogroms of Jews during the period of the British Mandate. In the tradition of returns to Jaffa, upon encountering the outcome of long-established processes of de-Arabizing the place and its history, Tamari and friends "treat themselves to a sumptuous meal by the sea in order to forget."[20] Sadly, the travesties of history are warded off in one of Jaffa's famous fish restaurants—a must for any tourist visiting any of the old port cities of Acre, Haifa, or Jaffa.

Such visits were not rare during the years following the signing of the Oslo Accords and before the eruption of the Second Intifada in 2001. Reality has changed since then, and, accordingly, so have relations between Israelis and Palestinians. Turki's, Hammami's, and Tamari's journeys suggest that virtual realizations of returning to Palestine may seem to reveal similar experiences of estrangement. Nonetheless, they also demonstrate the different directions whereby Palestinians have taken their identity. Turki's memoir explores the making of a Palestinian American identity, while Hammami's and Tamari's respectively live in East Jerusalem and under the Israeli military occupation in the West Bank. The homeland exists in the stories and memories, while Israeli reality has rendered its geographical location unrecognizable for these "returnees" who, in turn, discover, upon arriving there, that they also have become unrecognizable unto themselves. That is, Israel has erased Palestine as such, and exile has altered Palestinians as such. Turki's possibly bitter or ironic attitude expresses the current consequences of this equation, of how he regards himself as a Palestinian today. Diasporas will teach that exile is home: "Forty-five years of exile are homeland enough. Anywhere where one is free to watch one's favorite movies, reread one's favorite classics, listen to one's favorite music, support one's favorite unpopular causes, and, above all, do one's work without fear of retribution, is homeland enough. . . . And I need not die in Haifa, Safad, or Jaffa. Washington will do. I have lived there longer than in any other part of the world. Nor, when I'm dust and forgotten, should it be of any consequence to anyone where my remains are buried."[21] Journeys to the "homeland" do certainly refer to a transnational leitmotif rather than a local one. Most Palestinian travelers adhere to comprehensive itineraries upon their journeys in order to visit as many locations as possible. Nonetheless, it is the local settings of a certain village, house, or backyard, extensively narrated in exile, that facilitate the traveler's relationship to the place.

In *I Saw Ramallah*, Barghouti extensively reformulates this relationship to foreground the dominance of exile in his Palestinian identity.[22] Upon arriving in Ramallah and traveling to his hometown, Deir Ghassanah, for the first time since returning "home" from twenty years of exile, Barghouti makes a long, comprehensive confession regarding the deep gap between the Palestine he has carried with him since his exile in 1967 and the one he encounters upon his return in 1996: "I have completely forgotten what the road to Deir Ghassanah looks like. I no longer remember the names of the villages on both sides of the twenty-seven kilometers that separate it from Ramallah. Embarrassment taught me to lie. Each time Husam asked me about a house, a landmark, a road, an event, I quickly replied 'I know.' The truth is I did not know. I no longer knew." It is not only a tragic personal confession of ignorance to surroundings that in memory and imagination have served as the location of "home" for decades but also one of loss. Barghouti lies to maintain at least the appearance of his familiarity with the homeland. His self-reflection may seem subversive in the national context, but I also think it candidly represents the majority of Palestinian exiles and refugees and, more poignantly as Barghouti observes, their descendants:

> It is over. The long Occupation [the existence of Israel] that created Israeli generations born in Israel and not knowing another "homeland" created at the same time generations of Palestinians strange to Palestine; born in exile and not knowing nothing of the homeland except stories and news. . . . The Occupation has created generations without a place whose colors, smells, and sounds they can remember; a first place that belongs to them, that they can return to in their memories in their cobbled-together exiles. There is no childhood bed for them to remember, a bed on which they forgot a soft cloth doll, or whose pillows—once the adults had gone out of an evening—were their weapons in a battle that had them shrieking with delight. This is it. The Occupation has created generations of us that have to adore an unknown beloved: distant, difficult, surrounded by guards, by walls, by nuclear missiles, by sheer terror.
>
> The long Occupation has succeeded in changing us from children of Palestine to children of the idea of Palestine.[23]

Barghouti's interpretation of Palestine as an idea rather than a tangible location at the end of this confession transforms the absence of a tangible successful nation-state into an abstract notion that Palestinians may aspire to both rediscover and reinvent, but with caution. Barghouti dissociates it from the notion of an authentic "homeland," insofar as the real Palestine, he explains, is a temporal configuration that can be retrieved neither through memory nor narration. Once tainted by displacement, the "homeland" will be forever lost to the exile. To bend Barghouti's words regarding a child's first sexual experience for my own purposes, "he who knows is not innocent." For Barghouti, "innocence" characterizes another Mourid Barghouti in a different Palestine at another time:

> I have lost and some I possess for a while and then I lose because I am always without a place. Nothing that is absent ever comes

> back complete. Nothing is recaptures as it was. 'Ein al-Deir is not a place, it is time. Evidence of the last rain that we can see on our shoes even though our eyes tell us it has dried. The thorns of the brambles trained our hands and our sides to bleed early when we were children returning home at sunset to our mothers. Do I want to scramble through brambles now? No, what I want is the time of scrambling. 'Ein al-Deir is specifically the time of Mourid as a child, and 'Ammi Ibrahim, a peasant and a hunter.[24]

Temporality is paradoxically the dimension through which Barghouti is able to maintain the idea of Palestine while recognizing its inaccessibility. In the present synchronous space, remnants of Palestine (for example, Deir Ghassanah in Barghouti's case) do not speak to who he has become in exile:

> It might have been a moment of pure happiness [the return to his hometown Deir Ghassanah], apart from that voice that scolded me, that said: "Wait a minute!" A cruel and hurtful thought: What does Deir Ghassanah know of you, Mourid? What do your people know of you? What do they know of the things that you have been through, the things that have shaped you, your acquaintances, your choices, the good and the bad in you throughout the thirty years that you have lived far from them? What do they know of your language? Your language that in some ways is similar to theirs and in some ways different, the language of your mind, of your speech, of your silence and isolation, your language in conflict and in contentment? They have not watched your hair turn grey. They do not know your friends or your habits, and if they did, would they like them? Your position on the concept of family, on women, on sex, literature, art, politics? They do not know the bad traits you rid yourself of and the others you acquired since you left them. They think you were not upset about the cutting down of the fig tree. They do not know Radwa or Tamim. They do not know all that has happened to you in their (your?) absence. You are no longer the child in first-year primary they used to see a long time ago, walking across this square on his way to multiplication tables or the dictation lesson.[25]

Upon returning "home," Barghouti is struck by his otherness. The person he has become in exile may seem and sound similar to his compatriots, but Barghouti recognizes that he definitively does not belong to the place in the way that he did as a child. He arrives "home," but as a foreigner who exists in a parallel exilic reality. A first-generation refugee of 1967, Barghouti articulates the unbridgeable distance decades of exile has developed between him and his "beloved" Palestine. It seems that only in exile may he return to dream of a "homeland" close to his heart.

Similarly, the arrival "home" represents the ultimate aim of the displaced individual's constant desire while in diaspora. However, as both Turki's and Barghouti's memoirs show, such "homecomings" do not realize a sense of fulfillment of individual and collective aspirations of the Palestinian *awdah* as wishfully expected. Rather, they bring the dispossessed face-to-face with their contemporary exilic identities. Barghouti makes this point early in his memoir. While waiting to pass the checkpoint at the King Hussein Bridge to enter the Territories for the first time in two decades, he already expresses sentiments of estrangement: "But I do know that the stranger can never go back to what he was. Even if he returns. It is over. A person gets 'displacement' as he gets asthma, and there is no cure for either."[26] Displacement is a chronic condition from the outset, Barghouti states. When once displaced, it will permanently mark an individual's identity. Hence, in this context, Barghouti's as well as Turki's arrivals "home" are already predetermined to fail, insofar as both authors became different creatures once they were the first time displaced and allowed only to claim Palestine "homeland," but no longer "home."

Beit Jala, Santiago, Michigan

As Turki's and Barghouti's narrations show, arriving in the "homeland," they encounter remnants of a past Palestine that, in return, bring them face-to-face with their own exilic identities. Such confessions of dispossession suggest that, to the Palestinian exile, configurations of "home" may no longer necessarily be located in the "homeland." It is, therefore, important to ask: In the absence of a chronotopical Palestine, where will future generations of Palestinians return to, and for what end, when the idea of "homeland" fails to house the notion of "home"? The Palestinian Latin American experience may offer some insights, insofar as it refers to one of the oldest Palestinian diasporas that came about several decades before the Nakba. It tells the story of a community that has "successfully" assimilated into near disappearance.

Historically, the complexities involved in returning to the homeland started to frame this particular group of Arabs' sense of identity at the turn of the twentieth century. Whereas the population in historical Palestine more or less successfully negotiated various forms of national identification against the backdrop of severe local political changes, immigration from Palestine to the Americas sowed the seeds for the discourse of *al-awdah illa al-watan* (the return to the homeland) that would eventually dominate the Palestinian narrative after 1948. As sociologist Cecilia Baeza explains, during the early decades since Arabs first started to arrive in the Americas in the 1870s, immigrants from Palestine identified through four loci: hometown (Jerusalem, Bethlehem, Beit Jala, Taibeh, and so on), region (the Levant), religion (mostly Christian, particularly emphasizing their relation to the Holy Land), and their Arab roots. References to Palestine were sporadic, even rare. However, the establishment of the British Mandate after World War I brought about basic changes in Palestinian immigrants' sense of self-identification because the new administration in Palestine started to complicate the process of traveling back and forth between the two continents. Whereas, during the Ottoman rule, émigrés had been able to travel home with relative ease, the Mandate began issuing Palestinian passports based on its new citizenship laws. The Arab émigrés who had acquired citizenship in their Latin American host countries and were not present during the transition from Ottoman to Mandate rule had to apply for visas to enter Palestine. Such barriers triggered an acute awareness of a political connection to the homeland among Palestinian émigrés in the Americas. The difficulties in being able to return to Palestine brought this previously marginal locus for identification to the heart of how Palestinians began to see themselves abroad. Baeza points out that during the 1920s, several organizations started to incorporate the term "Palestine" into their names, and soccer clubs such as Club Deportivo Palestino went as far as using the colors of the Palestinian flag for the players' soccer jerseys.[27] The history of Palestinians in Latin America shows that the idea of returning, or being unable to return, to the homeland was deeply embedded in the crystallization of their (trans)national identity before it became a fundamental tenet in the Palestinian national movement subsequently to the establishment of the State of Israel. Eventually, the historic events that dispossessed and displaced 750,000 Palestinians also perpetuated the immigrant status of hundreds of thousands of Palestinians in Latin America. Hence, the Nakba refers not only to mass expulsion and the destruction of hundreds of villages but also to the transformation of immigrant communities in the Americas into diasporic ones.

Today, as Baeza reports, a recent wave of Chileans of Palestinian origin are engaging on journeys to the "homeland," (re)discovering a heritage relatively lost among their and previous generations.[28] Meruane's memoir *Volverse Palestina* is, at the moment, the most comprehensive circulating text of such a journey of (re)discovery, describing the author's first-time visit to Beit Jala—her grandfather's location of origin. Belonging to the Latin American Palestinian experience, Meruane, born in Chile, is, like other Palestinians there, completely assimilated, and stories of Palestine are merely part of a heritage that is both culturally and linguistically remote. During her journey to Beit Jala, she explicitly stresses this distance, from the outset, by way of dissociating herself from any direct relation to the idea of *al-awdah*. For Meruane, "return" is borrowed: "*Return.* I am assaulted by that verb every time I think about the possibility of Palestine. I tell myself it wouldn't really be returning, just visiting a land I've never been to before, a land of which I have no images of my own. Palestine has always been a murmur in the background, a story I tell myself to save a shared origin from extinction. It would not be my return, I repeat. It would be a return borrowed from someone else, made in someone else's place. My grandfather's, maybe. Or my father's." Having never set foot in Palestine before, Meruane's "return" transforms into a rite of initiation—a process of "becoming"—playing on the ambiguity of the Spanish reflexive verb "volverse" that captures both senses: while *returning* to Palestine, she figuratively *becomes* Palestinian. Meruane not only narrates this paradoxical process that represents what many descendants of Arab immigrants undergo when visiting Palestine but also speaks out for a generation that is breaking away from their parents' sense of defeat. Her father had never wanted to return to the patrimony that he, like other Palestinians in Latin American countries, could never properly inherit: "There was no turning back for him. No turning back for so many Palestinians who no longer could or no longer wanted to return, who had even forgotten the Arabic word for it—Palestinians who had come, like my grandparents, to feel like any other Chilean."[29] Meruane views this radical break from Palestine as a traumatic one in the consciousness of her father's generation—a break that has both framed her generation's Chilean identity and motivated them to "return" to (re)discover their roots.

Therefore, Meruane's personal narrative tells the story of many third-generation immigrants who do find it in themselves to cautiously relate to their parents' location of origin. However, this relationship is borrowed from memories and narrations that she does not emotionally internalize in the way that may on several occasions have prevented her father from undertaking a similar journey upon arriving at the borders of the Gaza Strip from the Egyptian side and at the borders of the West Bank from the Jordanian side without resolving to cross them. He would perhaps not have been able to endure traumas of security checkpoint interrogations by Israeli soldiers; or, as Meruane suspects, he may have decided to avoid the situation of arriving at his family's former house without having brought the key: "There, on the other side, stands the heritage he has never been able to properly inherit. Maybe he dreads the idea of getting to that house without having a key, of being forced to knock on the door of a home that has been stripped of his family and filled with strangers."

Nonetheless, despite her grandparents' and parents' respective realizations of their inability to ever return home, Meruane sets out to make this journey, "borrowing" their heritage and compromised desire for *al-awdah*. In preparation for the trip, Meruane conducts a failed online research of her origins. Turning to her father and aunts, she discovers that they are also acutely uncertain of too many details in order for her to properly narrate their lineage, distancing them further from an authentic relation to their heritage, even in the post-1948 transnational consciousness. They do not belong to any recognizable Palestinian category, but have merely ceased to exist as such, turning into an inextricable part of the Chilean people. Meruane makes this point by way of questioning the authenticity of her roots in relation to the current inhabitants of Beit Jala: "He [her father], like many Chilestinians of his generation, maintain firm ties with Beit Jala but never makes a show of it. Their donations have added up to the existence, over there, of a school named Chile. A plaza named Chile. The daily needs of Palestinian children, real Palestinians, if Palestine can still be said to be real."[30] Her parents, like so many immigrants from Palestine of their generation, still maintain ties with Beit Jala, most visibly through occasional donations to build institutions for the locals, whom Meruane refers to as "real Palestinians" in a place that is only questionably Palestinian to whom she and her family have become in Chile after so many years.

Nonetheless, as the title of Meruane's memoir implies, the journey to Palestine transforms her. Already at Heathrow Airport, her final stop before actually arriving in Israel—Palestine, Meruane is subjected to security checks by Israeli agents. As Rashid Khalidi has described, humiliating airport security checks are an experience to which all Palestinians can testify. For Meruane, this encounter is her first direct contact with a distant heritage that gradually starts to assume a more tangible form:

> My Palestinian heritage, which I had to defended only as a difference in Chile when, on occasion they called me Turk, in Heathrow had acquired weight and presence. It was a thick scar that I was

> now eager to show off. I wanted to bare it, to wave it at the female officers who had made me pull down my pants, unbutton my shirt, turn around, remove my machine. To give them the scar instead of that device, which they took with gloved hands, promising to give it right back. To set the scar down next to the sugar pills that I was also carrying with me, for emergencies. Why not try one, I said to the bomb expert, they're orange-flavored. But then I found I was not the only one who bore that mark: in the room they'd just moved me to, there were other young people, dark like me, curly-haired. Thick, unruly brows above damp-coal eyes.[31]

As she advances toward her goal, Meruane finds herself further transformed. She arrives in Tel Aviv/Jaffa and continues to Jerusalem and then Beit Jala, where she meets with relatives and gets the opportunity to familiarize herself with distinct localities and explore her family roots. However, rather than arriving at definitive conclusions regarding her relationship to the Palestinian heritage, Meruane leaves things open, as if postponing a kind of decision she has to make. Perhaps such deferrals have come to characterize the Palestinian experience of "homecoming." In this sense, certainly, Meruane's journey seems similar to Barghouti's and Turki's, although she is a third-generation immigrant belonging to a different Palestinian story. She does not bring a key, and although she expresses a desire to visit her grandparents' former house, her hosts effortlessly convince her to go shopping in Bethlehem instead, leaving such a crucial stop in her Palestinian journey unfulfilled. As Meruane states, "The visit is put off till next time, and I fear that visit will never take place but that my desire to see my grandfather's house will leave me forever bound to the possibility of Beit Jala." She links herself to Palestine through maintaining the desire to see her grandfather's house rather than actually going to see it—an experience, if realized, that may have left her disappointed and permanently cut Meruane off from her heritage.

In the short story "Autocartography: The Case of Palestine, Michigan" (1996), Anton Shammas offers an insightful epilogue to my argument on the relationship between homeland and the consequences of displacement for second- and third-generation exiles or immigrants such as Meruane. Protagonist "A" is planning a trip to Palestine—a location she refers to as "home" although she has never visited there. "A" is aware of the complexities in defining her prospective journey as a "homecoming," and the large part of the story presents an interior monologue debating these problems. She explains from the outset that "going back" is different from "going home." Whereas the former refers to going to a location where the returnees have lived before, the latter may refer to arriving at a place that they have previously never been to—although it is as if they had, suggesting that "home" refers to a place a person has cultivated a connection to through narrations rather than personal memories. To "A," going home is problematic in an exclusively Palestinian context: "So A wanted to go home to Palestine. The problem was—outside here imagined memories and imagined space, as created by her Palestinian father in the postnostalgic world of Dearborn, Michigan—there was, there is, no Palestine to go to."[32] As a daughter of a Palestinian refugee, "A's" decision to go "home" raises a complex question regarding motive since her apparent home now is in Motown, Michigan, and Palestine has ceased to exist as such—an outcome that she, and more disconcertingly her father and grandmother, is repeatedly reminded of through the Arabic mantra "rahat Falasteen" ("Palestine is gone").

Nonetheless, as the narrator artfully explains, identity is a kind of noise, and Palestinian noise has been disarranged all too long. In Zionist discourse, it went from being altogether absent to configured as the roar of barbarians: "First, it was the noise of absence in the famous Zionist slogan, 'Land without a people to a people without a land.' Or, the noise of Caliban in Herzl's Judenstaat: 'We shall form part of Europe's fortified wall against Asia, and fulfill the role of cultural vanguard facing the barbarians.'"[33] Since World War II, Palestinian noise was muffled, as it constantly had to pass through the black hole of the Holocaust until the First Intifada in 1987 when it became unprecedentedly audible to the world—an event that leads "A" to consider traveling to the "homeland" for the first time. However, Palestine continues to stay off the maps, and "A's" idea of "home" is merely a combination of an imagined geography and her grandmother's and father's tales about the place. Like Meruane, "A" senses that this place does not belong to her in the way it does to her parents and grandparents. Therefore, if the "homeland" had become inaccessible, then, "A" thinks, she should create her own Palestine, and upon discovering several locations in the United States named Palestine—one in Michigan—she imagines a home with a real address where Palestinians like herself could buy land and settle down. As a result, "A" feels she may now postpone the journey home.

Shammas's story foregrounds a second-generation exile's attachment to her current location of residence and willingness to search for alternative ways of interpreting her national heritage. To "A," the "homeland" is a mobile idea that could for many Palestinians, and their descendants, be peacefully and conveniently realized in a number of locations in the United States—far away from the turmoil of that tiny infamous spot in the Middle East and both geographically and culturally closer to her current address in Michigan. Having recognized the possibility of such an endeavor—although she may never actively pursue it—"A" finds it adequately consoling. She indefinitely delays her journey, content with the discovery of a prospective space for maintaining her Palestinian heritage. It does not need to materialize. The mere possibility suffices.

I think the story is telling of how Palestinians in the West relate to their national roots. As mentioned, the concept of *al-awdah* may connote identical visions of "homecoming" within the various local contexts of displacement, insofar as Palestinians from around the globe more or less unanimously converge on this historic right. However, the rendering of the distinct local conditions that respectively delineate this position significantly diverges. In refugee camps, Palestinians live under atrocious conditions and would probably contemplate the possibility of returning to the "homeland" with more pragmatic urgency than any other Palestinian group. In the occupied territories, the possibility of virtual "returns" materialized following the 1993 Oslo Agreements through organized three-day tours that took them to the Galilee, the Lebanese borders, Tel Aviv, and Jaffa, as Israeli director Ra'anan Alexandrovich documents in his film *The Inner Tour* (2000). The motives for such journeys were unique in the Palestinian context, particularly compared to those reasons driving exiles and immigrants from Western countries, such as Turki and Meruane, to engage on similar journeys. Palestinians living under more privileged circumstances than those individuals in the refugee camps or the occupied territories do not urgently search for the "homeland," but may consider occasionally visiting there, assured that they will return to their exile where they may, like "A," continue to imagine a Palestine that is characteristically closer to their current relatively stable lives.

One particular concept configures as the single basic universal national tenet that seemingly addresses collective aspirations and needs of all Palestinian communities despite location: *al-awdah*. The hope of returning to Palestine has since 1948 epitomized the people's rootedness in the land and configured as the grail of Palestinian aspiration. Rather than cementing "this fundamental plank of the Palestinian case," as Ghada Karmi has it, the Oslo-invented Palestinian Authority has repeatedly turned it into a bargaining chip in its numerous failed negotiations with the respective Israeli governments. But it has also since, as I have argued here, served as a token for demarcating the cultural nuances developing among displaced Palestinian communities around the globe. My point in bringing these various texts together has been to show how the universality of a fundamental Palestinian national principle develops in various directions within the polylingual category I have demarcated in this chapter. Whereas the concept of "return" may remain intact in respective diasporic contexts, insofar as surviving first-generation refugees continue to transmit memories and narrations of the lost "homeland," processes of transnational intertextuality reveal differences between the various portrayals of "returning home." The leitmotif of return is merely one among several themes that has to be examined both locally and transnationally in order to mark the similarities and distinctions that continue to evolve since the historic dispersion of the Palestinian people. The initial context for my discussion is based on dismantling the misconception of Palestinians' cultural homogeneity and emphasizing the idea that the Nakba perpetuated previous and produced several new distinct and problematic realities that have increasingly proliferated during the past decades.

Conclusion

> But maybe, out of polite arrogance, he might have finished with a paraphrase of Borges: "Which of the two of us has written this book I do not know."
>
> —Anton Shammas, *Arabesques*

When, at the end of *Arabesques*, Anton Shammas the protagonist finally meets with Michael Abyad at Larry Ataya's country house in Iowa City, Shammas the author sets up a unique cultural moment whereby Palestinians who have traversed different paths come together face-to-face. The Israeli-Palestinian protagonist encounters his diasporic counterpart, and, as they relate their intersecting family histories, the reference to Almaza's son Anton Shammas who died in infancy—and who, in his death, becomes the current Anton's namesake and Michael's fictional alter ego—points to an additional Palestinian trajectory: the Latin American experience. Shammas the author captures these distinct narratives at the opening paragraph of Michael's account:

> My parents, as they would say in Israel, belonged to the founding fathers of Arab Haifa. They had no children. In January 1928 they go to Beirut, where they adopt an infant only a few days old. A year later they return to Haifa and pass him off as their son. That was the year that Almaza, Jiryes Shammas's wife, came to work as a maid in our house, after Uncle Jiryes—if you will pardon me calling him Uncle—had sailed for Argentina and her son, Anton, had died. You probably know the story. I'm raised by Almaza, and during my childhood I hear about Anton, the baby who died before he

> was a year old. I hear about him, and sleep on his pillow, and even have his dreams. In '48 we escape to Beirut, and Almaza comes along with us. (257–58)

The diasporic Palestinian recounts his family history to the Israeli-Palestinian and alludes to the Latin American Palestinian who died "before he was a year old." While this fascinating conversation takes place in one room of Ataya's house, Shammas the author does not disregard the presence of the Palestinian living under Israeli military occupation. Ataya is also hosting Paco from the territories, who, during his stay, seems to be joined at the hip to the Israeli writer Bar-On. It appears that, already in the mid-1980s, Shammas the author anticipates the consequences of the multiple itineraries of Palestinian displacement, as well as the concomitant development of manifold Palestinian identities. He succeeds in creating a situation that defines the multifaceted character of the relations among today's variegated Palestinian communities.

More significantly, the Borgesian twist at the end is not merely an aesthetic means of tying up the several plotlines of the novel into a mystical Conwayan Knot. Rather, it leads to a string of inevitable questions, upon realizing the repercussions of Palestinian displacement: Are Palestinian citizens of Israel narrating their counterparts living under occupation or under siege in the territories and in Gaza? Are refugees writing their compatriots living under Israeli jurisdiction? Are Palestinians in the United States chronicling the experiences of their fellow nationals in the homeland? Is the diaspora writing the homeland, or is it the other way around? Among the various contexts "outside" Israel-Palestine, which diaspora are we referring to? Moreover, among the divisions "inside," is every group writing its own story and, if so, in which language? And, finally, who—among these distinct groups—is narrating "the nation"?

Throughout the writing of *Being There, Being Here*, I have mentally kept returning to *Arabesques* to recall the point of departure for my argument on Palestinian literature. Any study, however, on the multiple literary itineraries of Palestinian displacement will always be far from comprehensive, insofar as these itineraries continue to develop, even at this moment, as I am writing these sentences. The unfolding of the consequences of displacement and concomitant artistic productions are ongoing processes, and any attempt at criticism is bound to fall short. Subject to the ebb and flow of war and politics in the Middle East and beyond, the various contexts of displacement "inside" and "outside" Israel-Palestine are in a constant flux. Writers, filmmakers, and artists continue to create from multiple locations of displacement in the pervasive absence of a chronotopic Palestinian nation-state. However, rather than document the ontological existence of a single Palestine, we should acknowledge the emergence of several epistemic Palestines—similarly grounded in memories and narrations of the past—that are constantly coming into being, as Palestinians everywhere distinctively fathom the present and envision the future. It is, nonetheless, my hope that the writing of this book has brought these developing story lines into a challenging and fruitful dialogue, which might frame future studies of Palestinian arts and letters in the context of an increasingly globalized world.

I do not consider *Being There, Being Here* as a niche study of Palestinian literature, but rather a critical attempt at exploring the manifold long-term cultural and literary consequences of the Palestinian Nakba. The amalgamation of literary texts representing various Palestinian trajectories from around the globe in different languages expands the scope of the linguistic and cultural framework whereby it is possible to express and interpret today's increasingly diverse Palestinian experiences. Along these lines, I have focused on specific thematic sites that I believe reveal this proliferation across borders, generations, and languages. For the remainder of this chapter, I wish to present a thought experiment to highlight the poignancy of my perspective. In chapter 5, I suggested we hypothesize that Israelis have realized that the nation-state framework could not possibly comprehend the distinctive cultural outcomes of two millennia of persecution and, therefore, decided to migrate to the various diasporas, while Palestinians from around the globe could now peacefully return to build their nation in all of Palestine. In such a fictional reality—"Palestine 2048"—it would, first of all, be necessary to account for the cultural consequences of the various experiences of displacement. Second, we would need to relinquish any sentiments regarding the idea of a "unified Palestinian people" that—as I have argued from the outset of this book—has not only pervaded the national script during decades of various displacements and consequent cultural diversification but also misrepresented the reality of Palestinian society prior to 1948.

The hypothesis of Palestine 2048 raises a number of questions—probably more than I will be able to explore here. However, I will try to highlight those cruxes I find important for developing an awareness of how the cultural repercussions of displacement might inform the continued production of criticism in the field of Palestine studies. Would this new nation-state be an economically viable democracy, or would it take to the authoritarian models implemented by its Arab neighbors? Of course, at this point it is impossible to reply to such a question, and it will be the least of my concerns in this exercise. Nonetheless, I think it is important to keep this general distinction in mind while exploring culturally relevant issues. For the sake of argument, we will envision Palestine 2048 as a democratic nation that would allow freedom of expression for the various Palestinian groups arriving in the homeland. And the official language would be Arabic, although a large number of "returnees" would probably prefer the language(s) they have brought with them from the various diasporas. Internally, the different groups would make cultural and political distinctions among themselves.

Palestinians who have endured decades living under different forms of military occupation would behave differently than those individuals who "enjoyed" Israeli or Jordanian citizenship, who would then, again, behave differently from the more than a million Palestinians who have arrived from the refugee camps. Also, returnees from developed Western countries would be different not only among themselves, depending on context, but also from the rest of the Palestinian population—both economically and culturally. How may the institutions of this nation accommodate these varieties and nuances? Which elites would emerge and attempt to hegemonize the nation in their image? Would parliamentarian representation be based upon these distinctions, or would the emergence of the sovereign nation marginalize these backgrounds?

As speculated earlier, would Palestine go through processes of culturalization based on complex intertextualities of narratives of prior displacement? Would the citizens of Palestine constantly remind each other of their recent past? Palestinian citizens would not merely be Palestinian, but their past displacement would be an integral part of their identity. One citizen would be defined as once having been Israeli, the other as having lived in the camps. The now past siege and occupation would probably define the status of the Gazans and Palestinians from the West Bank towns, and the Americans and Europeans would, perhaps, find it difficult to relinquish their Western ways.

Pre-Nakba origins, passed down through memory and narration, would certainly play a significant role in Palestinians' motivation to return and their subsequent social status citizens in the homeland. However, it is necessary to acknowledge that these elements are part of a heritage that has served to formulate the national script and framed nostalgic cravings during displacement in the past seventy years. Images of fig, olive, and orange trees embody the Palestinians' connection to the land, but would not suffice to account for the complexities of the new reality. It is, rather, the contexts developed between 1948 and 2048 that would be impacting Palestinian self-conceptions pervading this current Palestine. This condition may lead to considerations of authenticity: Who is the "real" Palestinian? The former American and European as well as Israeli citizens would be relegated to the lowest step on the cultural ladder, insofar as they are quantitatively the smallest groups and may have become too Westernized or "Israelized." A fierce competition for authenticity would develop between the two largest groups—the former refugees (particularly the ones from the camps) and the former occupied populations of the West Bank and, more notoriously, the Gazans. These groups would configure as the most powerful constituents, since they have endured the more difficult conditions during Israel's reign than those who ended up under more privileged circumstances. The traumatic experiences of the respective refugee camps and the occupation would probably serve as effective political leverage for construing the shape of the new Palestinian identity. National pride would be based upon stories of steadfastness (*summud*) and resistance (*muqawama*) along the steep uphill journey toward Palestinian independence in 2048.

The Israeli Palestinians and their Western counterparts would bring less leverage to this site and, as a result, play a secondary role in the making of the new Palestine, although economic leverage would perhaps cast the "Americans" in a more privileged position than the other "less authentic" Palestinians. The Israeli experience would become a mark of Cain for the 1.57 million citizens who, for seventy years, partook in the Israeli reality. They learned Hebrew, interacted with their Jewish compatriots, participated in the Israeli economy, and expressed loyalty to the state—despite their objections to its national character—and the majority remained relatively silent, while only a few protested against the oppressive policies of consecutive Israeli governments toward their Palestinian brethren. The creation of the "good Arab," in the Israeli context, is probably something that will forever be held against Israel's Palestinian citizens. Needless to argue here, this concept is not straightforward and does not refer to a one-dimensional attitude. Rather, it points to the complex social roles that this particular minority had resorted to in order to preserve a national identity while engaging the Israeli reality. The chronotopical dynamics of this duality have pushed these Palestinians beyond any national context that may comprehensively frame their sense of selfhood. Similarly, respective dualities have also irreversibly altered the identities of other Palestinian groups. However, in the Israeli context, it is the largely tense but mostly civil engagement between a Jewish majority and an Arab minority that has framed this experience. As Palestinian intellectuals and politicians in Israel have been asked on numerous occasions, would they be willing to relinquish their Israeli citizenship in exchange for living in the occupied territories, or elsewhere, to realize their Palestinian identity? The majority have always declined, giving the impression that they enjoyed life in Israel, which was probably the case for many. In a modern Palestinian state, such an experience would probably seem irredeemable, and the former Arab citizens of Israel would, as citizens of Palestine, ironically assume the position of a suspicious fifth column.

Considerations regarding past experiences of displacement and their impact on notions of national authenticity, alongside the quantitative sizes of the various groups and their economic status, will determine the shape of the new Palestinian society and its identity for several generations to come. I am summoning these issues in order to problematize the expected melting-pot policy that would frame Palestinian culture. All is not equal in the making of the Palestinian, and the influential forces in the government along with those individuals running the cultural institutions would naturally privilege characteristics associated with the powerful groups and marginalize others, mostly associated with the less powerful ones. Such divisions would not be exclusively determined by narratives of displacement, as I have argued so far, but also be determined by religious and geographical affiliations, not to mention social class.

Demographically, Palestine 2048 would constitute a large Muslim majority dominating the cultural space as well as several minorities—Christian, Druze, Circassian, and Jewish (if it would be possible to revive the identity of the Palestinian Jew, despite the historic adversarial contentions that came about during Israel's reign). The Palestinian population would be drawn to Jerusalem and the coastal cities rather than to the peripheral rural societies in the Galilee and the Bedouin societies of the Beer al-Sabeaa area, insofar as the majority of today's population is more urbanized and educated than their predecessors who inhabited the land before 1948. To turn to matters of cultural production: In Palestine 2048, what themes will artists, filmmakers, and literary writers address? Insofar as notions of exile, diaspora, nostalgia, occupation, and discrimination subsist now as part of history rather than pervade the immediate present, where will artistic creation head toward? Would the artist now be free from the tentacles of the tragic "monster Palestine"? Would the filmmaker now feel free to produce a romantic comedy, undisrupted by political traumas? And will the next generation's Habiby write about the tragicomic troubles of urbanization and alienation in Palestine rather than about the Israeli invasion? Which symbol will now replace the Handala, if anything? What settings would frame the story in the future of Hany Abu-Assad's next film? Who is the new Palestinian protagonist? Will the Palestinian story ever cease to be political?

Minority voices will target the hegemonic establishment rather than Israel, whose presence in Palestinian cultural productions has been ubiquitous since before 1948. In 2048 Israel has, for better or for worse, become a thing of the past. Or, perhaps, it will continue to haunt the Palestinian. Rather than look inward, the artist will be trapped in the Israeli stasis. As William Faulkner once put it, "The past is never dead. It's not even past." Israel may be gone, but then, again, it will be forever inextricable to the making of the Palestinian experience for upcoming generations. The historic multidimensional Jewish state will pervade self-conceptions of the respective groups in Palestine for many decades to come. Particularly during the early years, the aforementioned social divisions, based on histories of displacement, will determine the structures of the Palestinian reality, insofar as these histories were roughly formed by the level and type of engagement of the respective groups vis-à-vis Israel.

Will Israel and Israeli characters serve as the ultimate antagonists in the Palestinian story? Or will their absence leave room for artists and writers to grapple with representations of immediately urgent matters, such as the devastating patriarchy governing Arab society, women's social status, state corruption, religion, gay marriage, and the identities of the seemingly new Palestinians who have returned to reclaim their land? Will the new Palestinian peasant be wearing thimble hats while working the soil with pickaxes? Who will assume the role of the Palestinian double, insofar as the Jew is no longer immediately available? Who will Abulhawa's Ismael or Kashua's

Amir metamorphose into? Will the new Palestinian settings be the product of the artists' attempts at weaving the remnants of a previous Israeli architecture, which in itself was the product of attempts at covering up a Palestinian presence, into the making of the new reality? Or will they try to revive the pre-Nakba architecture in the modernization of the cities' new skylines? Will Palestinians attempt to eliminate any trace of a previous Israeli presence, or will they integrate this history into the creation of their new reality? Will they recognize that the Israeli experience, in its multiple variations, was a formative experience, or will they suppress it, leaving it to cancerously grow in the collective subconscious?

These questions and others come to mind while pondering the idea of Palestine 2048, which would house Palestinians, following the existence of the State of Israel for more than seventy years. Displacement has not only geographically divided and culturally changed Palestinians in multiple ways but also generated different political ambitions. Moreover, as I hope I have demonstrated throughout this book, it has variedly defined Palestinian literatures across borders, generations, and languages.

Notes

Bibliography

Index

Notes

Preface

1. Joseph Conrad, *A Personal Record*, 26; Hilo Glazer, "The Exclusive Israeli Communities That Shun Arabs, Mizrahim, and Anyone Else 'Incompatible,'" *Ha'aretz*, December 7, 2017, https://www.haaretz.com/israel-news/.premium.MAGAZINE-exclusive-israeli-towns-shun-arabs-and-anyone-else-incompatible-1.5628067.

Introduction

1. When page numbers appear parenthetically in the text, I cite from the translations for the sake of convenience.

2. Nathalie Handal, "The Shape of Time: New Palestinian Writing."

3. The term "host nation" is obviously problematic in the Israeli Palestinian context since Israel's Arab citizens do not configure as their diasporic Palestinian compatriots in their current locations of residence. Rather, in this particular context, Israel is the outcome of a European settler-colonial project that landed on Palestine's indigenous population in the twentieth century and has since shaped this community's Palestinian identity.

4. Throughout I will interchangeably employ the terms "Israeli Arabs," "Israel's Arab citizens," "the Arabs of Israel," "Israeli-Palestinians," and "the Palestinians of Israel" to refer to this group of Palestinians. My purpose is to highlight the complexity of arriving at a clear definition of this community, insofar as they inextricably belong in both the Israeli and the Palestinian contexts. Moreover, upon asking dozens of Arab individuals carrying Israeli citizenship of all ages and classes how they define themselves, the aforementioned terms were variedly employed by the respondents.

5. See Cecilia Baeza, "Palestinians in Latin America: Between Assimilation and Long-Distance Nationalism."

6. To refer to the national narrative as scripted might suggest that I view such narratives as static fictional constructs. I am well aware that, historically, multiple

competing factions and ideologies have constituted the idea of Palestinian nationhood. Scripting does not refer to a process of essentializing the national narrative. Rather, it suggests that the dynamics of nationalism is steered by design—politics as well as popular needs and ambitions, among others. However, with the intention of radicalizing my critical approach in this study, I employ the term "national script" for the purpose of referring to the seemingly immutable landmarks of the Palestinian national narrative: the Nakba, the revival of nationalism in 1967, the Right of Return, and so on.

7. Ola Awad, president of the Palestinian Central Bureau of Statistics, presented these numbers in a brief on the status of the Palestinian people at the end of 2018 on December 31.

8. Sari Hanafi, "Rethinking the Palestinians Abroad as a Diaspora: The Relationship between the Diaspora and the Palestinian Territories," 169–70.

9. Rashid Khalidi, "The Formation of Palestinian Identity: The Critical Years, 1917–1923," 171–73. Khalidi points to the various Palestinian cultural and regional elements that entered into the process of constructing a unified national identity. See also Salim Tamari, *Mountain against the Sea: Essays on Palestinian Society and Culture*, 22–36. Tamari presents a fascinating study of the cultural divide that developed between mercantile coastal communities and mountain-dwelling peasant societies in Palestine. Also, his study addresses the relationship between inland village communities and the urban centers that dominated them through absentee landlordism.

10. See Lauren Banko, *The Invention of Palestinian Citizenship, 1918–1947.* Banko meticulously describes the administrative shift from the Ottoman imperial reality to the British Mandate and how it shaped the realities of local Arabs and incoming Jews in Palestine following World War I. See also Joseph Massad, *The Persistence of the Palestinian Question: Essays on Zionism and the Palestinians*, 114–28. In Massad's discussion of the refugee problem, he argues that consecutive Israeli governments have systematically engineered the fragmentation of the Palestinian people. He sees today's geographical divisions as the "successful" outcome of Israeli policies toward the Palestinians.

11. Julianne Hammer, *Palestinians Born in Exile: Diaspora and the Search for a Homeland*, 3; Ghada Karmi, "After the Nakba: An Experience of Exile in England," 55.

12. Ghassan Kanafani, *The 1936–39 Revolt in Palestine*, 26–34.

13. This study focuses on the cultural and lingual consequences of Palestinian displacement primarily following the Nakba of 1948 and to a lesser degree on those consequences following the waves of immigration from Ottoman Palestine to the Americas starting during the 1870s. Therefore, my brief review of the development of Palestinian Arabic literature focuses on the post-Nakba decades. This is

not to claim that literature did not exist in Palestine before 1948. To the contrary, as Salma Khadra Jayyusi recounts, fiction and political poetry by figures such as Ibrahim and Fadwa Tuqan, Abu Salma, Abd al-Karim al-Karmi, and Mutlaq Abd al-Khaliq already started to emerge at the turn of the twentieth century (7–16).

14. Ibrahim Taha, *The Palestinian Novel: A Communication Study*, 14–21.

15. For criticism in English, see Hammer, *Palestinians Born in Exile*, 65–68. See also Barbara McKean Parmenter, *Giving Voice to Stones: Place and Identity in Palestinian Literature*, 70–85.

16. Parmenter, *Giving Voice to Stone*, 23.

17. For commentary in English, see Ahmad Sa'di and Lila Abu-Lughod, *Nakba: Palestine, 1948, and the Claims of Memory*, 12–13.

18. Ghassan Kanafani, *Resistance Literature in Occupied Palestine, 1948–1966*, 3–4. I'm relying here on Sulafa Hijjawi's English translation for the purpose of convenience.

19. Kanafani, *Resistance Literature in Occupied Palestine*, 8.

20. Hilary Kilpatrick, "Tradition and Innovation in the Fiction of Ghassan Kanafani," 64; Salah D. Hassan, "Nation Validation: Modern Palestinian Literature and the Politics of Appeasement," 16; Bashir Abu Manneh, *The Palestinian Novel: From 1948 to the Present*, 30–31.

21. Rather than listing the titles of dozens of novels, I want to foreground here young authors who have taken the Palestinian novel in different directions, significantly diverging from the national script: Adania Shibli's *Masaas* (*Touch*, 2010), Raji Bathish's *Ghurfa Fi Tel Aviv* (*A Room in Tel Aviv*, 2007), and Alaa Hlehel's *Carla Bruni Asheektee al-Seriyah* (Carla Bruni, My Secret Lover, 2012) and *Au Revoir Akka* (2014).

22. Salah D. Hassan argues that Salma Khadra Jayyusi's *Anthology of Modern Palestinian Literature* (1992) breaks off from Kanafani's demarcations in its prioritization of exilic over local texts. Hassan explains that a national anthology, while participating in canon formation and asserting a literary tradition, also accommodates historical contingencies that characterize the contemporary circumstances of its production. That is to say, whereas Kanafani's definition appears as a cultural extension to the heyday of the PLO's resistance activity, Jayyusi's *Anthology* defines the conditions and considerations that made the signing of the Oslo Accords possible (22).

23. Jayyusi, *Anthology of Modern Palestinian Literature*, 3–5.

24. See Ami Elad-Bouskila, *Modern Palestinian Literature and Culture*, 9. Elad-Bouskila points to only two groups in the modern Palestinian canon. One group includes writers belonging to the various communities living outside Israel in the Arab countries or abroad in Europe and the United States. The second group includes the Arab population living within the borders of Israel. Elad-Bouskila's

division may appear critically sufficient, but I do not think that it accurately depicts the diversity among the various communities in the way Jayyusi's model does.

25. David Damrosch, *What Is World Literature?*, 24–25; Lital Levy and Allison Schachter, "Jewish Literature/World Literature: Between the Local and the Transnational," 94.

26. Liisa Malkki, "*National Geographic*: The Rooting of Peoples and the Territorialization of National Identity among Scholars and Refugees," 24.

27. Ruba Salih and Sophie Richter-Devroe, "Palestine beyond National Frames: Emerging Politics, Cultures, and Claims," 6.

1. Palestinian Writings in the World

1. I employ the term "culturalization" instead of "culture" to emphasize the process of the making of culture in the Israeli case. Since the State of Israel is only a few decades old, I don't believe it is sufficient to speak of the identity of an Israeli culture. Rather, the realization of the Jewish "Right of Return" has brought together diverse Jewish diaspora cultures that, while competing for hegemony in the Israeli context, are both colliding and merging, ultimately setting in motion a process of "culturalization." I will further explain this argument in chapter 5 with relation to Palestinians' discourse on "return."

2. I have chosen to focus on Yasir Suleiman's presentation of the polarizing argument with regard to Arab Francophone writing because it clearly depicts the complexities of hybridization and postcolonial literature. I do, however, think it necessary to also reference here comparisons to Anglo-African and Anglo-Indian literature in the postcolonial context. For commentary, see Madhu Krishnan, *Contemporary African Literature in English: Strategies of Address and Cultural Constraints*; and Alan G. Johnson, *Out of Bounds: Anglo-Indian Literature and the Geography of Displacement.*

3. It is pertinent to point out that the British Mandate established, for better or for worse, a separate education system for the incoming Jewish settlers. See Rachel Elboim-Dror, "British Educational Policies in Palestine."

4. Ellen L. Fleischmann, *The Nation and Its "New" Women: The Palestinian Women's Movement, 1920–1948.*

5. Geoffrey Nash, *The Anglo-Arab Encounter: Fiction and Autobiography by Arab Writers in English*, 18.

6. Edwar al-Kharrat, "Egyptian Heart, French Tongue, a Personal Testimony," 10.

7. Edwar al-Kharrat, "In Search of an Identity for Francophone Literature."

8. Yasir Suleiman, "The Betweenness of Identity: Language in Trans-national Literature," 16.

9. I do not employ the term "postcolony" to refer to a state of Palestinian decolonization, and I fully agree with Joseph Massad's coinage of the "postcolonial colony" regarding Israel insofar as I find it impossible to separate the postcoloniality for Israelis from their colonization of Palestinians. Here the "postcolony," however, refers to the current state of affairs with regard to Palestinians' attitude in aspiring for the establishment of an independent and sovereign nation.

10. Suleiman, "Betweenness of Identity," 17.

11. Edward Said, "The Anglo-Arab Encounter," in *Reflections on Exile, and Other Essays*, 410; Suleiman, "Betweenness of Identity," 24.

12. Hilary Kilpatrick, "Arab Fiction in English: A Case of Dual Nationality," 46–49.

13. Such processes did not exclusively start with the invention of the internet. Palestinian exiles and refugees have, since their displacement, preserved and circulated memories of places, families, and traditions through oral narration. Nonetheless, these processes have assumed more sophisticated forms and acquired a wider reach through online social networks and the likes. The iNakba trilingual (Arabic, Hebrew, and English) mobile application, founded by Zochrot—an Israeli (both Arab and Jewish) nongovernmental organization—is one among several forums for sharing and archiving Palestinian localities from before 1948 and genealogical charts of the families and populations uprooted from these localities. It serves as a powerful site, not only for educating diasporic upcoming Palestinian generations who have never set foot in Israel-Palestine but also for Israelis who grew up through educational curricula that effectively work for the elimination of historic traces of anything Palestinian.

14. See Pnina Werbner, "Migration and Transnational Studies: Between Simultaneity and Rupture."

15. See Anat Ben-David, "The Palestinian Diaspora on the Web: Between Deterritorialization and Re-territorialization," 459–72. Ben-David's research has been particularly valuable in mapping the online traffic among web-based networks of Palestinian communities in Germany, France, Italy, Austria, Australia, the United States, Canada, Spain, Argentina, Chile, and Uruguay. See also Miriyam Aouragh, *Palestine Online: Transnationalism, the Internet and the Construction of Identity*, 1–39. Aouragh's extraordinary research traces the online history and development of the Palestinian identity between the diaspora and at "home" since the signing of the Oslo Accords in 1993.

16. Werbner, "Migration and Transnational Studies," 108; Aouragh, *Palestine Online*, 47.

17. Aouragh, *Palestine Online*, 32.

18. Gilles Deleuze and Felix Guattari, *Kafka: Toward a Minor Literature*, 16, 18.

19. Waïl S. Hassan, *Immigrant Narratives: Orientalism and Cultural Translation in Arab American and Arab British Literature*, 17; Lisa Suhair Majaj, "On Writing and Return: Palestinian-American Reflections," 118.

20. See Anja Kublitz, "The Ongoing Catastrophe: Erosion of Life in the Danish Camps" and "From Revolutionaries to Muslims: Liminal Becomings across Palestinian Generations in Denmark." Kublitz's research is groundbreaking in mapping the trajectory of Palestinian refugees in Denmark—from the Galilean village to the camps in Lebanon to the welfare system in Denmark.

21. Hassan managed to publish two poetry collections before his untimely death at the age of twenty-four on April 30, 2020. His first collection, published in 2013, became one the most best-selling books in the history of Danish letters and is one of the early ethnic Danish texts that succeeded in becoming mainstream. Hassan's poetry and his appearances on television turned him, at the age of nineteen, into a controversial public figure who uncompromisingly critiqued both the Danish establishment and his own community.

22. Ahmad Mahmoud, *Sort Land: Fortællinger fra Ghettoen*, 138, 139 (my translations).

23. Tarek Omar, "Nydanske Forældre: Vi her Begået alt for Mange Fejl."

24. A. Mahmoud, *Sort Land*, 138 (my translation). In recognition of Yahya Hassan's literary status, during the summer of 2014, he was invited to the annual Palestinian literature festival PalFest through the Danish-Palestinian writing exchange program Words without Borders. However, owing to security concerns, his poetry reading took place in a small café in Bethlehem before the festival officially kicked off, and it was not mentioned in the program listings along with the other authors presenting their works (*Copenhagen Post*, June 2, 2014). Moreover, in May 2015, one of Hassan's poems, "Father My Unborn Son," was published in the literary magazine *Words without Borders*, for a special issue titled "New Palestinian Writing," edited by Palestinian poet Nathalie Handal.

25. Both Shammas and Kashua reside in the United States today. Whereas Shammas retreated from the Israeli public in the '80s and has permanently moved to Michigan, Kashua's departure during the third Gaza war in 2014 has yet to be determined as temporary or permanent.

26. Anton Shammas, *Arabesques*, 168; Anton Shammas, "Your Worst Nightmare."

27. Chana Kronfeld, *On the Margins of Modernism: Decentering Literary Dynamics*, 23–24, 10–12.

28. See, for example, Hannan Hever, *Producing the Modern Hebrew Canon: Nation Building and Minority Discourse*. See also Rachel Feldhay Brenner, "The Search for Identity in Israeli Arab Fiction: Atallah Mansour, Emile Habiby, and Anton Shammas." See also Gil Hochberg, "To Be or Not to Be an Israeli Arab:

Sayed Kashua and the Prospect of Minority Speech-Acts"; Catherine Rottenberg, "*Dancing Arabs* and Spaces of Desire"; and Batya Shimony, "Shaping Israeli-Arab Identity in Hebrew Words: The Case of Sayed Kashua."

29. Anthony Giddens, *The Consequences of Modernity*, 64.

30. Françoise Lionnet and Shu-mei Shih, *Minor Transnationalism*, 5.

31. See also Jan Nederveen Pieterse, "Hybrid Modernities: Mélange Modernities in Asia," 75.

32. Edward Said, "Globalizing Literary Study." See also Timothy Brennan, "From Development to Globalization: Postcolonial Studies and Globalization Theory," 122–23. Brennan distinguishes between "process" and "policy" in his explanation of the cultural and material ambiguities of the term "globalization."

33. See Amal Amireh and Lisa Suhair Majaj, *Going Global: the Transnational Reception of Third World Women Writers*, 2–4. Amireh and Majaj employ the term "material apparatuses" to explain the multidirectional "migration" or "cultural flow" between the first and third worlds.

2. The Anglophone Palestinian Novel

1. Nouri Gana, *The Edinburgh Companion to the Arab Novel in English: The Politics of Anglo Arab and Arab American Literature and Culture*, 12.

2. See Carol Fadda-Conrey, *Contemporary Arab-American Literature: Transnational Reconfigurations of Citizenship and Belonging*; and W. Hassan, *Immigrant Narratives.* See also Steven Salaita, *Arab American Literary Fictions, Cultures, and Politics* and *Modern Arab American Fiction: A Reader's Guide.*

3. Steven Salaita, "Scattered Like Seeds: Palestinian Prose Goes Global," 48.

4. Abu Manneh, *Palestinian Novel*, 31; Nicolas Bourriaud, *Relational Aesthetics.*

5. See Eitan Bar Yosef, *The Holy Land in English Culture, 1799–1917: Palestine and the Question of Orientalism.*

6. James L. Gelvin, *The Israel-Palestine Conflict: One Hundred Years of War*, 148–51.

7. Mara Naaman, "Invisible Ethnic: Mona Simpson and the Space of the Ethnic Literature Market," 380.

8. Ibrahim Abu-Lughod, "Review: The Pitfalls of Palestiniology," 403–4.

9. Fawaz Turki, *Exile's Return: The Making of a Palestinian-American*, 118.

10. Ahmad Sa'di, "Representations of Exile and Return in Palestinian Literature," 233.

11. W. Hassan, *Immigrant Narratives*, 122.

12. Samia Serageldin, "Perils and Pitfalls of Marketing the Arab Novel in English," 440; W. Hassan, *Immigrant Narratives*, 136.

13. Ezzedine C. Fishere, *Embrace on Brooklyn Bridge: A Novel*, 12.

14. M. Lynx Qualey, "Why Red-Line-Crossing Novelist Ezzedine C. Fisher Doesn't Fear Trolls."

3. (Tres)passings

1. Kashua writes in Hebrew. For this chapter I use the available English translation for the purpose of convenience.

2. In an interview with Neri Livne, a reporter from one of Israel's major newspapers, *Ha'aretz*, Kashua explains, "To write in Arabic in the way I speak it, which is the Palestinian-Israeli dialect, just isn't possible. Only literary Arabic is used for writing and I don't know it well enough" (*Ha'aretz*, January 5, 2004, http://www.haaretz.co.il/misc/1.937524). In an interview with *Publishing Perspectives*, Abulhawa refers to her inability to write in Arabic, "I want to be accepted as a Palestinian writer even though I write in English. That I cannot write in my mother tongue is a sad condition of the 'shatat' (diaspora) and 'manfa' (exile)" (http://publishingperspectives.com/2012/03/the-many-lives-and-languages-of-a-palestinian-novel/).

3. For the sake of convenience, I refer here to Adam Yale Stone's translation of the interview published in *Journal of Palestine Studies* in 2012.

4. Almog Behar, "Mahmoud Darwish: Poetry's State of Siege," 189.

5. Mahmoud Darwish, *Memory for Forgetfulness*, x.

6. I should point out that in this interview, Darwish expresses a deep sense of estrangement in the occupied Palestinian territories. He does not consider his "return" to be authentic, insofar as he possesses no memories that may connect him to the place. Darwish felt he was living in exile there in a "political homeland."

7. Mahmoud Darwish, "'Exile Is So Strong within Me, I May Bring It to the Land': A Landmark 1996 Interview with Mahmoud Darwish by Hilit Yeshurun," 53.

8. Lital Levy, *Poetic Trespass: Writing between Hebrew and Arabic in Israel/Palestine*, 3.

9. Salaita, *Modern Arab American Fiction*, 134–39.

10. Salaita, "Scattered Like Seeds," 46.

11. It seems impossible to bring up the issue of Palestinian exile today without referring to at least one of Said's many writings on the topic. His article "Between Worlds" (1998, in *London Review of Books*), his memoir *Out of Place* (2000), and his collection of articles *Reflections on Exile, and Other Essays* (2002) present Said's comprehensive meditations on his experiences as an exile.

12. David Grossman, *The Yellow Wind*, 125; Karen Grumberg, *Place and Ideology in Contemporary Hebrew Literature*, 126.

13. Said, *Out of Place*, 53.

14. Following the publication of *Arabesques*, Gerald Marzorati arrives in Israel to interview Shammas for the *New York Times*. During their many talks, Shammas describes the difficulties he had to confront upon moving from Fassuta to Haifa at a relatively young age. Kashua's autobiographical *Araveem Rokdeem* (*Dancing Arabs*, 2002) describes the protagonist's consistent anxieties as he gradually learns to navigate the Israeli Jewish environment when he moves to a prestigious boarding school in Jerusalem.

15. The comatose character is a relatively familiar figure in Arabic literature. For example, in Lebanese author Elias Khoury's *Bab a-Shams* (*Gate of the Sun*, 1998), Yunes, an aging Palestinian freedom fighter, lies in a coma and serves as the silent recipient of Khalil's stories of Palestinian exile. In my opinion, Kashua takes this motif one step further, insofar as Amir, rather than merely talking to Yonatan, makes the radical move of actually taking over his Jewish counterpart's identity.

16. From Zahalka's speech in the Israeli Knesset on September 8, 2015; my translation.

17. It is worth noting that Mapai played no small role in suppressing the identity of the "Arab Jew" and inventing the category of the "Mizrahi" Jew to eliminate traces of Arab culture within the Israeli society. Batya Shimony discusses this phenomenon in Israeli society extensively in her article on Kashua.

18. Salaita, "Scattered Like Seeds," 50.

19. Homi K. Bhabba, *The Location of Culture*, 62–64.

20. Shimony, "Shaping Israeli-Arab Identity in Hebrew Words," 159.

21. Susan Sontag, *On Photography*, 4.

22. Sontag, *On Photography*, 4.

23. Sontag, *On Photography*, 14.

4. Sexual Politics and Nationhood between Exile and the Homeland

1. Rhoda Ann Kanaaneh, *Birthing the Nation: Strategies of Palestinian in Israel*; Manal Shalabi, "The Sexual Politics of Palestinian Women in Israel"; Julie Peteet, *Gender in Crisis: Women and the Palestinian Resistance Movement*; Amal Amireh, "Between Complicity and Subversion: Body Politics in Palestinian National Narrative"; Ruba Salih, "Bodies That Walk, Bodies That Talk, Bodies That Love: Palestinian Women Refugees, Affectivity, and the Politics of the Ordinary."

2. Nancy El Gendy, "Trickster Humour in Randa Jarrar's *A Map of Home*: Negotiating Arab American Muslim Female Sexuality," 1.

3. See Nira Yuval-Davis, *Gender and Nation*, 26–67.

4. See Rabab Abdulhadi, "The Palestinian Women's Autonomous Movement: Emergence, Dynamics, and Challenges," 655–56. Abdulhadi identifies the three-dimensional "superwoman," representing glorified martyrdom and nurturance;

the "fertile mother," representing the reproduction of the nation; and, third, as the signifier of national honor, she asserts that these three concepts of womanhood highlight the tension between national aspiration and the desire to preserve conventional social structures. The Palestinian woman was expected to be a militant and an activist as well as a mother and a wife, while also serving as a symbol of the nation's honor. That is to say, her activism is contrasted with the more traditional role of motherhood. She both maintains her maternal status and becomes a "soldier" in the demographic war against Israel, echoing the mission David Ben Gurion assigned to Jewish women in the war against the local Arab population.

5. Ipshita Chanda, "Feminist Theory in Perspective," 489.

6. Abdulhadi, "Palestinian Women's Autonomous Movement," 654.

7. Peteet, *Gender in Crisis*, 172–74.

8. Amireh, "Between Complicity and Subversion," 749–52.

9. This oft-quoted phrase is of uncertain origin and unknown primary source. The various uses of this phrase usually aim to describe the immorality of the Zionist settlement in Palestine insofar as there was knowledge of an existing population. In 2012, Shai Afsai claims, in his analysis of Palestinian British author Ghada Karmi's *Married to Another Man: Israel's Dilemma in Palestine* (2007), that this phrase is a fabrication and, ultimately, based in anti-Zionist propaganda. Nonetheless, despite the dubious status of its authenticity, I have decided to allude to it here since—even if a fabrication—it represents a telling metaphor for the gendering of the nation.

10. Amireh, "Between Complicity and Subversion," 751.

11. Sheila Katz, *Women and Gender in Early Jewish and Palestinian Nationalism*, 84.

12. Ghazi al-Khalili, *The Palestinian Women and the Revolution*, 77.

13. Fleischmann, *Nation and Its "New" Women*, 3.

14. Abdulhadi, "Palestinian Women's Autonomous Movement," 654.

15. Amireh, "Between Complicity and Subversion," 758–59.

16. See Edward Said, *After the Last Sky*, 271. See also Lila Abu-Lughod, *Veiled Sentiments*, 88–90.

17. Amireh, "Between Complicity and Subversion," 761.

18. Valentine Moghadam, *Modernizing Women: Gender and Social Change in the Middle East*, 10.

19. Gil Z. Hochberg, "No Pride in Occupation: A Roundtable Discussion."

20. Majaj, "On Writing and Return," 116.

21. Majaj, "On Writing and Return," 117.

22. Majaj, "On Writing and Return," 116.

23. Dina Jadallah, review of *A Map of Home*, by Jarrar, 112.

24. Nirit Anderman, "The Palestinian Women behind a New Wave of Great Israeli Cinema," *Ha'aretz*, October 29, 2016, https://www.haaretz.com/israel-news/culture/movies/.premium-the-palestinian-women-behind-a-new-wave-of-great-israeli-cinema-1.5453589.

25. Tamari, *Mountain against the Sea*, 8–12.

26. When my wife and I went to watch *Bar Bahar* for the second time in Haifa, we were joined by my wife's ostensibly progressive communist colleague and her husband. Throughout the screening, she seemed uncomfortable, and while leaving the theater after the show, she expressed her dislike and commented that these girls (the actresses) did not seem to understand what they were doing. After all, they would still need to come back to society and lead a "normal" life. This incident, indeed, does not represent any comprehensive view of *Bar Bahar* and its reception. It is, nonetheless, telling of how even left-oriented individuals affiliated with the local Communist Party censure liberal portrayals of female sexuality as a glaring red line.

5. When the Exile Brings a Key

1. The Handala is the signature drawing by Palestinian cartoonist Naji Ali. It depicts a poor ten-year-old boy, defiant, rough, barefooted, and with his back turned to the world. This seemingly simple drawing alludes to several Palestinian motifs of displacement. Ali speaks of having given birth to a ten-year-old boy who will always remain at this age—the same age as when Ali himself became a refugee; he is dirty and poor, Ali continues, like the children of the refugee camps; his hands are folded behind his back in defiance against any US-mediated settlement for the Israeli-Palestinian conflict.

2. Sari Hanafi, "Virtual and Real Returns," 132. Hanafi, the former director of the Palestinian Refugee and Diaspora Center, divides the waves of return to the occupied Palestinian territories during the '90s into two: the first forced movement was caused by the outbreak of the Gulf War and uprooted 350,000 Palestinians from Kuwait and other Gulf countries, of whom only 37,000 arrived in the territories; the second wave followed the launch of the peace process and allowed for the return of Palestinians from Arab countries such as Egypt, Jordan, and Tunisia. My article does not relate to these groups that had somehow succeeded in maintaining the right to return to the occupied territories while in diaspora, but rather to Palestinians who were allowed to visit only temporarily as tourists.

3. My simplistic summary of the origins of the Palestinian plight is not to claim that the Palestinian national narrative started to come about only as a result of the founding of the State of Israel in 1948. To the contrary, historically, I position my understanding of the beginnings of a Palestinian national consciousness

among historical theses such as the ones presented by Baruch Kimmerling, Rashid Khalidi, Beshara Doumani, and recently Hillel Cohen.

4. Because of the abundance of textual narratives of Palestinian returns, I have had to leave out prominent memoirs such as Ghana Karmi's *Return: A Palestinian Memoir* (2015) and Salman Abu Sitta's *Mapping My Return: A Palestinian Memoir* (2016).

5. Alfred Schütz, "The Homecomer," 370, 374–75; Werbner, "Migration and Transnational Studies," 107.

6. Richard Kearney, *Poetics of Modernity*, xii.

7. Linda Hutcheon, *A Poetics of Postmodernism: History, Theory, Fiction*, 14.

8. Prior to the Yom Kippur War in 1973, the ultimate aim of the PLO was the total liberation of Palestine and the return of all displaced Palestinians. Following the war, the PLO started to consider the possibility of setting up an "authority" on any liberated part of Palestine. In 1988, at the closing of the nineteenth session of the Palestine National Council meeting in Algiers, the majority of the representatives adopted the Declaration of Independence of the State of Palestine. This document, penned by the renowned Palestinian poet Mahmoud Darwish, configured the most comprehensive expression of the PLO's view regarding a peace settlement in the Middle East. It expressed Palestinians' recognition of Israel's right to exist, denunciation of terrorism, and the declaration of an "independent Palestinian State" on the 1967 territories.

9. See Ghada Karmi, "The Right of Return: A Forgotten Issue." Karmi presents a comprehensible historical survey of how the "Right of Return" has configured as a sacred pillar in the Palestinian consciousness while consistently impeding the progress of any settlement between Israelis and Palestinians.

10. Salim Tamari, "The Local and the National in Palestinian Identity," 3–4.

11. Mahmoud Darwish, "Hagalut kol-kach Hazakah Betokhee, olai 'Avea ota 'Artzah," 172 (my translation).

12. Adam Shatz, "A Poet's Palestine as a Metaphor," *New York Times*, December 22, 2001.

13. Palestinian-Israeli writer Emile Habiby organized for Darwish a two-day permit by the Israeli government so that he could visit the Galilee and that they could meet. Tragically, Habiby died in a car accident shortly before Darwish's arrival. Instead of a meeting that would have gone down in the history of Palestinian literature as a major literary event, Darwish attended and eulogized Habiby at his funeral.

14. Darwish, *In the Presence of Absence*, 109, 121, 124.

15. See Sidra DeKoven Ezrahi, *Booking Passage: Exile and Homecoming in the Modern Jewish Imagination*. Ezrahi discusses the impact of the theological

framework on literary configurations of exile and return in the Jewish context. I think it is important to note this basic difference between Jewish and Palestinian representations of "return." In the Palestinian context, the national call for "homecoming" is rooted in a political-historical injustice, whereas the Jewish "return" is founded on a religious calling.

16. Turki, *Exile's Return*, 4.

17. Turki, *Exile's Return*, 5; Rema Hammami and Salim Tamari, "Virtual Returns to Jaffa," 69.

18. Turki, *Exile's Return*, 6.

19. Hammami and Tamari, "Virtual Returns to Jaffa," 69.

20. Hammami and Tamari, "Virtual Returns to Jaffa," 67.

21. Turki, *Exile's Return*, 273.

22. For the purpose of convenience, I will refer to Ahdaf Soueif's excellent translation of Barghouti's memoir rather than the original Arabic text throughout this article.

23. Mourid Barghouti, *I Saw Ramallah*, 61–62.

24. Barghouti, *I Saw Ramallah*, 88, 87.

25. Barghouti, *I Saw Ramallah*, 84–85.

26. Barghouti, *I Saw Ramallah*, 4.

27. Baeza, "Palestinians in Latin America," 64.

28. See Cecilia Baeza, "O 'refúgio' e o 'retorno' entre os Palestinos do Chile: Narrativa identitária e discurso militante," 309–13.

29. Lina Meruane, *Volverse Palestina*, 17 (translated from Spanish by Andrea Rosenberg).

30. Meruane, *Volverse Palestina*, 17, 19.

31. Meruane, *Volverse Palestina*, 26.

32. Anton Shammas, "Autocartography: The Case of Palestine, Michigan," 466.

33. Shammas, "Autocartography," 469.

Bibliography

Abdel-Fattah, Randa. *Does My Head Look Big in This?* Tuggerah: Pan Macmillan Australia, 2005.

Abdulhadi, Rabab. "The Palestinian Women's Autonomous Movement: Emergence, Dynamics, and Challenges." *Gender and Society* 12, no. 6 (1998): 649–73.

Abulhawa, Susan. *The Blue between Sky and Water.* New York: Bloomsbury, 2015.

———. *Mornings in Jenin.* New York: Bloomsbury, 2010.

Abu-Lughod, Ibrahim. "Review: The Pitfalls of Palestiniology." *Arab Studies Quarterly* 3, no. 4 (1981): 403–11.

Abu-Lughod, Lila. *Veiled Sentiments: Honor and Poetry in Bedouin Society.* Berkeley: Univ. of California Press, 1986.

Abu-Lughod, Lila, and Ahmad S. Sa'di. *Nakba: Palestine, 1948, and the Claims of Memory.* New York: Columbia Univ. Press, 2007.

Abu Manneh, Bashir. *The Palestinian Novel: From 1948 to the Present.* Cambridge: Cambridge Univ. Press, 2016.

Abu Sitta, Salman. *Mapping My Return: A Palestinian Memoir.* Cairo: American Univ. in Cairo Press, 2016.

Allen, Diana. *Refugees of the Revolution: Experiences of Palestinian Exile.* Stanford, CA: Stanford Univ. Press, 2014.

Alyan, Hala. *Salt Houses.* London: Hutchinson, 2017.

Amireh, Amal. "Between Complicity and Subversion: Body Politics in Palestinian National Narrative." *South Atlantic Quarterly* 102, no. 4 (2003): 747–72.

Amireh, Amal, and Lisa Suhair Majaj. *Going Global: The Transnational Reception of Third World Women Writers.* New York: Garland, 2000.

Aoudé, Ibrahim G. "Maintaining Culture, Reclaiming Identity: Palestinian Lives in the Diaspora." *Asian Studies Review* 25, no. 2 (2001): 153–67.

Aouragh, Miriyam. *Palestine Online: Transnationalism, the Internet and the Construction of Identity.* New York: I. B. Tauris, 2012.

Appadurai, Arjun. *Modernity at Large: Cultural Dimensions of Globalization.* Minneapolis: Univ. of Minnesota Press, 1996.

Baeza, Cecilia. "O 'refúgio' e o 'retorno' entre os Palestinos do Chile: Narrativa identitária e discurso militante." In *Entre o velho e o novo mundo: A diáspora Palestina desde o Oriente médio* à América Latina, edited by Leonardo Schiocchet, 297–322. São Paulo: Chiado, 2015.

———. "Palestinians in Latin America: Between Assimilation and Long-Distance Nationalism." *Journal of Palestine Studies* 43, no. 2 (2014): 59–72.

Bakhtin, Mikhail M. *The Dialogic Imagination.* Edited by Michael Holquist. Translated by Caryl Emerson and Michael Holquist. Austin: Univ. of Texas Press, 1981.

Banko, Lauren. *The Invention of Palestinian Citizenship, 1918–1947.* Edinburgh: Edinburgh Univ. Press, 2016.

Barghouti, Mourid. *I Saw Ramallah.* Translated by Ahdaf Souief. Cairo: American Univ. in Cairo Press, 2000.

———. *I Was Born There, I Was Born Here.* Translated by Humphrey Davies. London: Bloomsbury, 2012.

———. *Ra'aytu Ramallah.* Cairo: American Univ. in Cairo Press, 1997.

———. *Wulidtu Hunak, Wulidta Huna.* Beirut: Riad El-Rayyes Books, 2009.

Bar Yosef, Eitan. *The Holy Land in English Culture, 1799–1917: Palestine and the Question of Orientalism.* Oxford: Oxford Univ. Press, 2005.

Behar, Almog. "Mahmoud Darwish: Poetry's State of Siege." *Journal of Levantine Studies* 1 (2011): 189–99.

Ben-David, Anat. "The Palestinian Diaspora on the Web: Between De-territorialization and Re-territorialization." *Social Science Information* 51, no. 4 (2012): 459–74.

Bernard, Anna. *Rhetoric and Belonging: Nation, Narration, and Israel/Palestine.* Liverpool: Liverpool Univ. Press, 2013.

Bhabba, Homi K. *The Location of Culture.* 1994. Reprint, New York: Routledge, 2004.

Bourriaud, Nicolas. *Relational Aesthetics.* Dijon: Les Presse du Reel, 1998.

Brah, Avtar. *Cartographies of Diaspora: Contesting Identities.* London: Routledge, 1996.

Brennan, Timothy. "From Development to Globalization: Postcolonial Studies and Globalization Theory." In *Cambridge Companion to Postcolonial Literary Studies*, edited by Neil Lazarus, 120–38. Cambridge: Cambridge Univ. Press, 2004.

Brenner, Rachel Feldhay. "The Search for an Identity in Israeli Arab Fiction: Atallah Mansour, Emile Habiby, and Anton Shammas." *Israel Studies* 6, no. 3 (2001): 91–112.

Chanda, Ipshita. "Feminist Theory in Perspective." In *A Companion to Postcolonial Studies*, edited by Henry Shwarz and Sangeeta Ray, 486–507. Oxford: Blackwell, 2005.

Conrad, Joseph. *A Personal Record*. Edited by Zdzislaw Najder and J. H. Stape. Cambridge: Cambridge Univ. Press, 2008.

Dabbagh, Selma. *Out of It*. New York: Bloomsbury, 2012.

Dallal, Shaw. *Scattered Like Seeds*. Syracuse, NY: Syracuse Univ. Press, 1998.

Damrosch, David. *What Is World Literature?* Princeton, NJ: Princeton Univ. Press, 2003.

Darraj, Susan Muaddi. *A Curious Land: Stories from Home*. Amherst: Univ. of Massachusetts Press, 2015.

———. *The Inheritance of Exile: Stories from South Philly*. Notre Dame, IN: Univ. of Notre Dame Press, 2007.

Darwish, Mahmoud. *Dhakira lil-Nisyan*. *Al Karmel* 21–22 (1987): 4–96.

———. "'Exile Is So Strong within Me, I May Bring It to the Land': A Landmark 1996 Interview with Mahmoud Darwish by Hilit Yeshurun." *Journal of Palestine Studies* 42, no. 1 (2012–13): 46–67.

———. *Fi Hadrat 'al-Ghiyab*. London: Riad al-Rayyes Books, 2006.

———. "Hagalut kol-kach Hazakah Betokhee, olai 'Avea ota 'Artzah." *Hadarim* 12 (Spring 1996): 172–98.

———. *In the Presence of Absence*. Translated by Sinan Antoon. New York: Archipelago Books, 2011.

———. *Journal of an Ordinary Grief*. Translated by Ibrahim Muhawi. New York: Archipelago Books, 2010.

———. *Memory for Forgetfulness*. Translated by Ibrahim Muhawi. Berkeley: Univ. of California Press, 1995.

———. *Yawmiyyat 'al-Huzn 'al-Adi*. Beirut: Dar al-'Awda, 1973.

Daswani, Girish, and Ato Quayson. *A Companion to Diaspora and Transnationalism*. Oxford: Blackwell, 2013.

Davis, Rochelle. "Mapping the Past, Re-creating the Homeland: Memories of Village Places in Pre-1948 Palestine." In *Nakba: Palestine, 1948, and the Claims of Memory*, edited by Lila Abu-Lughod and Ahmad H. Sa'di, 53–76. New York: Columbia Univ. Press, 2007.

Deleuze, Gilles, and Felix Guattari. *Kafka: Toward a Minor Literature* [1975]. Translated Dana Polan. Minneapolis: Univ. of Minnesota Press, 1986.

Doumani, Beshara. *Rediscovering Palestine: Merchants and Peasants in Jabal Nablus, 1700–1900*. Berkeley: Univ. of California Press, 1995.

Ebileeni, Maurice. "Breaking the Script: The Generational Conjuncture in the Anglophone Palestinian Novel." *Journal of Postcolonial Writing* 55, no. 5 (2019): 628–41.

———. "Ha-poetica shel Ha-masaa Ha-Filistini Ha-Bayta." *OT* 7 (Spring 2017): 67–92.

———. "Literary Trespassing in Susan Abulhawa's *Mornings in Jenin* and Sayed Kashua's *Second Person Singular*." *Comparative Literature* 69, no. 2 (2017): 222–37.

———. "Palestinian Writings in the World: A Polylingual Literary Category between the Local and Transnational Realms." *Interventions: International Journal of Postcolonial Studies* 19, no. 2 (2017): 258–82.

Elad-Bouskila, Ami. *Modern Palestinian Literature and Culture*. London: Frank Cass, 1999.

Elboim-Dror, Rachel. "British Educational Policies in Palestine." *Middle Eastern Studies* 36, no. 2 (2000): 28–47.

Ezrahi, Sidra DeKoven. *Booking Passage: Exile and Homecoming in the Modern Jewish Imagination*. Berkeley: Univ. of California Press, 2000.

Fadda-Conrey, Carol. *Contemporary Arab-American Literature: Transnational Reconfigurations of Citizenship and Belonging*. New York: New York Univ. Press, 2014.

Fanon, Frantz. *Black Skin, White Masks* [1952]. Translated by Richard Philcox. New York: Grove Press, 2008.

Fawal, Ibrahim. *On the Hills of God*. Louisville, KY: NewSouth Books, 1998.

Fishere, Ezzedine C. *Embrace on Brooklyn Bridge: A Novel* [2011]. Translated by John Peate. New York: Hoopoe, 2017.

Fleischmann, Ellen L. *The Nation and Its "New" Women: The Palestinian Women's Movement, 1920–1948*. Berkeley: Univ. of California Press, 2003.

Gana, Nouri. *The Edinburgh Companion to the Arab Novel in English: The Politics of Anglo Arab and Arab American Literature and Culture*. Edinburgh: Edinburgh Univ. Press, 2015.

Gelvin, James L. *The Israel-Palestine Conflict: One Hundred Years of War*, 3rd ed. Cambridge: Cambridge Univ. Press, 2014.

Gendy, Nancy el-. "Trickster Humour in Randa Jarrar's *A Map of Home*: Negotiating Arab American Muslim Female Sexuality." *Women: A Cultural Review* 27, no. 1 (2016): 1–19.

Giddens, Anthony. *The Consequences of Modernity*. Stanford, CA: Stanford Univ. Press, 1990.

Gikandi, Simon. "Globalization and the Claims of Postcoloniality." *South Atlantic Quarterly* 100, no. 3 (2001): 627–58.

Grossman, David. *Ha-Zman Ha-Tsahov*. Tel Aviv: Hakibbutz Hame'ohad, 1987.

———. *Sleeping on a Wire: Conversations with Palestinians in Israel*. Translated by Haim Watzman. New York: Farrar, Straus & Giroux, 1993.

———. *The Yellow Wind* [1988]. Translated by Haim Watzman. New York: Picador, 2002.

Grumberg, Karen. *Place and Ideology in Contemporary Hebrew Literature*. Syracuse, NY: Syracuse Univ. Press, 2012.

Habiby, Emile. *The Secret Life of Saeed the Pessoptimist* [1974]. Translated by Salma Khadra Jayyusi and Trevor LeGassick. Brooklyn: Interlink Books, 2003.

———. *'Al-Waqa'i' al-ghariba fi 'ikhtifa' Said Abi 'al-Nahs 'al-mutasha'il*. Jerusalem: Ṣalaḥ al-Din, 1977.

Hammad, Isabella. *The Parisian*. New York: Grove Press, 2019.

Hammad, Suheir. *Born Palestinian, Born Black*. New York: Writers and Readers, 1996.

Hammami, Rema, and Salim Tamari. "Virtual Returns to Jaffa." *Journal of Palestine Studies* 27, no. 4 (1998): 65–79.

Hammer, Julianne. *Palestinians Born in Exile: Diaspora and the Search for a Homeland*. Austin: Univ. of Texas Press, 2005.

Hanafi, Sari. "Rethinking the Palestinians Abroad as a Diaspora: The Relationships between the Diaspora and the Palestinian Territories." *HAGAR: International Social Science Review* 4, nos. 1–2 (2003): 157–82.

———. "Virtual and Real Returns." In *Crossing Borders, Shifting Boundaries: Palestinian Dilemmas*, edited by Sari Hanafi, 131–56. Cairo: American Univ. in Cairo Press, 2008.

Handal, Nathalie. *The Invisible Star (La estrella invisible): Bilingual Edition*. Granada: Valparaíso Ediciones, 2014.

———. "The Shape of Time: New Palestinian Writing." *Words without Borders*, May 2015. http://www.wordswithoutborders.org/article/the-shape-of-time-new-palestinian-writing.

Hasbúns, Rodrigo. *Los affectos*. Barcelona: Literatura Random House, 2015.

———. *El lugar del cuerpo*. Madrid: Alfaguara, 2012.

Hassan, Salah D. "Nation Validation: Modern Palestinian Literature and the Politics of Appeasement." *Social Text* 21, no. 2–75 (2003): 4–24.

Hassan, Waïl S. *Immigrant Narratives: Orientalism and Cultural Translation in Arab American and Arab British Literature*. Oxford: Oxford Univ. Press, 2011.

Hassan, Yahya. "Father My Unborn Son." *Words without Borders*, May 2015. http://wordswithoutborders.org/article/father-my-unborn-son.

———. *Yahya Hassan*. Copenhagen: Gyldendal, 2013.

Hever, Hannan. *Producing the Modern Hebrew Canon: Nation Building and Minority Discourse*. New York: New York Univ. Press, 2002.

Hochberg, Gil Z. *In Spite of Partition: Jews, Arabs, and the Limits of Separatist Imagination*. Princeton, NJ: Princeton Univ. Press, 2007.

———. "No Pride in Occupation: A Roundtable Discussion." *GLQ: A Journal of Lesbian and Gay Studies* 16, no. 4 (2010): 599–610.

———. "To Be or Not to Be an Israeli Arab: Sayed Kashua and the Prospect of Minority Speech-Acts." *Comparative Literature* 62, no. 1 (2010): 68–88.

Hutcheon, Linda. *A Poetics of Postmodernism: History, Theory, Fiction*. London: Routledge, 1988.

Jabra, Jabra Ibrahim. *Hunters in a Narrow Street: A Novel* [1960]. Reprint, London: Lynne Rienner, 1996.

Jadallah, Dina. Review of *A Map of Home*, by Randa Jarrar. *Arab Studies Quarterly* 32, no. 2 (2010): 109–13.

Jarrar, Randa. *Him, Me, Muhammad Ali: Stories.* Louisville, KY: Sarabande Books, 2016.

———. *Love Is an Ex-Country.* New York: Catapult, 2021.

———. *A Map of Home.* New York: Penguin Books, 2008.

Jayyusi, Salma Khadra. *Anthology of Modern Palestinian Literature.* New York: Columbia Univ. Press, 1992.

Jebreal, Rula. *Miral* [2004]. Translated by John Cullen. New York: Penguin Books, 2010.

Johnson, Alan G. *Out of Bounds: Anglo-Indian Literature and the Geography of Displacement.* Honolulu: Univ. of Hawaii Press, 2011.

Kanaaneh, Rhoda Ann. *Birthing the Nation: Strategies of Palestinian Women in Israel.* Berkeley: Univ. of California Press, 2002.

Kanafani, Ghassan. *'Adab 'al-Muqawama fi Filstin 'al-Muḥtalla, 1948–1966.* 1968. Reprint, Cyprus: Rimal, 2013.

———. *A'ed 'illa Haifa.* 1969. Reprint, Beirut: Dar al-Awdah, 1985.

———. *The 1936–39 Revolt in Palestine.* New York: Committee for Democratic Palestine, 1972.

———. *Resistance Literature in Occupied Palestine, 1948–1966.* Translated by Sulafa Hijjawi. Baghdad: Ministry of Culture, 1968.

———. "Returning to Haifa" [1969]. In *Palestine's Children: Returning to Haifa, and Other Stories*, translated by Barbara Harlow and Karen E. Riley. London: Lynne Rienner, 2000.

Karmi, Ghada. "After the Nakba: An Experience of Exile in England." *Journal of Palestine Studies* 28, no. 3 (1999): 52–63.

———. *Return: A Palestinian Memoir.* London: Verso, 2015.

———. "The Right of Return: A Forgotten Issue." *Middle East Monitor* 1 (September 2015). https://www.middleeastmonitor.com/articles/guest-writers/20747-the-right-of-return-a-forgotten-issue.

Kashua, Sayed. *Araveem Rokdeem.* Ben Shemen: Modan, 2002.

———. *Dancing Arabs.* Translated by Miriam Shlesinger. New York: Grove Press, 2004.

———. *Goof Sheni' Yaheed.* Jerusalem: Keter, 2010.

———. *Let It Be Morning.* Translated by Miriam Shlesinger. New York: Grove Press, 2010.

———. *Second Person Singular*. Translated by Mitch Ginsburg. New York: Grove Press, 2012.

———. *We Yehye Boker*. Jerusalem: Keter, 2006.

Kassem, Fatma. *Palestinian Women: Narrative Histories and Gendered Memory*. London: Zed Books, 2011.

Katz, Sheila. *Women and Gender in Early Jewish and Palestinian Nationalism*. Gainesville: Univ. Press of Florida, 2003.

Kearney, Richard. *Poetics of Modernity*. Atlantic Highlands, NJ: Humanities Press, 1995.

Khalidi, Rashid. "The Formation of Palestinian Identity: The Critical Years, 1917–1923." In *Rethinking Nationalism in the Arab Middle East*, edited by Israel Gershoni and James Jankowski, 171–91. New York: Columbia Univ. Press, 1997.

———. *Palestinian Identity: The Construction of Modern National Consciousness*. New York: Columbia Univ. Press, 1997.

Khalifeh, Sahar. *Bab 'el-Saha*. Beirut: Dar al-Adaab, 1994.

Khalili, Ghazi al-. *The Palestinian Women and the Revolution*. Acre: Dar al-Aswar, 1977.

Khamis, Khulud. *Haifa Fragments*. Victoria: Spinifex Press, 2015.

Kharrat, Edwar al-. "Egyptian Heart, French Tongue, a Personal Testimony." *Alif: Journal of Comparative Poetics* 20 (2000): 8–24.

———. "In Search of an Identity for Francophone Literature." *Al Arabi Mag* 515 (2001): 76–79.

Khoury, Elias. *Bab 'al-Shams*. Beirut: Dâr al-Adâb, 1998.

———. *Gate of the Sun* [1998]. Translated by Humphrey Davies. New York: Picador, 2006.

Kilpatrick, Hilary. "Arab Fiction in English: A Case of Dual Nationality." *New Comparisons* 13 (1992): 46–55.

———. "Tradition and Innovation in the Fiction of Ghassan Kanafani." *Journal of Arabic Literature* 7 (1976): 53–64.

Kimmerling, Baruch, and Joel S. Migdal. *Palestinians: The Making of a People*. Cambridge, MA: Harvard Univ. Press, 1994.

Krishnan, Madhu. *Contemporary African Literature in English: Strategies of Address and Cultural Constraints*. New York: Palgrave Macmillan, 2014.

Kronfeld, Chana. *On the Margins of Modernism: Decentering Literary Dynamics*. Berkeley: Univ. of California Press, 1996.

Kublitz, Anja. "From Revolutionaries to Muslims: Liminal Becomings across Palestinian Generations in Denmark." *International Journal of Middle East Studies* 48 (2016): 67–86.

———. "The Ongoing Catastrophe: Erosion of Life in the Danish Camps." *Journal of Refugee Studies* 29, no. 2 (2015): 229–49.

Levy, Lital. *Poetic Trespass: Writing between Hebrew and Arabic in Israel/Palestine*. Princeton, NJ: Princeton Univ. Press, 2014.

Levy, Lital, and Allison Schachter. "Jewish Literature/World Literature: Between the Local and the Transnational." *PMLA* 130, no. 1 (2015): 92–109.

Lionnet, François, and Shu-mei Shih. *Minor Transnationalism*. Durham, NC: Duke Univ. Press, 2005.

Lloyd, David. *Nationalism and Minor Literature: James Clarence Mangan and the Emergence of Irish Cultural Nationalism*. Berkeley: Univ. of California Press, 1987.

Mahmoud, Abdel Aziz. *Hvor Taler Du Flot Dansk*. Copenhagen: Politiken, 2016.

Mahmoud, Ahmad. *Sort Land: Fortællinger fra Ghettoen*. Copenhagen: People's Press, 2015.

Mahmoud, Lena. *Amreekiya*. Lexington: Univ. Press of Kentucky, 2018.

Majaj, Lisa Suhair. "On Writing and Return: Palestinian-American Reflections." *Meridians* 2, no. 1 (2001): 113–26.

Maleh, Layla al-. *Arab Voices in Diaspora: Critical Perspectives on Anglophone Arab Literature*. Amsterdam: Rodopi, 2009.

Malkki, Liisa. "*National Geographic*: The Rooting of Peoples and the Territorialization of National Identity among Scholars and Refugees." *Cultural Anthropology* 7, no. 1 (1992): 24–44.

Mansour, Atallah. *In a New Light* [1966]. Translated by Abraham Birman. London: Valentine, Mitchell, 1969.

Massad, Joseph A. *The Persistence of the Palestinian Question: Essays on Zionism and the Palestinians*. New York: Routledge, 2006.

Mattar, Hisham. *Anatomy of Disappearance*. New York: Dial Press Trade Paperbacks, 2012.

Meruane, Lina. *Volverse Palestina*. New York: Penguin Random House, 2014.

Moghadam, Valentine. *Modernizing Women: Gender and Social Change in the Middle East*. Boulder, CO: Lynne Rienner, 1993.

Moore, Lindsey. "A Conversation with Selma Dabbagh." *Journal of Postcolonial Writing* 51, no. 3 (2015): 324–39.

Mufti, Aamir. *Forget English: Orientalisms and World Literatures.* Cambridge, MA: Harvard Univ. Press, 2016.

Naaman, Mara. "Invisible Ethnic: Mona Simpson and the Space of the Ethnic Literature Market." In *The Edinburgh Companion to the Arab Novel in English*, edited by Nouri Gana, 363–85. Edinburgh: Edinburgh Univ. Press, 2013.

Nash, Geoffrey. *The Anglo-Arab Encounter: Fiction and Autobiography by Arab Writers in English.* Bern: Peter Lang, 2007.

"Number of Palestinians in the World Is 11.8 Million, Says Statistic Bureau." *Palestine News Network* 2 (January 2014). http://www.imemc.org/article/66665.

Omar, Tarek. "Nydanske Forældre: Vi her Begået alt for Mange Fejl." *Politiken* 1 (June 2014). https://politiken.dk/debat/art5519901/Nydanske-forældre-Vi-har-begået-alt-for-mange-fejl.

Parmenter, Barbara McKean. *Giving Voice to Stones: Place and Identity in Palestinian Literature.* Austin: Univ. of Texas Press, 1994.

Peteet, Julie. *Gender in Crisis: Women and the Palestinian Resistance Movement.* New York: Columbia Univ. Press, 1991.

———. "Problematizing a Palestinian Diaspora." *International Journal of Middle East Studies* 39, no. 4 (2007): 627–46.

Pieterse, Jan Nederveen. "Hybrid Modernities: Mélange Modernities in Asia." *Sociological Analysis* 1, no. 3 (1998): 75–86.

Qasim, Mahmoud. *Arab Literature Written in French.* Cairo: Public Egyptian Authority of Books, 1996.

Qualey, M. Lynx. "Why Red-Line-Crossing Novelist Ezzedine C. Fisher Doesn't Fear Trolls." *Bookriot*, June 2, 2017. https://bookriot.com/2017/06/02/why-red-line-crossing-novelist-ezzedine-c-fishere-doesnt-fear-trolls/.

Ray, Sangeeta, and Henry Schwarz. *A Companion to Postcolonial Studies.* Oxford: Blackwell, 2000.

Rottenberg, Catherine. "*Dancing Arabs* and Spaces of Desire." *Topia: Canadian Journal of Cultural Studies* 19 (Spring 2008): 99–114.

Rum, Etaf. *A Woman Is No Man.* New York: HarperCollins, 2019.

Saadawi, Nawal el-. *A Daughter of Isis: The Autobiography of Nawal el Saadawi.* New York: Zed Books, 1999.

Sa'di, Ahmad. "Representations of Exile and Return in Palestinian Literature." *Journal of Arabic Literature* 46 (2015): 216–43.

Said, Edward. *After the Last Sky*. Boston: Faber and Faber, 1986.

———. "Between Worlds." *London Review of Books* 20, no. 9 (1998): 3–7.

———. "Globalizing Literary Study." *PMLA* 116, no. 1 (2001): 64–68.

———. *Orientalism*. 1978. Reprint, New York: Vintage, 1994.

———. *Out of Place: A Memoir*. New York: Vintage Books, 1999.

———. *Reflections on Exile, and Other Essays*. Cambridge, MA: Harvard Univ. Press, 2002.

Salaita, Steven. *Arab American Literary Fictions, Cultures, and Politics*. New York: Palgrave Macmillan, 2006.

———. *Modern Arab American Fiction: A Reader's Guide*. Syracuse, NY: Syracuse Univ. Press, 2011.

———. "Scattered Like Seeds: Palestinian Prose Goes Global." *Studies in the Humanities* 30, nos. 1–2 (2003): 46–59.

Salih, Ruba. "Bodies That Walk, Bodies That Talk, Bodies That Love: Palestinian Women Refugees, Affectivity, and the Politics of the Ordinary." *Antipode* 49, no. 3 (2017): 742–60.

Salih, Ruba, and Sophie Richter-Devroe. "Palestine beyond National Frames: Emerging Politics, Cultures, and Claims." *South Atlantic Quarterly* 117, no. 1 (2018): 1–20.

Schulz, Helena Lindholm (with Julianne Hammer). *The Palestinian Diaspora: Formation of Identities and Politics of Homeland*. London: Routledge, 2003.

Schütz, Alfred. "The Homecomer." *American Journal of Sociology* 50, no. 5 (1945): 369–76.

Serageldin, Samia. "Perils and Pitfalls of Marketing the Arab Novel in English." In *The Edinburgh Companion to the Arab Novel in English*, edited by Nouri Gana. Edinburgh: Edinburgh Univ. Press, 2013.

Shalabi, Manal. "The Sexual Politics of Palestinian Women in Israel." In *Displaced at Home: Ethnicity and Gender among Palestinians in Israel*, edited by Rhoda Ann Kanaaneh and Isis Nusair, 153–68. Albany: State Univ. of New York Press, 2010.

Shammas, Anton. *Arabesqot*. Tel Aviv: Am Oved, 1986.

———. *Arabesques* [1986]. Translated by Vivian Eden. Berkeley: Univ. of California Press, 2001.

———. "An Arab Voice in Israel." *New York Times Magazine*, September 18, 1988.

———. "Autocartography: The Case of Palestine, Michigan." In *The Geography of Identity*, edited by Patricia Yaeger, 466–75. Ann Arbor: Univ. of Michigan Press, 1996.

———. "Kitsch 22." *Tikkun* (September–October 1987): 22–26.

———. "Your Worst Nightmare." *Jewish Frontiers* 56, no. 4 (1989): 8–10.

Sharabi, Hisham. *Embers and Ashes* [1978]. Translated by Issa J. Boullata. Northampton, MA: Olive Branch Press, 2008.

Shimony, Batya. "Shaping Israeli-Arab Identity in Hebrew Words: The Case of Sayed Kashua." *Israel Studies* 18, no. 1 (2013): 146–69.

Sikseck, Ayman. *El Yaffo*. Tel Aviv: Yediot Sphareem, 2010.

Snaije, Olivia. "The Many Lives and Languages of a Palestinian Novel." *Publishing Perspectives* 21 (March 2012). http://publishingperspectives.com/2012/03/the-many-lives-and-languages-of-a-palestinian-novel/.

Søgaard, Jannie Iwankow. "Yahya Hassans digte er mest for midaldrende etniske danskere." *Kristeligt Dagblad* 28 (November 2013).

Sommer, Doris. "Language, Culture, and Society." In *Introduction to Scholarship in Modern Languages and Literatures*, edited by David G. Nicholls, 3–29. 3rd ed. New York: Modern Language Association of America, 2007.

Sontag, Susan. *On Photography*. London: Penguin Books, 1979.

Suleiman, Yasir. "The Betweenness of Identity: Language in Trans-national Literature." In *The Arab Diaspora: Voices of an Anguished Scream*, edited by Ian Richard Netton and Zahia Smail Salhi, 11–25. London: Routledge, 2006.

Taha, Ibrahim. *The Palestinian Novel: A Communication Study*. London: Routledge, 2010.

Tamari, Salim. "The Local and the National in Palestinian Identity." In *Israeli and Palestinian Identities in History and Literature*, edited by Kamal Abdel-Malek and David C. Jacobson, 3–8. London: Macmillan Press, 1999.

———. *Mountain against the Sea: Essays on Palestinian Society and Culture*. Berkeley: Univ. of California Press, 2009.

Touqan, Fadwa. *A Mountainous Journey*. Translated by Olive Kenny. St. Paul, MN: Graywolf, 1990.

Turki, Fawaz. *The Disinherited: Journal of a Palestinian Exile*. New York: Monthly Review Press, 1972.

———. *Exile's Return: The Making of a Palestinian-American*. New York: Free Press, 1994.

———. *Soul in Exile: Lives of a Palestinian Revolutionary*. New York: Monthly Review Press, 1988.

Vinson, Pauline Homsi. "Arab American Coming of Age." *Al-Jadid* 13–14, nos. 58–59 (2007–8): 45–46.

Werbner, Pnina. "Migration and Transnational Studies: Between Simultaneity and Rupture." In *A Companion to Diaspora and Transnationalism*, edited by Ato Quayson and Girish Daswani, 106–24. Oxford: Wiley Blackwell, 2013.

Yuval-Davis, Nira. *Gender and Nation*. London: Sage, 1998.

Index

Maurice Ebileeni is a lecturer in the English Department at the University of Haifa. He is the author of *Conrad, Faulkner, and the Problem of Nonsense*, and his work on Palestinian literature and culture has appeared in *Comparative Literature*, the *Journal of Postcolonial Writing*, *Interventions: International Journal of Postcolonial Studies*, and the Hebrew-language *Ot*.